Cultural studies:
a critical introduction

Cultural Studies: A Critical Introduction is a wide-ranging and stimulating introduction to cultural studies from its beginnings to the global field that it is becoming today. It begins by describing cultural studies' social and theoretical histories and contexts, and then presents a series of short essays on important areas, designed to provoke discussion and raise questions. Each thematic section examines and explains a key topic.

Sections include:

- The discipline
- Time
- Space
- Media and the public sphere
- Identity
- Sexuality and gender
- Value

Cultural Studies: A Critical Introduction will be very useful in classrooms but will also appeal to anyone with an interest in keeping up or familiarising themselves with cultural studies in its contemporary forms.

Simon During is Professor of English at the Johns Hopkins University. He is editor of *The Cultural Studies Reader* (2nd edition, Routledge 1999) and most recently author of *Modern Enchantments: The Cultural Power of Secular Magic* (2003).

Cultural studies:
a critical introduction

Simon During

LONDON AND NEW YORK

First published 2005
by Routledge
2 Park Square, Milton Park, Abingdon, Oxon, OX14 4RN

Simultaneously published in the USA and Canada
by Routledge
270 Madison Avenue, New York, NY 10016

Routledge is an imprint of the Taylor & Francis Group

© 2005 Simon During

Typeset in Perpetua by Taylor & Francis Books
Printed and bound in Great Britain by MPG Books Ltd, Bodmin, Cornwall

British Library Cataloguing in Publication Data
A catalogue record for this book is available from the British Library

Library of Congress Cataloging in Publication Data
During, Simon, 1950–
  Cultural studies : a critical introduction / Simon During
     p. cm. Includes bibliographical references.
  1. Culture – Study and teaching. 2. Culture. I. Title.
  HM623.D87 2005
  306'.071–dc22
                          2004015958

ISBN 0–415–24656–3 (hbk)
ISBN 0–415–24657–1 (pbk)

Contents

CONTENTS

Acknowledgments

I want to thank Loren Glass, Ted Striphas and Graeme Turner for their insightful comments on an earlier version of this manuscript: Ted's detailed response in particular proved invaluable. And to acknowledge the support I received from the Centre for Critical and Cultural Studies at the University of Queensland while writing. The project itself was Rebecca Barden's idea (thanks!) and Lisa paid a price for me taking it on: all that time in the study. So too did Nicholas I suspect. The work itself is dedicated to those readers who I hope will take something from it and go on to make it obsolete.

Introduction

This book is not quite the usual introduction to cultural studies – an academic field that we can define, without messing about, as the engaged analysis of contemporary cultures. Cultural studies is *engaged* in three different senses. First, in the sense that it is not neutral in relation to the exclusions, injustices and prejudices that it observes. It tends to position itself on the side of those to whom social structures offer least, so that here 'engaged' means political, critical. Second, it is engaged in that it aims to enhance and celebrate cultural experiences: to communicate enjoyment of a wide variety of cultural forms in part by analysing them and their social underpinnings. And third, and this marks its real difference from other kinds of academic work, it aims to deal with culture as a part of everyday life, without objectifying it. In fact cultural studies aspires to join – to engage in – the world, itself.

Most introductions to cultural studies focus on the discipline's historical development, usually tracing it from its beginnings in Britain in the 1960s as a mix of left-wing sociology, adult education and literary criticism, to its current dissemination across much of the global academy, and they go on to provide an account of its basic methods and interests. But the bulk of this book, while it does not ignore questions of disciplinary history and method, consists of a series of short essays on the discipline's core topics, designed to stimulate discussion and thought in the classroom, although not only in the classroom. It is not aimed at absolute beginners (although I'd hope some novices will find it stimulating) but more at those who are feeling their way further into the subject on the basis of some preliminary study, as well as at old hands intrigued by what I hope is a fresh take on the field.

I have chosen to structure the book as a series of essays on specific topics because my experience in class has shown me that the most effective way to teach cultural studies is to

1

draw on students' cultural interests, and to show how academic work can extend those interests and offer critical insight into them. The short essay is an ideal way of doing that. In broader terms, this is a book designed to get students into cultural studies by showing how the discipline helps us to understand and orientate ourselves towards a wide range of institutions, media, concepts and formations – from television to multiculturalism; from cultural heritage to queer politics. To reach this point, however, in its first section, the book begins by providing a brief overview of the discipline's past and present; its interactions with other related academic disciplines; its connections to changes in tertiary education; as well as some of the key debates that have shaped it.

Part 1

THE DISCIPLINE

Going global

Perhaps the most remarkable feature of cultural studies today is the way that it is becoming global – along with trade, finance, communications and the university system as a whole. It's taught, in one form or other, in most national academic systems. Which means that, wherever you are coming from, there will be people in the field working on material that belongs to 'another culture' than your own. This presents a challenge. On the one hand, as the discipline is globalised it becomes harder to take any particular cultural context as standard, let alone as universal. The horizons of dialogue, exchange and research are extended. This fits in well with the discipline's orientation, since it has never claimed scientific objectivity and rarely assumes that it possesses analytic methods that hold good across different cultures. On the other hand, to the degree that regional cultures are in fact analysed around the world in terms of a set of methods and theories first developed in the West, the discipline becomes complicit in the logic by which regional differences are reduced under the guise of accepting them as differences. And the sheer variety of topics and histories brought into the discipline through globalisation, along with the consequent loss of shared references and competencies, threatens to disrupt its capacity to draw practitioners into a shared project.

The notion that the amount and specialisation of culture- and knowledge-prodution had made a single and comprehensive overview of society impossible was already commonplace in the eighteenth century (see Barrell 1992). In cultural studies these days, however, that sense is felt less in terms of loss than of confusion. For example, in a 1998 volume of the flagship journal *Cultural Studies*, one can find a traditional literary-critical essay on *Hamlet* and Marx; a sociological essay on consumerism and the

Louvre; an archivally based piece on colonial science in South India; a feminist critique of the theory of cultural 'hybridity'; an essay on Bob Marley and black transnationalism; a contextualising historical essay on Fu Manchu, the Chinese baddie hero of a number of popular early twentieth-century novels by 'Sax Rohmer'; an essay on breast cancer and the 'public body' in the USA; as well as self-reflective essays on the discipline itself.

Faced with all this, it is easy to feel like an intellectual tourist dropping into topics which may be enticing in their sheer exoticness but towards which one has little interest or responsibility. No wonder outsiders sometimes roll their eyes at cultural studies' ambitions and shapelessness. One answer to this is to think of cultural studies' teachers and students as agents for connections between globally dispersed events and flows more or less vaguely in the interests of a transnational movement against exploitation and centrism. But it has to be said that that kind of academic *noblesse oblige* risks increasing the gap between what such topics mean to cultural studies and what they mean on the ground – where what humanities academics think hardly matters. More to the point, it risks the engagement in culture that is one of the field's defining features.

Culture today

For all that, diffusion is not the key to global cultural studies. Mobility is. The kind of cultural formations of most interest to the discipline are becoming increasingly mobile everywhere. This is true in the literal sense that they tend to move across distances and borders, but also in the sense that their relations with their social and material settings (the economy, politics, education, technology and so on) change so quickly and thoroughly, although at different paces and in different ways in different places. It's also true in the sense that sectors and genres internal to cultures are interacting so dynamically with one another. Culture is not a thing or even a system: it's a set of transactions, processes, mutations, practices, technologies, institutions, out of which things and events (such as movies, poems or world wrestling bouts) are produced, to be experienced, lived out and given meaning and value to in different ways within the unsystematic network of differences and mutations from which they emerged to start with. (Again this model strikes a less than contemporary note: the basis of such an understanding of culture first appears in the German philosopher Friedrich Nietzsche's work at the end of the nineteenth century.)

For cultural studies today, cultural objects are simultaneously 'texts' (that is, they have meaning) *and* events *and* experiences, produced out of, and thrown back into, a social force field constituted unevenly by power flows, status hierarchies and opportunities for many kinds of transportation, identification and pleasure. They are also social institutions, some based in the state, others in the market or in so-called civil society. Cultures travel across geographical borders; they merge and separate; they cross and disrupt political and social divisions, and also, sometimes, strengthen them. Cultural technologies are born and die. Capital and fashions ebb and flow through different cultural forms. Some genres become specialised and 'extreme', others sweep the world.

So it often seems as if, because 'culture' no longer refers to a specific set of things and because cultural markets are so pervasive, it – and hence cultural studies – can be just about anything (see Readings 1996, 17). Certainly as we shall see it often threatens to exceed its limits and take over alternative concepts such as society. Despite all this, cultural studies does not in fact cover culture with equal attention to all its modes. It has mainly directed itself to a particular set of cultural formations – those that connect most directly to its mainly secular, middle-class, leftist, youngish (or wannabe young) more or less Eurocentric practitioners. Hence, it has tended to neglect, for instance, religion; food; sport; hobby-sports such as fishing and train-spotting; middle-brow and 'kitsch' culture, especially that part which is family-based and of most interest to the middle aged such as home improvement and gardening. For different reasons it has neglected high culture itself.

Then, too, study of culture itself belongs to culture. We cultural studies practitioners are making culture, even if from within a fairly highly organised institution – the education system – and even if our political ends, which some would describe as the democratisation of culture, impose upon us certain constraints. At any rate cultural studies' concept of 'culture' breaks with the concepts of culture that have been dominant in the past. In particular, in losing its intimate connection with traditional high arts, the discipline tends to regard all cultural practices and objects as value-equivalent. Indeed it is a child of a society where such a levelling view has an economic function, namely the increase of cultural consumption of all kinds. Nor does it adhere to the idea promulgated by followers of the great, eighteenth-century German philosopher Immanuel Kant hold – that at culture's core lies the aesthetic: the domain of activities that are 'ends in themselves' and not of use for some other purpose, as, for instance, are food or buildings. Likewise the older, anthropological sense of 'culture' is exhausted, by which the term referred to the inherited, primarily non-modern and uncontested values, beliefs and practices that organise individuals' relations to, and participation in, communities.

Method

Once these older concepts of culture begin to retreat, and once culture is treated globally, method becomes a real problem for the academic study of culture. What kind of concepts and practices should we bring to our material? Interviews? Statistical analysis? Philosophical conceptualising? Political critique? Close readings of 'texts' (which might include songs, TV shows as well as novels)? In fact it is difficult to say much more about cultural studies method except that, in a very general way, it is both a theoretical and empirical discipline, and, at its best, is both at the same time. It need not be organised around method partly because commercial, globalised culture is so diffuse and fluid, and generates so many positions from which to engage it, and because, in cultural studies, theories and methods themselves adhere to the logic of fashion (if mediated by the education system), passing through it continually. For all that, cultural studies does consistently drift back towards the interpretative and empathetic methods of traditional hermeneutic disciplines, including the literary criticism to which (as we shall see) it owes so much – methods which, paradoxically, disavow the rigidity of method.

When, nonetheless, the concept of 'method', drawn from the social sciences (and routinely demanded in academics' research-funding applications), *is* made central to cultural studies' identity, it quickly becomes highly generalised. In his excellent book, *Inside Culture*, Nick Couldry, for instance, places method, which he thinks of as a 'path of reasoning', at the heart of cultural studies, since it provides the shared values or 'common framework with which we can recognise that we are in dialogue' (Couldry 2000, 143). This is obviously to differ from those who (like myself) think of cultural studies as basically anti-methodological, but it is worth noting where this stance takes Couldry. For him, cultural studies has a tripartite method: it is materialist and reflective (that is, it continually examines its own development and processes); it is anti-positivist (that is, it does not believe that culture can be accounted for in objective facts); and it is theoretically eclectic. In a sense this is to give the game away since it does not spell out a method unique to cultural studies. The claim that cultural studies is method-based expresses a particular orientation within it – or maybe just a hope.

Given this it seems natural to ask: if a discrete and stable set of methods do not characterise cultural studies, and if culture is so totalising and fluid a concept, where does cultural studies find its centre of gravity? One response is to contend that the theory established during the period of cultural studies' emergence (rather than method as such) provides a *lingua franca* for the global cultural studies community: the common ground from which debate, teaching and research can proceed, albeit without being an overarching monopoly. And there can be little doubt that much cultural studies shares an overlapping set of proper name references (Raymond Williams, Antonio Gramsci, Michel de Certeau, Stuart Hall, Michel Foucault, Edward Said, Paul Gilroy and so on) as collected in the standard textbooks, although many of these names mean more in Anglophone or French cultural studies than they do in, say, Asian cultural studies.

Another, more rewarding response would be to say that cultural studies is united not by a discrete set of theoretical references but by dual impulses which are vaguer than a method: a will to interpret the culture within the protocols of academic knowledge (providing evidence and citations for arguments; referring to well-recognised general concepts; implicitly or explicitly placing one's work within the disciplinary field; exposing one's writing to debate, and engaging in debate with others, etc.) as well as a (political) drive to connect with everyday life as lived outside the academy, and especially as lived by those with relatively little power or status. Indeed cultural studies at its best deals mainly with quite non-technical terms such as 'popular culture', 'racism', 'globalisation', 'heterosexuality' – words which have good equivalents in various languages and which are actively used outside the academy. But even here cultural studies' globalism can cause problems: some of these terms at least (multiculturalism, queer) have different circulations, references and connotations in different parts of the world, and these slight differences are easily lost sight of. Certainly too much insistence on cultural studies' own 'common culture' is likely to fall prey to the difficulties that always befall the quest for unity and coherence – the passing over of internal differences, the retreat into generality and abstraction, and the almost invisible transformation of supposed common features into regulatory norms.

The fallback position on defining cultural studies is nominalist: cultural studies is just what names itself as, and is recognised as, cultural studies. But we don't have to be quite so minimalist: I would point to two further features which help characterise the field, one which is recognised by Nick Couldry, the other which is not. The first characteristic feature of cultural studies is that it is, as I say, an *engaged* study of culture. By engagement – let me repeat – I mean a sensitivity to the ways in which culture is (in part) a field of power-relations involving centres and peripheries, status hierarchies, connections to norms that impose repressions or marginalisations. But I also mean a commitment to celebrating or critiquing cultural forms (often in relation to the social field in which they are produced), to producing accounts of culture that can be fed back into cultural production and/or to producing new connections between various cultural forms and people (mainly, of course, students) in 'ordinary life'.

It is because cultural studies is engaged that it belongs to the humanities rather than to the social sciences which claim to analyse their objects *objectively*. And it is because it is engaged that it can so easily become a factor in cultural production itself. Cultural studies has become an element in cultural work across many fields. For instance, the young black British artists of the 1980s – Chila Burman, Sonia Boyce, Isaac Julien, Keith Piper – who were engrossed by the theory being then produced by Homi Bhabha, Kobena Mercer, Paul Gilroy and others (McRobbie 1999, 6). Angela McRobbie has also noted that many of the young journalists working on the new magazines of the nineties aimed at young women had some training in media and cultural studies, which helped provide the framework in which they negotiated their workplace (McRobbie 1999, 28). American novelists such as Don Delillo and Jonathan Franzen are familiar with contemporary cultural theory, and to some degree undertake to instantiate it in their novels. Indeed in countries such as Australia and the UK, cultural studies is providing the basic understanding and interpretation of contemporary culture and society in art, design

9

and even fashion schools, and, as such, is presupposed in much work in these fields, especially in avant-garde work. The political sense of engagement merges surprisingly easily into this more neutral, almost economic sense of engagement.

The second ideal feature of cultural studies (which is recognised by Couldry) is that it ought to be self-reflective. It needs continually critically to examine itself, and in particular its relations to the educational system on the one side, and the non-academic cultural institutions on the other. This self-reflection is not so much a matter of method as an institutional requirement. Cultural studies needs to manage constant shifts in relations between its own home – the university – and transformations in the wider culture outside, and that need, presented to it by the sheer fact of its existence and its will to survival in the educational system, constitutes part of its project as it jostles older disciplines and long-established understandings of culture and education. This self-reflection routinely takes the form of an examination of its own history. Is cultural studies a specific discipline or does it exist across or outside established disciplines? Is it, for instance, better regarded not as a discipline but as a critical practice? In cultural studies such questions have not been secondary, they have helped to generate the discipline itself.

Disciplinarity

So questions about method and coherence quickly slide into questions of disciplinarity, debate over which remains fierce. Tony Bennett, for instance, has argued strongly that the incapacity to form a proper discipline will be regarded as institutional failure (Bennett 1998b, 533–534), while the consensus among those who came to the field early was that it ought to remain outside the constraints of disciplinarity. From that point of view, disciplinarity restricts the variety of topics, interests, positions, contexts and methods that the field can accommodate. There is no clear answer to this debate, partly because the status and function of disciplinarity in the humanities is changing. Let us remind ourselves that academic disciplines in the humanities and social sciences have never been unitary formations: they integrate various methods, objects of inquiry and professional interests. There is an important sense in which all disciplines are inter-disciplines. Once established they are compelled to emphasise differentiation and autonomy yet they remain joined to one another by at least some shared interests and methods – one can take the complex entanglements of and disjunctions between literary studies and history as an example. Discrete disciplines also remain connected through sub-disciplines that permeate across and connect their boundaries: social theory for instance belongs simultaneously to sociology and to cultural studies.

More importantly, disciplines are not simply defined by their intellectual projects: as Bennett recognises, they are institutions linked to units (departments, schools, faculties) in universities. It is difficult to generalise about disciplinarity and university systems since different countries have very different university systems (with different funding and governance arrangements) as well as different disciplinary investments. Here we strike at once the difficulty in making clear and true statements about such matters on a global scale. And disciplinarity is itself becoming downgraded in the university system: there is evidence that, worldwide, managers of what we can call, following Simon Marginson and Mark Considine, the 'enterprise university' are less and less focussed on disciplines (Marginson and Considine 2000). So increasingly disciplines flourish elsewhere than the university department or programme itself – and especially in journals and conferences. That's where academics and graduate students interact away from the classroom or departmental common spaces, and that's where cultural studies forms itself as a discipline. And, importantly, these sites are increasingly transnational.

The academic setting

So cultural studies is a discipline that has emerged in an administrative context which does not actively encourage disciplinarity. University managers do not see themselves as providing the settings for the flourishing of disciplines but rather, on the one side, as producing knowledge through research ultimately as a resource for national productivity, and, on the other, meeting the vocational needs of their students, now usually figured as consumers of education. Behind them, governments are typically concerned both to increase participation rates in post-compulsory education and to ensure that public funding is used in the national economic interest rather than for social purposes such as equality.

Thus universities are being administered with an emphasis on efficiency, productivity and accountability. Such moves squeeze the humanities (along with social and pure sciences), encouraging, in their case, departmental amalgamations, interdisciplinarity and courses which offer, at least putatively, clear pathways into employment. This favours cultural studies as against the older disciplines, and there can be no doubt that the rise of cultural studies has been in part the result of the post-1970s university managerialism, and the social forces behind it. There is, of course, a tension here: from within cultural studies, the discipline's rise is consistently narrated in terms of its struggle against elitism, Eurocentrism and cultural conservatism; yet from the outside it often looks like a beneficiary of the new market-orientated political economy and economistic models of university governance. Both views are justifiable: this is the first of the discomforting harmonies between cultural studies and neo-liberalism that we will encounter in this book – which provides evidence for cultural studies itself being, what ever else it is, a product of the hyper-fluid economy and culture of contemporary global markets.

I have said that the enterprise university is a worldwide phenomenon, but that needs qualification since the globalising of the university is creating new hierarchies within the international academy. In particular, the US academy, backed by the USA's military and ideological might, seems to be becoming more and more dominant. In the Anglophone world, but also to some degree in Asia and Latin America, theories and sub-disciplinary formations prosper to the degree that they are disseminated from and sanctioned by elite US universities. Yet, in those elite universities there are few anti-disciplinary pressures, and the traditional humanities remain strong, still in the business of distributing cultural capital to the most favoured social groups or to indi-viduals given the opportunity to join such groups. So cultural studies has not flourished institutionally in these universities, nor indeed in British or European elite universities. Where it does formally exist in the more rarefied sectors of the global university system (as in Harvard's Center for Cultural Studies), it tends to name a site where different disciplines meet: it gestures at a cross-disciplinarity rather than at even an inter-disciplinarity. There's a slight tension at work here. Cultural studies is no longer a marginal field – after all it has risen partly on the logic of neo-liberal governmental policies – but it remains shut out of the highest reaches of the global university system, which are largely protected from those policies.

Nor, of course, does the globalisation of cultural studies mean that it is positioned institutionally in the same way around the world, although most Anglophone accounts fail to register this sufficiently (see Stratton and Ang 1996). Indeed the humanities themselves don't everywhere take the form familiar from within the North American/European/British ex-colonies nexus. In Latin America they are usually covered by the term 'Facultad de Letras' (and because the politics of ethnicity has historically been relatively weak there, they have, for instance, taken relatively little interest in 'multiculturalism' and more interest in concepts such as 'hybridity'). In Asia, culture is studied largely in language or social science departments (see Yudice 2001, 218–219). Specifically, in the People's Republic of China, where the politics of resistance cannot easily be made academic, cultural studies is often dismissed as merely theoretical (although there is also great interest in it). This is one reason that in Asia especially cultural studies work depends more heavily on non- or quasi-academic settings than it does in, say, Britain. And certain key concerns of metropolitan cultural studies traditions are less apparent in the so-called 'third world', where the question of Westernisation, modernisation, and autonomous national identity and nation-building loom large. And also where academic secularity is less taken for granted.

In continental Europe itself, cultural studies, when thought of as the politically engaged study of culture, especially popular culture, is not as well established as it is in the Anglophone world. There, the use of cultural hierarchies to supplement economic hierarchies in the articulation of class structures (best described by the French sociol-ogist Pierre Bourdieu in his classic *Distinction*) remains too well entrenched. And in France in particular what Marc Fumaroli calls the 'cultural state' – the state that directs and promotes culture – is more developed than in any other capitalist country (see Fumaroli 1991). The post-war triumph of social welfarism across the European continent, along with the perceived threat of American cultural domination has meant that cultural values have not been the object of contest that they have been in the USA and UK. In Europe, anti-Americanism also plays its part in preventing academic disciplines asserting an affirmative relation to commercial culture. More specifically, in Germany critical theory, aimed primarily at critiquing capitalist culture, dominates; and in France the stand-off between speculative (as represented by Jean Baudrillard) and critical, empirical approaches to culture (as represented by Bourdieu) seems to delimit the field. So although French theorists have provided cultural studies with core concepts and methods, the discipline has not flourished in France. French thinkers such as Michel de Certeau and Foucault are especially important to the discipline because of the radical and unsettling thrust of their thought, but the cultural traditionalism that stimulated their radicalism is apparent in cultural studies' relative inconspicuousness in France.

But I will have more to say about differences in cultural studies globally in sections to come. Before that we need to have a stronger sense of the enterprise culture which is taking charge of globalising processes across the board.

Further reading

Chen 1998; Couldry 2000; Denning 2004; Hall, Morley and Chen 1996; Morley 2000.

Enterprise culture

Cultural studies reflects on itself so obsessively not just because it lacks a generally acknowledged set of methods, or because globalisation is dispersing and mobilising it, but also because, despite everything, it remains mystified about its own conditions of emergence. As already noted, those conditions are not quite adequately described in the often-told epic story of heroic dissident British intellectuals (Richard Hoggart, Raymond Williams, Stuart Hall, the Birmingham school) battling for democratisation against elitism and hegemony in the sixties and seventies. Or more global versions of this story such as Michael Denning's account of cultural studies as a product of the transnational 'new left' encounter with the explosive popular culture of the sixties (Denning 2004, 76–90). After all we have begun to see how university managerialism finds common cause with cultural studies. And to see how cultural studies is entwined with a new configuration of capitalist culture. But we need now to examine more carefully what that configuration – which I will call enterprise culture – actually is.

Enterprise culture is associated first with a rapid increase in the social presence of culture, economically, governmentally and conceptually – its positive re-weighting, as stock analysts might say. Contemporary societies have become, some authorities claim, 'culture-societies' (Schwengell 1991; Schulze 1992). Certainly the percentage of workers in cultural industries has increased markedly over the past decades, in Australia, for instance, by 23 per cent in the nineties alone. According to a recent UNESCO report, international trade in cultural goods has increased by a factor of 5 over the last twenty years (UNESCO 2001a, 4). Entertainment is said to be the USA's biggest export now. A large number of middle-class people in their twenties and thirties, making the difficult move from the education system to the workplace, are involved in some kind of creative work, which in many developed nations is supported by some kind of unemployment benefit (in some countries, creative workers and would-be creative workers have their own form of the dole) (see McRobbie 1999, 3–6). In most places in the world, every decade (and sometimes every year) there are, in relation to population growth, more television channels broadcasting longer hours, more movies, more books, more comics, more magazines, more tourist resorts, more lifestyle choices, more commodities sold on the basis of design, more records, more fashion brands, more computer games, more access to the World Wide Web, more sporting events, more celebrities in relation to total population than there ever were before.

This has had a profound impact on old high culture, which has become just another province within this larger field rather than its pinnacle. High culture is increasingly dependent on state subsidies – where it competes both with community arts and its cousin, the avant-garde. It confers less and less status upon its devotees. For almost everyone in Anglophone society, rich or poor, to go on an exotic adventure tour, for instance, offers more prestige than a familiarity with, say, George Eliot's novels or Jacobo Tintoretto's art or Felix Mendelssohn's music. So the academic disciplines that provided the skills fully to appreciate and contextualise Eliot, Tintoretto and Mendelssohn lose ground to disciplines which aim rather to provide entry into the cultural industries. In fact cultural studies often appeals to students for whom the old hierarchy of distinction, by which high culture possessed more cultural capital than popular culture, is not so much wrong and to be resisted as meaningless.

What exactly is this new enterprise culture? It's another term that points in two directions – first, to 'enterprise' and 'entrepreneurialism' as a rubric covering a wide band of social and economic activities, and, second, to the entrepreneurialisation of culture conceived more narrowly – in effect, as the totality of leisure activities. Both forms of enterprise culture emphasise the concept of the 'career' in which the old category of labour is replaced by one of self-organised, economically productive cultural agency. In this context, cultural studies is under pressure to present itself as preparing students with the skills required to embark on particular careers and at the same time productively to participate in the culture. From the entrepreneurial as well as from the leftist point of view, it is harder and harder to defend academic training as a site of scholarship for its own sake or as the preserver of received cultural standards. From the perspective of entrepreneurialism, academic study too seems to be a branch of the business of culture.

At another level, enterprise culture emphasises a set of specific personal and ethical qualities: self-sufficiency, appetite for risk, individualism, creativity and sense of adventure as well as self-control, financial expertise and management skills. Such an ethic is not confined to leisure activities of course (although it's there in adventure sports, etc.). It belongs to the world of work, which, especially in its salaried forms, is now saturated in culture also. The enterprise-culture ethic covers an accounting career almost as well as it does one in the arts, property or even academia. It is in these terms

that employers try to manage the cultures of their workplaces, since the cultural identities that workers bring to the workplace are seen to be either irrelevant or divisive –
except maybe where they instantiate 'diversity'.

Productivity depends on team spirit, the capacity to respond to the unforeseen, on
being 'proactive' rather than 'reactive'; on mood, pleasure, identification with
company aims, or to put it in more philosophical terms, on the sense that existential
wants are being satisfied at work: in a word – on culture. Work 'culture' also helps
displace the old Marxist understanding of labour as 'alienated', that is, a failing fully to
express an individual's needs and potential. And this emphasis on culture allows individual workers to accept specific protocols (e.g. performance reviews) set by
companies with a minimum of resistance. One persuasive school of thought, drawing
on the work of Michel Foucault, sees this turn to enterprise culture in the workplace as
a new form of 'governmentality' or 'governmental rationality' aimed at changing the
subjectivities of workers so that their lives themselves are perceived and executed as
enterprises (du Gay 1996, 56–58). But that paradigm risks losing sight of what attracts
people into enterprise culture: not just the promise of reward (behind which lies the
fear of failure), but the excitement of a challenge, the enticement of self-responsibility.

No easy political judgement of entrepreneurial culture is possible. The arguments
that it creates new subjects who possess less capacity for resistance or criticism of
society as a whole than did the social welfare or liberal ideologies that entrepreneurialism has largely replaced, or that it masks a radical increase in employment insecurity
and burn-out, or that it is mainly addressed to the relatively rich, while true, do not
end the story. Entrepreneurialism has encouraged (admittedly mainly relatively rich)
people to bring their talents to market and, more specifically, has enabled the increase
of cultural activity since the eighties. In the UK it has eased access to cultural industries
and other workplaces for those from outside the Oxbridge axis (partly because training
in these fields is relatively cheap, and there exist fewer barriers to entry than to the
professions); it has increased options about how and when to work; it has required
creative workers to take their audiences and their requirements increasingly seriously.
It has its own utopianism since it proposes a society of energetic individuals, both
supportive of (as consumers) and competitive with (as producers) one another,
fulfilling their personal dreams. And no less to the point, in the arts it is not as though it
has been destructive of an older system in which quality was systematically higher. (Of
course there exist exceptions to this, such as British television, where the move into
outsourcing of product and a greater attention to ratings even at the BBC has led to the
production of less well-thought-out and original programming, according to its own
audiences.)

In enterprise culture, cultural industries are routinely regarded as economic
contributors, as employers, as attractors of tourism and business, as agents in urban
regeneration, for instance. Which means that governments (in the vernacular sense)

get increasingly involved. Nations can themselves be branded culturally, as in Tony Blair's short-lived attempts to label Britain 'Cool Britannia' in 1998. Hobbies can quickly turn into small businesses, often with support from government agencies encouraging entrepreneurialism. Jobs in arts administration and project management, whose aim is to drum up business for cultural enterprises, proliferate. Furthermore entrepreneurialised culture is open to governmental intervention not just in order to encourage business by fixing conditions for funding ('accountability'), but once again in order to shape ways of life and values. Culture is regarded as a means through which governments can manage different communal values and traditions in society (Bennett 2001, 17). So, for example, multiculturalism became official policy in Australia during the 1980s while Mrs Thatcher mandated Shakespeare on the British school curriculum in the same decade. Once again it is possible to exaggerate the newness of this: in eighteenth-century London the economic benefits of a healthy theatre were often remarked upon, and government regulated the field (and censored product) much more stringently than today.

Culture wars

If entrepreneurialism has become the dominant cultural mode over the past twenty years or so, at least in the West (but not only – think of Singapore), and has begun to incorporate cultural studies into itself via the enterprise university, this does not mean that all other senses of culture have withered away. Multiculturalists and (as they say in the USA) 'minorities' use culture routinely in a more traditional sense, partly because, as Paul Gilroy contends, those who have been excluded from formal politics as well as many forms of economic activity take culture in that sense most seriously (see Gilroy 1987). But two other moments in which culture is conceptualised in different terms than it is in enterprise culture are worth drawing attention to immediately.

The first is Samuel Huntington's influential intervention into geopolitical theory in his *The Clash of Civilisations* (1997). Huntington argued that after the fall of the Soviet state, the dualistic politics of the Cold War, in which democratic capitalism was pitted against communism, has been replaced by the competition between five different blocs, each clustered around a 'core' state, distinguished this time not by economic – political orientation but, more profoundly, by culture. Huntington's understanding of culture shares much with traditional anthropology. For him, cultures are inherited and more or less immutable. Each society has a single culture. Each individual is wholly shaped by the single culture that they inherit. It is the very opposite of the mobile, fluid, market-directed, entrepreneurial, globalised culture that I have been invoking and to which contemporary cultural studies belongs. It's no accident that Huntington polemicises for monoculturalism, urging the USA to resist the 'divisive siren-calls of multiculturalism' (Huntington 1997, 40). A politics of cultural purity and its

17

obverse – the insistence on the sheer otherness of different cultures – is being promul-gated here, a politics which mirrors that of conservatives the world over. An account such as that of Huntington, which traps us into sealed traditions whose relation to one another is finally marked by incomprehension and suspicion, helps to reveal the progressive force in the cultural-studies and entrepreneurial concept of a mobile, fluid, commercialised culture.progressive force in the cultural-studies and entrepre-neurial concept of a mobile, fluid, commercialised culture.

The second important area in which 'culture' retains a rather different sense than the one it has within enterprise culture is that of the so-called 'culture wars' of the Anglophone West, whose heyday was the late eighties and early nineties, but which are by no means over. In fact there have been various culture wars, of which we can usefully distinguish three. The first is centred on questions of morality and censorship, with champions of 'permissiveness' or liberalism squaring off against guardians of decency and 'family values'. The second is centred on the risks to traditional heritage and cultural value posed by commercial culture. And the third is focussed on the threat to consensus and unified heritage implied by multiculturalism and migration. (We might add a fourth culture war, fought daily almost everywhere outside the USA: that between Americanisation and its enemies).

Each of these debates will be dealt with in more detail in the chapters that follow, though it is important to note that they are not simply different fronts of one war – there are many migrant proponents of multiculturalism, for instance, who oppose permissiveness. But the point that it is important to make here is that just as Huntington replaces questions of political and economic dominance with questions of culture in the realm of geopolitics, the conservative side in these various culture wars places questions of culture at centre stage inside the nation-state. It is as if, as political differences between the left and the right on traditional issues – welfarism and economic policy for instance – shrink, culture is thrust forward in its place as a stake for divisive debate. It is also as if, when schisms between Christian confessions (Protestantism and Catholicism) lose their venom, contests over secular culture replace them. In fact, each of the cultural wars is a response to the rise of enterpre-neurialised culture and the decline of culture considered as a set of standards. Again cultural studies has, almost without exception, resisted the conservative side in each of these fronts, in another example of its connection simultaneously to enterprise culture and to progressivism.

Further reading

Du Gay 1997; Lewis 1990; Lury 1996; Marginson and Considine 2000; McRobbie 1999; Readings 1996.

Genres and genealogies

.I have been writing so far mainly as if cultural studies was unified, even if it lacks a unifying method. But in fact cultural studies exists in very different forms, and the term 'cultural studies' is used in a variety of ways. As we have begun to see, different nations have developed different kinds of cultural studies. But there have also developed different cultural–political positions, different intellectual trajectories, different disciplinary alliances and different accounts of the cultural studies intellectual. Among these different forms, let me at once distinguish three national inflections of Anglophone cultural studies – British, American and Australian.

Given my insistence that cultural studies is globalising itself rapidly and needs to be understood in terms of new global flows it may seem odd that here I am, once again, emphasising the discipline's most established Anglophone national traditions. My reasons are, sadly, pragmatic and reflect political and commercial realities as much as intellectual ones. I do want to argue for British cultural studies having a particular importance to the field. But this is a book written in English and aimed primarily at American, Australian and British readers; my own competence and range is limited (I wish I knew more about the background of the kind of work that is now appearing in the *Journal of African Cultural Studies* for instance); and if cultural studies is appearing in different forms and out of different genealogies in many localities it can't be denied that the work which circulates most widely tends to refer back to what has been produced in the old Anglophone imperial nations. Flows of knowledge are by no means unidirectional – from the centre out – but it's not as if centres don't exert a centripetal force even on the resistance to Eurocentrism. To argue otherwise is merely wishful thinking.

British cultural studies

My own idealised sense of the field as the engaged, simultaneously theoretical and empirical study of contemporary culture from below or from the margins is basically borrowed from British cultural studies, which, as I say, has often (and for good reason) been regarded as the mother lode of the discipline globally. Most of all it was in the UK that culture became defined as simultaneously a way of life, a set of texts and an instrument of social division. And in Britain, the cultural studies academic has been consistently figured as something like an 'organic intellectual', that is, as a representative member of an oppressed or relatively powerless group – in the early days as marked by class, and later by gender, race or sexuality, later still by membership of a taste community or a subculture. He or she has a commitment to education as a tool for progressivist politics (British cultural studies emerges out of the worker's education movement) and is armed with theoretical and interpretative concepts that will enable an expanded understanding of any particular text or cultural situation.

The history of British cultural studies has been argued over repeatedly, and I don't intend to go through these debates again in detail here (see Turner 1996; Dworkin 1997; Steele 1997). But it is important to remember that cultural studies in Britain emerged from a Centre (at the University of Birmingham) funded by the owner of Penguin Books, which was at that time popularising quality literature and which was first headed up by Richard Hoggart, whose *The Uses of Literacy* (1957) became one rallying-point for the new field. At this point cultural studies was in dialogue with a form of literary criticism developed by F.R. Leavis. Leavisism (as it was called) asserts that language contains residual meanings that have not been wholly incorporated into debased modern commercial culture; it retains trace elements able to express more communal and harmonious ways of living. In a word, language remains a bulwark against modern mechanisation (Mulhern 2000, 18). For Leavis, this was most true of literary language, so that literary criticism, based on immersion in great literature, was the strongest basis for cultural critique – however puzzling such a view might seem to us today.

It was Raymond Williams who rejected the notion that literary language contains this kind of ethical capital and turned attention away from literature to culture. In *Culture and Society* (1958) he analysed the history in which 'culture' had long been imagined as a transcendent bulwark against modern society's commercialisation and democratisation. He showed how, in the period between Edmund Burke and Leavis (i.e. between about 1760 and 1960), the concept of absolute culture became narrower and narrower, its defenders less and less connected to powerful social forces and the rhetoric in praise of it more and more shrill. A sense of culture as 'ordinary' had been lost. So his project was to reconnect culture in the sense of art and literature with the culture of the ordinary (partly out of a so-called 'new left' rejection of official Leninist Communist Party doctrine which privileged the Communist Party itself above the ordinary worker). This marks *the* key moment in the emergence of British cultural studies.

The problem with *Culture and Society* is that Williams himself was unable to jettison culture as defined in the conservative movement after Burke because he shared its negative views of the organisation of modern society. *Culture and Society* ends by arguing that we need an expanded notion of culture as 'a whole way of life' (a phrase coined by T.S. Eliot, now given a radical twist, that would be developed further by Williams in his next book, *The Long Revolution*), but also, misguidedly as it turned out, that working-class solidarity might create its own democratic variation of high culture against capitalist, market-orientated modernity.

Later in his career, as he outlined what he called his 'cultural materialism', Williams' main theme became the relations between the political, the economic and the cultural. Cultural materialism developed out of a multifaceted critique of the Marxian base/superstructure theory. That theory states that changes in the 'super-structure' (i.e. culture and 'ideology' in the sense of social values and stereotypes) are determined by changes in the 'base' (i.e. the economy). Against that, Williams argued that (shifts in) economic structures cannot explain (shifts in) cultural organisation and content in anything like the requisite amount of detail. Cultural forms and events are more various, the specific possibilities available to cultural workers more abun-dant than any reference to economic foundations can account for. Furthermore Williams embraced the line that the base/superstructure model under-emphasises the materiality of culture itself. For him, culture consists of practices that help shape the world: they too are material: 'The word is as material as the world', to cite a catchphrase of another of cultural studies' founders, Stuart Hall. And finally, Williams decried the separation of the base from the superstructure as such. For him, both are aspects of a larger social whole that continually interact with one another and constantly mutate.

In his early books Williams' theory remains based on the assumption that societies are interrelated wholes insofar as all social practices are also cultural practices, that is, practices that make collective meaning. But this kind of argument – labelled 'cultur-alism' – was under attack by the early seventies. Williams himself turned to the work of the pre-war Italian communist Antonio Gramsci to problematise his early 'organic' culturalism, especially Gramsci's concept of 'hegemony'. For Gramsci, hegemony helped to explain why class conflict was not endemic despite the fact that power and capital were so unevenly distributed and the working class (in Italy, particularly the southern peasantry) led such confined lives. Gramsci argued that the poor partly consented to their oppression because they shared certain cultural dispositions with the rich. Cross-class alliances or 'blocs' could form around interests in particular circumstances or 'conjunctures', the most important such hegemonic 'cultural front' being popular nationalism. Yet hegemony, especially as Williams glossed it, was not a mere belief, interest or 'ideology'. It covered (as he wrote), 'a whole body of practices and expectations, our assignments of energy, our ordinary understanding of the nature

21

of man and his world' (Williams 1980b, 38). Crucially, it offered the promise, and sometimes the opportunity, for change. Hegemony was bound to beliefs and passions so deep as to form the very substance of a practice of life.

During the seventies Gramscian thought battled with another Marxist mode of social analysis, dubbed 'structuralist'. Structuralist analyses abandoned the category of culture, and offered an account of society (heavily influenced by the revisionist French communist, Louis Althusser) as an assemblage of 'relatively autonomous' (i.e. only loosely connected and self-determining) institutions – the education system being the most important of these – which in turn produced forms of knowledge and value (so-called 'signifying practices') that, in the last instance, were organised so as to perpetuate capitalist relations of production.

The struggle between Gramscianism and structuralism gradually dissolved during the eighties. At that point Stuart Hall (who took over Raymond Williams' role as British cultural studies' most influential theorist and who had worked through these intellec-tual debates most carefully and articulately) was working with a model which took account of a pluralist, de-centred, 'post-Fordist' society, in which different social and cultural fields (economic, political, cultural) are in constant and constantly changing interaction with one another, without any field determining the others, although the economy continues to provide the constraints within which the others move (Hall 1996, 44). (This is the kind of model I invoke in slightly different terms above.) In this model, particular interactions between social and cultural fields are local, and need not have implications for society as a whole. Rather, each interaction has power effects insofar as it conditions individual lives. Furthermore, individuals have a number of different, often mutable identities rather than a single fixed identity, and this spread of identities, and the occasions for invention and recombination that it throws up, form a ground for political and cultural agency.

Indeed, leaving this particular theory aside, the understanding of individual and communal agency shifted over the years. Take as an example a relatively early work from the Birmingham school such as the collectively written *Policing the Crisis* (Hall *et al.* 1978). This showed that the media panic around a 1973 mugging in Handsworth by a young black man helped the state to inaugurate policies that controlled not so much crime but black male youth as such. It demonstrated that ideology – thought of as the set of generally accepted beliefs and stereotypes – was constructed by the interaction of different, and sometimes conflicting, forces, many with long and complex histories, and worked towards the hegemony of racist values and constraints on black people's lives. Here black youth were seen as subjects of ideology, policing, media scares and so on, rather than as players negotiating and opposing dominant forces in the social field.

This vision of victim passivity was to change in cultural studies of the eighties, when individuals came to be regarded as agents rather than as subjects of larger ideological and social structures. As a result, the 'politics of representation' became paramount. In this move, representation took on two meanings: it referred, first, to the way that particular social groups were represented, especially in the media, and the political gains to be won by critiquing such representations where they stigmatised; second, it referred to the way in which representative politics disempowered specific interests and identities and reduced political agency, especially that of minorities in the American sense.

The next step away from subaltern passivity for British cultural studies was towards 'ethnography' – that is, the study not of representations (such as TV shows or advertisements) or of institutions but the analysis of how culture is used and understood by actual individuals and groups. Ethnography takes two forms. It can be 'quantitative', which involves large-scale surveys and (usually) statistical analysis. However this kind of research ultimately belongs more to social sciences than to cultural studies. It can also involve interviews with small groups or individuals – so-called 'qualitative' research. By and large British (and Australian) cultural studies turned to this latter form of ethnography in the late seventies, in a move that marks its most profound break with predominantly textual and archival humanities disciplines such as literary criticism and social theory. At first, cultural-studies ethnography concentrated on how audiences of varying class, gender or ethnicity accepted or rejected the political slant of news programmes and the like. But partly because it soon became clear that the less-privileged members of society often preferred conservative programmes, it moved on to the impact of television, reading, music, etc. on the everyday life of consumers, drawing attention to the pleasures, evaluations, fulfilments, bondings and constraints involved in cultural life. By the nineties, much British cultural studies ethnography involved reporting on fans of particular genres, by researchers who were themselves fans as well as academics – in a word, organic intellectuals for taste subcultures.

While the trajectory of British cultural studies remains especially important to cultural studies, because it was in the UK that the contemporary field was first institutionally defined, it is fair to say that British cultural studies has now become just another province of global cultural studies. And it is now limited in particular by its increasing focus on Britain itself. As the discipline has globalised, and as universalising theories have become increasingly difficult to sustain, British cultural studies has tended to retreat into the culture of its own nation-state.

US cultural studies

Cultural studies has come to mean something rather different in the USA than in Britain, although versions of British cultural studies have been and are pursued in the USA, notably by James Carey (from within mass communications), by Lawrence Grossberg and, from within American Studies, by George Lipsitz (whose career begins in the labour movement) (see Carey 1983 and 1997; Grossberg 1997; Lipsitz 1990).

23

There have been many attempts to provide a specifically American genealogy for cultural studies (see as an example Grossberg 1996). Perhaps the most convincing effort has been that by Michael Denning, who attempted to corral the legacy of thirties Popular Front intellectuals for cultural studies, thinkers who certainly were crucial to the development of post-war American studies (Denning 2004, 136–142). (The 'Popular Front' was an anti-fascist alliance of left forces that included communist and non-communist activists and claimed to represent the popular will.) It is also possible to show that early twentieth-century pragmatists such as John Dewey paid serious and progressive attention to the relation with lived culture and social justice and actively sought to build institutions to expand cultural horizons among workers. This task was further developed by Marxian sociologists such as C. Wright Mills (whose doctoral thesis was on Deweyian pragmatism). Mills had a stronger grasp of class and power than Dewey; he popularised the term 'elite' and turned his attention (in a negative way) to 'mass culture'. This left-wing intellectual tradition continued to influence figures such as the seminal feminist Betty Friedan, who emerged from the labour movement in the sixties and whose work feeds into cultural studies as we know it today.

On a different track one could also make a strong case to bring the African American leader W.E.B. Du Bois into the stream of American cultural studies via sixties black-power intellectuals such as Le Roi Jones. Or it could be shown that, in journals such as *Politics* and *Partisan Review*, anti-communist, left-wing 'New York intellectuals' of the post-war years (notably Dwight Macdonald), who had loose connections with the Jewish exiles from Nazi Germany such as Max Horkheimer (of the Frankfurt School), paid attention to culture in ways which have some similarity to Leavis, Orwell and Hoggart in Britain. Or, finally, there were writers such as Robert Warshow, Manny Farber and Parker Tyler, who treated popular culture (and especially the movies) much more sympathetically than the *Partisan Review* crowd and who became mediators between journalism and the growing academic field of American Studies.

But the effort to promote an American lineage for cultural studies proper is a little strained, and invites the question 'Why bother?' Why draw national pride into the debate? The fact is that the forms of analysis developed by Williams and Hall (drawing upon work by Gramsci, Michel de Certeau, Althusser, Foucault, etc.) were unique and specific, and implicitly articulated against the humanist frameworks of the traditional left, including the American left. And these indigenous history-building accounts often slide over the fact that the traditional disciplines, armoured by an elaborate 'professionalism', are even stronger in the USA than they are in Latin America, Asia, Britain or Australia.

Today in the USA cultural studies is typically associated with 'minority' scholars, that is, with multiculturalism and the analysis of race and power. (Here, of course, 'minority' has a completely different referent than it did for F.R. Leavis, for whom 'minority culture' meant the beleaguered literary culture of those charged with resisting mass communication; and something else again for the French theorist Gilles Deleuze, for whom it meant something more like simply 'marginal'.)

While cultural studies in the USA can mean the study of popular culture, Rey Chow has argued that four rather different topics have been especially important in marking it out as American (see Chow 1998, 2–4). The first is the 'postcolonial' critique of Western representations of non-Western cultures, as pioneered by Edward Said in his book *Orientalism* (1978). The second, following Gayatri Spivak's path-breaking work, is a concern with the subaltern (that is, the powerless and dominated), and an analysis of how gender, race, cultural otherness and class combine to fix subalterneity (Spivak 1988). The third is an analysis of 'minority discourse', that is an attention to the expressive voices of subordinated 'others'. And last is the embrace of 'hybridity' (about which see pp. 150–2 below). In Britain and Australia such topics would as likely as not fall under a different disciplinary rubric. They might well be thought of as belonging to postcolonialism, multiculturalism or, perhaps, ethnic studies rather than simply to cultural studies.

In the USA cultural studies is less obsessed with America itself than British cultural studies is obsessed with Britain, perhaps because the USA is a global power and attracts more staff and students internationally. In this context, it is important to note that the USA is also where 'area studies' are strongest, that is the study of specific regions from an interdisciplinary point of view, which balance a sensitivity to the 'authority and authenticity of native experience' as Harry Harootunian puts it, with a potential usefulness for official foreign policy (Harootunian 2000, 41; see also Miyoshi and Harootunian 2002). These regions are supposed to form roughly discrete and coherent unities requiring development. Cultural studies, which emphasises the mobility of, and interactions between, different cultures, and which attempts to speak from below, productively problematises area studies even when it enters into dialogue with them – a problematisation that has been debated most effectively in journals such as *Public Culture*. Nonetheless the preponderance of area studies, along with the hierarchical nature of the US university system which is less state-managed than in most other countries, has helped sideline cultural studies there.

Australian cultural studies

Australian cultural studies emerges out of British rather than US cultural studies. It was imported by a stream of young British academics who went to Australia looking for jobs in the late seventies and early eighties (Tony Bennett, John Fiske, John Hartley, Colin Mercer and David Saunders among others). They found a thriving intellectual import culture, working outside or on the margins of the academy and focussed on the latest trends in Europe, notably what the latest Althusserians were doing or where Foucault was at, and whose most active figures included Ian Hunter and Meaghan

25

Morris. As it turned out, cultural studies went on to be more successful in the Australian academic system than in any other. This has meant that its claim to radical political value has been harder to maintain: it has quickly been normalised there.

Nonetheless, in an influential essay introducing the collection *Australian Cultural Studies: a Reader*, John Frow and Meaghan Morris argued that Australian cultural studies was characterised by its capacity to view 'imaginary social unities' as dangerous and 'to think of cultures as processes which divide as much as they bring together' (Frow and Morris 1993, ix). In this light Australian cultural studies carried out the work of demystification not dissimilar to that of older Marxian theories which placed class at the heart of all social formations and critiqued images of reconciled or unified culture as illusory, as products of false consciousness. For Frow and Morris, it is not class but migrant/settled and coloniser/colonised divisions that are at the core of the local discipline's concerns, pushing aside interests in, say, popular culture.

Whatever the case in the early nineties, it is hard to see it like that now, despite important work on migrant culture being produced by (for instance) Ien Ang (2001) and Ghassan Hage (1998) and a new generation of indigenous intellectuals – Tony Birch, Marcia Langton and Philip Morrissey for instance – who are articulating new understandings of contemporary aboriginal culture consequent to pioneering work by Stephen Muecke and Eric Michaels (whose *Bad Aboriginal Art* remains essential reading for anyone working in the field anywhere) (see Muecke 1992; Michaels 1994).

Nowadays Australian cultural studies is increasingly normalised, concentrating on cultural policy studies (discussed on pp. 73–7) and, often uncritically, on popular culture and the media. Indeed it is in Australia that the celebration of popular culture as a liberating force (about which more below) first took off through Fiske and Hartley's contributions. The young populists of the seventies now hold senior posts and what was pathbreaking is becoming a norm. The readiness of a succession of Australian governments to encourage enterprise universities has empowered the older tertiary technical training departments in such areas as communications, allowing them to have an impact on more abstract and theorised cultural studies in ways that appear to have deprived the latter of critical force. Furthermore, the structure of research funding, which asks even young academics to apply for grants, has had a conformist effect. Perhaps Australian cultural studies offers us a glimpse of what the discipline would be like were it to become relatively hegemonic in the humanities.

Local studies

These national versions of cultural studies need to be differentiated from the quasi-disciplines defined by their focus on specific nations or communities, such as Chicano/a Studies, British Studies and American Studies, all of which can be thought of as 'local studies'. Confusingly, local studies may have sub-formations which narrow their focus further – to just culture, as for instance Chicano/a Cultural Studies and British Cultural Studies. Thus a recent set of anthologies published by Oxford University Press under the titles *British Cultural Studies*, *American Cultural Studies* and so on do not really belong to cultural studies in the sense discussed here (cultural studies 'proper'); they simply introduce students to British and American culture from a number of social science and humanities perspectives. These academic formations have been developed because they can be packaged in the classroom economically and efficiently, often to students not majoring in the humanities or social sciences or to students in non-research institutions. For this reason, they have not achieved the status of established research-based disciplines. They have also tended to work with more essentialist notions of national identity and, often (as with Australian Studies), with an open nationalist bias. Among local studies, however, American Studies stands out: it has long been the most professionalised of these disciplines at the same time as having real roots in the left, although its national limits and tendency to resist theory have meant that its exchanges with cultural studies proper have been limited (Maddox 1999).

In some cases, however, cultural studies proper has emerged within local studies. Take cultural studies in Hong Kong as an example. It has been concerned mainly with the question of Hong Kong's exceptionalism: with analysing the way that Hong Kong's long history as a British colony, its fierce commitment to capitalism and the global export markets, and its role since 1997 as a mediating economy between the People's Republic of China (PRC) and the rest of the world has placed it on the border of the West and Asia (see Erni 2001; Chan 1995; Chew 2001). From an outsider's point of view Hong Kong cultural studies, as for British cultural studies, can seem a little parochial. But there can be no doubt that its local success as an academic discipline is a reflex to the need for the society to orientate itself in the world during unstable times, to maintain the kind of intellectual capital required to produce for audio-visual export markets, and, no less importantly, to give itself the conceptual tools with which to accommodate itself to, or (carefully) resist, the PRC.

In addition to such national and local streams of cultural studies (and I will deal with certain other cultural studies in the section on cultural studies' pasts below), it is important briefly to single out two further cultural-studies strands which are determined not by geography but by the discipline's relation to anti-elitism and to ordinariness.

Cultural populism

As we have begun to see, cultural populism is a strand of cultural studies especially associated with the Australian-based John Fiske and John Hartley (see Fiske 1989; Hartley 1992; for a critique, see McGuigan 1992 and Kellner 1995). It supposes that popular culture is not merely the opposite of high culture but also of dominant culture,

27

which means that, for it, championing the popular has political value (Mulhern 2000, 138). Thus, in a famous instance, in the late 1980s John Fiske spoke of the libratory force of Madonna's use of masquerade (Fiske 1987). From the perspective of radical populism, popular culture always acts against hegemony, thought of here as elitist domination. It inverts the various traditional 'minority' accounts of high culture, which regard high culture as a bulwark against a trivial mass culture. Such a position has become harder to maintain in the age of enterprise culture, not simply because high culture is losing relative value but because, as we have begun to see, popular culture has itself increasingly become dispersed into niches, and is increasingly hybridising itself and soliciting a wider range of audience responses (see pp. 193–202).

Everyday life

The strand of cultural studies concerned with everyday life emerges from an earlier twentieth-century intellectual tradition that attempted to theorise everyday life in order to understand – and to counteract – the upheavals of modern existence. Perhaps the first key moment here comes with French surrealism, the avant-garde movement which, during the inter-war period, aimed to reveal mysteries secreted in the mundane (mysteries in the spiritual sense rather than the Sherlock Holmes sense – although, as the surrealists knew, detective fiction tends to lead us into the heart of the everyday's dark side). At more or less the same time, the realisation that something of value could be wrested from the familiar, the routine, combined with a fear that everyday life itself was under threat from modernity helped motivate an amazing, large-scale organisation in Britain: the Mass Observation movement of the 1940s which called upon the community itself to record the routines of ordinary life across the nation (Highmore 2002).

Closer still to cultural studies, the French communist theorist, Henri Lefebvre, created everyday life as a category for academic social theory in the 1940s and in response to the surrealists. For him (as a receptive reader of the Hungarian theorist Georg Lukács and his pathbreaking work), the everyday is where workers' 'alienation' is lived out: divided, as life under capitalism is, between work and leisure. For Lefebvre, capitalist work, in its specialisation and repetition, cannot fulfil workers' full human potential (which is why they are 'alienated' from their true potential selves) and leisure becomes just an occasion for recuperation, for regaining the energy to go on working in order to keep capitalist profits rolling in. Indeed, for Lefebvre, everyday life is a product of capitalist modernity: previously life had been ritualised, touched by cosmic reverence as well as by an assured and participatory belief that vital traditions were being maintained – which meant that life was never ordinary in our sense today. Modern everyday life emerges in the emptiness of a rootless social order designed primarily to produce economically. Nonetheless, and for all that, it remains a space where people have a residual capacity to act freely, and where political domination peters out. Hence everyday life is ambiguous: it is less meaningful than it ought to be, but it is where autonomy and resistance to the system still have some kind of chance (see Lefebvre 1991).

Lefebvre's pioneering notion of everyday life is difficult to grasp because he calls upon it to concretise both the damage sustained by modern capitalist society and the possibilities for insubordination and transformation within modern capitalism. Certainly his 'everyday life' is a much more nuanced notion than that implied by Raymond Williams and Richard Hoggart's reverence for the 'ordinary' and their relatively straightforward efforts to locate cultural value and solidarity within ordinary life. The category of everyday life in later cultural studies has had to negotiate between the complex category it inherited from Lefebvre and the more simple category it inherited from Williams. And it has done so mainly via the work of Michel de Certeau, a Jesuit priest and historian of Christian mysticism, whose book, *The Practices of Everyday Life*, translated into English in 1984, had an enormous impact on cultural studies in the late eighties and early nineties. What was appealing about de Certeau for cultural studies theorists was that he depoliticised cultural resistance and extended the concept of individual agency. For him, individuals may practice all kinds of 'ruses' in their dealings with society. He argues that the networks of controls and meanings through which individuals pursue their social existence have become increasingly powerful and rationalised but still remain full of gaps. So there are still circumstances where it is possible to act outside of – or even against – the system's logics, even if these occasions are normally concealed. Such occasions are tactical (improvised from within everyday life) rather than strategic (determined by reason and planning from outside the flow of everyday life). They require what de Certeau calls 'arts of making' (*arts de faire*) which create something fresh, unexpected, expressive and usually defiant out of the forms of work or consumption that are demanded of us (de Certeau 1984, xii–xix): examples include an employee using her employer's resources and time for her own ends without formally stealing or cheating. De Certeau's framework was extended, in particular by the Australian theorist Meaghan Morris, to cover a range of still more casual cultural activities (Morris 1988 and 1998).

More recently another concept of life has emerged within cultural theory – Georgio Agamben's 'bare life'. Agamben's notion refers to anonymous biological life, and he uses it, following Foucault, to show how modernity may be understood as the increasing politicisation of the concept of life and of the capacity of sovereign power (that is, the state) to intervene in the lives of its citizens at the level of their most basic biological functions (Agamben 1998). It is not clear how useful this concept will be for cultural studies. A version of it can be found in Michael Hardt and Antonio Negri's bestseller *Empire*, which contends that, under current globalisation and deploying the new technologies, basic productive human life is at last on the threshold of overcoming the restraints of national difference and class oppression worldwide. But here 'life' is very remote from the everyday customs theorised by Williams. It is a metaphysical notion being called upon to do abstract political work, rather than a category expressed in quotidian existence, embedded in history and politics, which can provide a context for critical analysis and action (Hardt and Negri 2000).

Cultural studies and its disciplinary neighbours

Cultural studies also exists as an element alongside (and sometimes within) other, more securely institutionalised disciplines. In particular, it has complex and intimate relations with literary studies, media studies, anthropology, sociology, geography, history, political theory and social policy. I will deal with geography and history in the chapters on time and space (see Parts 2 and 3 respectively). So I want briefly to describe its relations with literary studies, sociology and anthropology here. Let us focus briefly first on literary studies. In English departments, especially those in the USA, 'cultural studies' has tended to become a successor to deconstruction, feminism, postcolonialism and the new historicism, just as if it were another way of 'doing literature'. In effect it means a more extensive set of objects for analysis – one which includes popular texts, alongside an understanding of literature as a cultural product. At its best, the 'cultural studies' turn has helped literary studies move on from the production of endless 'readings' of individual texts to examining reading as a form of life for different communities and individuals in different times and places. But of course it would be wrong to think that cultural studies is primarily a branch of literary studies. Not to put too fine a point on it, that way of thinking is finally an expression of literary studies' will-to-power.

Cultural studies has more difficult relations with sociology and anthropology. From sociology's side, cultural studies is often seen to be a primarily literary discipline, tinged with postmodernism and post-structuralism, light on empirical research and innocent of statistical analyses. From the cultural studies side, sociology aims at an impossible value-neutrality and too often falls prey to the positivist assumption that facts and data describe social reality independently of engagement and value. Sociology is also seen to deaden culture by disengaging from it. A great deal of sociology, from a cultural studies point of view, seems to consist of reductive abstractions. Recently sectors within cultural sociology have attempted to rationalise the cultural field by bringing overarching social theories to bear on it, in a conscious effort to supplant cultural studies' supposed anarchy (see Smith 1998). In fact however, some sectors of sociology have absorbed elements of cultural studies (let the chapter on Raymond Williams in Anthony Giddens' *In Defence of Sociology* [1996] stand as an instance of that) and much cultural studies is intertwined with sociology. For instance Paul Willis's *Learning to Labour* (1977), an important book arguing that working-class boys' resistance to schooling was a rational strategic response to the constraints into which they were born, has become a classic in both disciplines (Long 1997).

Cultural studies has had more impact on anthropology than on sociology, both because the classical objects of anthropologists' research – 'natives' whose societies and cultures are relatively unaffected by colonial or Western impacts – are being absorbed into global networks, and because today a supposedly scientific study of such cultures is politically insupportable. After all it implicitly places the 'native' in a position of passivity and subordination. Once 'other' cultures are regarded as integrated within Western modernity (which need not mean that they lose their specificity and agency), and once visiting scholars refuse to take the position of the objective scientist in relation to them, then anthropology becomes difficult to distinguish from cultural studies (see Marcus 2001; for good examples of cultural-studies-inflected anthropology, see Ivy 1995 and Tsing 1993). At this point, arguments between the two disciplines tend to occur over anthropology's claim that research should be based on a particular kind of fieldwork – so-called 'participant observation' – in which researchers share their subjects' life-worlds. But more fundamentally, anthropology seems by and large to have remained attached to the notion that the cultures and societies that it studies are autonomous and systematisable wholes (for a brief history and critique of this belief see Clifford 1988, 1–25). This is not the case for cultural studies, which, as we know, now deals with its objects (urban rap subcultures or television audiences for *Big Brother* for instance) as *loosely* bound together, both in continual process and in dynamic interaction with other formations, and about which the cultural studies academic may simultaneously hold a number of rather different positions. For all that, there is no doubt that the disciplines are becoming increasingly entwined.

Political theory and postmarxism

Cultural studies has also been developed by importing methods and ideas from less well-established fields, notably from political theory. Over the last decade or so, among the most important of such borrowings has been what is often called 'postmarxism', whose traces remain evident in much cultural studies with a theoretical bent. Postmarxist political theory was developed by theorists such as Ernesto Laclau, Judith Butler and Slavoj Zizek, who like those working within cultural studies itself, were jettisoning traditional Marxism with its emphasis on class struggle and the role of the proletariat, and its insistence on the determining power of economic relations. The movement emerged as a criticism of the last widely circulated Marxist theory – Louis Althusser's notion of 'ideology' (Sim 1998 and 2000). Althusser's formulation of ideology was characteristic of the sixties in that it insisted that the personal (or, better, the subjective) and the political could not be pulled apart. This was not an argument that the circumstances of our everyday life relations are constrained by structures open to political reform, but that our images of the world are themselves politically nuanced. The fact that we don't know or think that this is the case is a sign precisely of how powerful the politics which inflects our

31

sense of the real actually is. Because, for Althusserians, images, social stereotypes, unexamined norms, media stories and vernacular forms of discourse such as jokes communicate political values, politics is not confined to the institutions in which politicians work and which political scientists study. Politics is everywhere. Indeed, for Althusser, individual identity is itself a function of ideology. It is only by identifying with ideologically presented models of selfhood – 'subject positions' – that people acquire a social identity. We recognise ourselves in the images of people like us that are communicated to us through the media and elsewhere. These images beckon and seduce us (technically speaking, they 'interpellate' us) as they invite us to accept their version of who we are. And ultimately what draws subjects into this process of identification is their desire for wholeness and coherence, a desire driven by a lack of secure grounding in this world – which Althusser, following the French psychoanalyst Jacques Lacan, theorised in psychoanalytic terms.

At its heart, postmarxism remains Althusserian, although it has accepted the most commonly expressed critique of Althusser's work – that it reduces the agency and freedom of individuals by seeing them as reflexes of ideology. Then too Althusserian theory seems to imply a contradiction: the individual needs to pre-exist the processes of identification for those processes to work at all, so how can s/he be formed by them? For postmarxists such as Zizek, identities are never securely fixed. We may recognise ourselves as placed in relation to race, nation, ethnicity, religion, locality, gender, etc. but there is something left over once we are identified as black, female, Zambian, Protestant, etc. From this perspective we don't have identities, but rather processes of identification, and, once again, we are driven into these processes because social structures do not meet all the needs of subjectivity – needs which can never be wholly met, since subjectivity is constituted by the trace of the violence through which individuals are separated from their mothers and are motivated by *desire*. At the same time, ideology is fragmented. It becomes not a unified thing but a plethora of different images, discourses and subject positions which do not necessarily cohere or work to the same ends or agree on values or what gives pleasure.

So, the terms in which individuals make sense of themselves are insecure: self-groundings promise more than they can deliver (they have a 'surplus of meaning' as Lacan put it). This is true too of communities, which, when they claim unity, are imagined and fragile constructs, 'phantasmatic signifiers' presenting themselves as stable and coherent only by performative effort or constant ideological and psychic work through which differences are repressed and 'others' are excluded. This line of thought contains a rebuke to those forms of progressive politics that have presupposed, or aimed at, impossibly unified communities: a certain feminist dream that all 'women' share the same wants and needs for example. And it implies that political movements will always be alliances of impermanent and heterogeneous groups drawn together on specific occasions for specific objectives.

Postmarxism is a speculative mode of analysis based on a universalising account of subjectivity which often seems to be not much more than the rearrangement of standard concepts from the history of (Hegelian/psychoanalytic) European philosophy. But it feeds so deeply into cultural studies because it allows for an account of the relation between social structures, political power and subjectivity more complex than that available in the traditional social sciences. The postmarxist subject eternally slides across and between codes and structures, restlessly acting on the symbolic and political world in order to transform it because that world cannot fulfil desire. Politically, postmarxism is useful because it does not regard the subjects of politics (the collectivities who possess political will) as having fixed identities across time; nor, for postmarxism, is the aim of politics the institution of a stable regime based on eternally valid principles or rights. In its contingency and open-endedness, with its shifting alliances, postmarxist politics mirrors hyper-fluid culture. Another way of putting this would be to say that, in spite of itself, postmarxist theory, like cultural studies, mimics capitalism's restlessness and formidable powers of innovation and destruction. And that is why postmarxism and cultural studies can cross-fertilise one another.

Cultural studies in the public sphere

I have been concentrating on cultural studies' relations with other academic fields and disciplines. But of course it also has relations with non-academic institutions, including potential employers of students, cultural producers and the media. Of these the last has received most attention, and indeed debate about relations between cultural studies academics, journalists and so-called public intellectuals (that is, intellectuals with a significant media profile) have been intense. At stake has been the following question: How can cultural studies claim to be an engaged and, in Edward Said's term, worldly practice if it remains stuck in the fasts of the academy? There have been a number of suggestions that cultural studies academics have failed to fulfil their responsibility to the public, having taken flight into theory and jargon. From this point of view, academics need to lift their public profile, popularise themselves and make themselves available to the media.

Something like the opposite is sayable also: that cultural studies is too journalistic and needs to restore analytic and critical distance between it and its objects (Savage and Frith 1993). Still another position is that the academic cultural critic is essentially deluded: the position of distanced authority from which s/he writes is a chimera. And for those who take that line, it may seem that journalists, being closer to the day-by-day shifts in cultural production and being required to write for mainly non-academic readerships, are better placed to evaluate culture than academics, who necessarily remain committed to academic abstraction and analysis. Another, somewhat similar, argument is that intellectuals in general have been marginalised, that they are no longer

33

called upon to provide cultural leadership and that a great deal of contemporary theory (which makes of the world a more decentred and disordered place than it once was) is an expression of intellectuals' loss of power (Bauman 1988).

Once more there is no correct position in these kinds of debates. By what criteria, for instance, could one judge whether we have too few – or too many – public intellectuals? (I personally incline to the 'too many' side insofar as public intellectuals often function as a source of cheap copy for the media, filling space that would be better set aside for well-researched but more expensive stories by journalists themselves.) Or how might one balance, on the one side, the various limits and pressures under which journalists operate as employees of media conglomerates whose product – the story – is required to help their managers meet returns on capital targets by delivering audiences to advertisers, against, on the other side, the pressures and limits that produce self-perpetuating, academic, critical rhetoric, whether this be, say, rhetoric deploring commodified culture or rhetoric celebrating hybridity and the crossing of borders?

In this situation it is difficult to do anything but fall back on almost banal principles. It is desirable to encourage the circulation of different voices and discourses, academic and non-academic, in the interests of social justice. It is especially desirable to encourage media commentary (whether by journalists or academic intellectuals) which attempts to connect social questions to cultural ones in ways that encourage a wide variety of expressive capabilities (which is one way of defining much of cultural studies). After all the mainstream media is not especially good at this, precisely because it has an economic interest in maintaining a distance between criticism and commercial leisure products. But, in general, it seems to me that cultural studies' primary commitment must be to the education system rather than to its big competitor, the media, and this is a topic that will exercise us further in the section on politics (see p. 39–42)

Cultural studies' pasts

We know that, given the absence of a strong methodological base and given its ambiguous status as a university discipline, cultural studies is drawn to reflect upon itself. Almost obsessively, it mulls over its own history. But the global dispersion of cultural studies both in a disciplinary sense and in a geographical sense means that that history has been radically dispersed. There can now be no single history of cultural studies. In particular, the notion that cultural studies began with the work of Hoggart and Williams, while it remains a reference point for most textbooks in cultural studies (including this one), cannot be regarded as having a linear relation to much of the work that goes under the name of cultural studies around the world today. Moreover too great an attention to that history smothers other traditions in other national cultural studies, a problem especially acute in those regions of the world which continue to have least access to international journals, publishers and conferences, Africa and Latin

America for example (see Wright 1998; Kaliman 1998). Why, once one thinks globally, should not Fernando Ortiz, the US-based Cuban theorist of 'transculturation' and the African diaspora, be an ancestor of cultural studies alongside Raymond Williams (see Oritz 1998)? Or, if it comes to that, why not Octavio Paz, José Enrique Rodó, Alfonso Reyes and many others – all the more so given that many of these Latin American cultural commentators (who by and large were not professional academics) have helped form the intellectual personality of theorists such as Néstor García Canclini (an Argentinean, educated in Paris, now working in Mexico) who do participate in today's global cultural studies academy.

Given this dispersion of cultural studies' history, it seems useful to make a distinction between precursors, sources and past practitioners. Past practitioners can be dealt with most summarily: they belong to the institution of contemporary academic cultural studies itself and have played a role not only in developing concepts, methods and case studies but may have provided guidance and patronage to later students and scholars. The most influential of these has been Stuart Hall, whose students and junior colleagues, working around (and beyond) the Anglophone world, were primary agents of the institutionalisation of cultural studies proper.

Precursors are those who have produced work similar in some way to contemporary cultural studies but in different institutional settings and often with relatively little acknowledgment. They have a proleptic relation to institutionalised cultural studies –that is to say they can now be seen to prefigure a field that they themselves could not imagine. Radical thinkers such as C.L.R. James, Franz Fanon, George Orwell and Fernando Ortiz who worked as activists and journalists are particularly important precursors because they provide an image of engaged cultural commentary upon which the shadow of the academy did not fall. Thus, to take George Orwell as an example: one of Orwell's projects (at his best) was to expose the invisibility of the working classes in dominant British (which for him meant pretty much English) culture, and to demonstrate that the commercial popular culture produced for the working class expresses a basic will to survival and, beyond that, a stoic yet boisterous defiance (Orwell 1961, 461 and 1970, 194). A version of Orwell's argument will later enter academic cultural studies under the guise of cultural populism. In Orwell, however, it was expressed through a socialist journalist's day-by-day commentary for a wider readership, rather than inside the autonomy, rigour, will-to-theory and restricted circulation of an academic field of study.

The concept of the 'source' of cultural studies is more vexed than that of the precursor or the practitioner. At one level, sources are the academic theorists who have provided the concepts that have been used in one branch or another of cultural studies, although their own overall project and disciplinary orientation falls outside the field. One can think of many names here, most French: Roland Barthes, Michel Foucault, Gilles Deleuze, Michel de Certeau, Antonio Gramsci, the post-Marxists. But beyond such names, cultural studies is the heir of wider streams in the humanities.

35

In Germany, for instance, one hears the line that the true founder of cultural studies is Johann Gottfried von Herder, who first used the concept of *Kultur* against the rationalism and universalism of 'Enlightenment' thinkers of the eighteenth century. Herder elaborated the notion that different societies possess different cultures (determined by local conditions and environments), through which they make sense of themselves and the world they inhabit, and through which they articulate their humanity. Here then, we find an early and very influential moment in the anthropological account of culture. While any suggestion that Herder founded cultural studies is non-historical and loaded in that it is dismissive of the specificity of contemporary cultural studies, it should not wholly be dismissed. One of the problems with cultural studies is that it has been too divorced from the long tradition of thought on culture and society, that it hasn't often placed itself even within the lineage that first developed the concept of culture and the disciplined study of the subject (see Kittler 2000 for a corrective to cultural studies' truncated historical sense of itself). After all, cultural studies retains strong traces of Herder's affirmation of culture as collective expression.

A notable exception to this amnesia is Francis Mulhern's provocative book *Culture/Metaculture* (2000), in which the notion of 'meta-culture' is introduced in order to describe the discourses in which cultures 'speak of themselves' (Mulhern 2000, xvi). Mulhern's argument is that the contemporary discipline of cultural studies has failed to recognise that it is repeating the patterns of older modes of cultural critique (he uses the German term *Kulturkritik*) even as it overturns cultural critique's social position and values by replacing the norms of high culture with those of popular culture. Through a historical summary of cultural critique, Mulhern reminds us how powerful and widespread the notion was that capitalist culture, based on the market, could only be protected from fragmentation and superficiality if guided by those with sufficient education and leisure to retain a disinterested, serious and informed relation to the cultural tradition. But for Mulhern, cultural studies aims to win for itself and for popular culture the authority once given to figures such as Matthew Arnold, F.R. Leavis and T.S. Eliot without, ultimately, changing the rules of the game. In both cases, culture is supposed to carry out the work of reform that, in truth, only politics can perform. Indeed, for Mulhern, culture's energy requires a distance from politics: the 'discrepancy' between them is what allows culture to possess whatever social power it does.

So, for Mulhern, Arnold, Leavis and Eliot are unacknowledged sources of cultural studies. This is arguable, even within British cultural studies (which is what Mulhern is addressing). Except maybe among a few cultural populists, cultural studies does not aim to replace high culture's supposed power to order social anarchy with popular culture's supposed capacity to undermine inherited social hierarchies. Rather, it attempts to show how certain cultural forms have supported social divisions and exclusions, and to encourage a culture which operates differently: a mobile, non-hierarchical, diverse, less normative culture, sometimes in the interests of a new kind of non-formalised politics –

which is a very different project. But Mulhern's insistence that figures such as Arnold and Eliot are predecessors of cultural studies at least reminds us that whom you regard as a cultural studies 'source' depends on your interpretation of the discipline's project.

Further reading

Dworkin 1997; Frow and Morris 1993; Highmore 2002; Long 1997; McGuigan 1992 and 1996; Miller 2001; Sim 2000.

1 . 4

Problems

Another useful way of approaching cultural studies is by considering the debates about method and interest that have divided the field internally. After all, it is largely around such debates that the field has articulated itself. Of these, the three most important are: (1) the debate over the claim that culture (and hence cultural studies) has strong political force; (2) the debate over the determining power of economic structures on cultural formations; and (3) the debate over the role that individual experience should play in cultural studies analysis. Let us address each in turn.

Cultural studies and politics

Despite (or because) British cultural studies emerged as a deviation from the new left of the sixties, with its distance from orthodox Marxism and organised labour (Stuart Hall was at one time editor of the British Marxist journal *New Left Review*), some of its strongest critics – such as Francis Mulhern – have come from what is now the 'old' new left. Such critics are particularly angered by the notion, prevalent both in cultural studies and postmarxism, that culture *is* politics. It is this idea that, more than anything, forms the basis of cultural studies' claim to be not so much an academic discipline but a 'critical practice' with political force. Obviously this claim invites scepticism: how can sitting in a classroom chatting about television compare as a political activity with leafleting on behalf of a candidate? And it's the complacency implicit in cultural studies' claim to political heft that helps give rise to the perception that there exists a template for cultural studies thinking which will produce the same kind of politically correct rhetoric on almost any topic (see Morris 1990).

In fact criticism of cultural studies' political ambitions points to three quite distinct modes of the discipline: cultural populism, which (as we have seen) treats popular culture as being counter-hegemonic; identity politics, which affirms collectivities formed around ethnic, sexual or local identities; and ideology-critique, which (against cultural populism) ascribes real political value to critical readings of those representations which seduce audiences into accepting dominant norms. To give an example of one form of the last mode: in an interesting recent essay about Bob Marley, Michelle Stephens argues that, as Marley's recordings became increasingly important to a major record company's catalogue, his image was de-politicised. His Rastafarianism and reputation as a ganja-smoking, sexualised 'rude boy' was downplayed as was his resistance to colonialism. As his political edge and rebelliousness was blanded out, he became a 'legend' as a family man and 'natural mystic' (Stephens 1998; Gilroy 1987, 169). Such a reading claims political force in that it let us see how commercialisation carries restricted norms.

We have already encountered Francis Mulhern's attack on cultural studies' political claims, for which the concept of politics in cultural studies is merely gestural or, as he puts it, 'phatic' (Mulhern 2000, 150). For him, the self-attribution of political force by cultural studies academics expresses nothing other than a desire; formal politics remains the arena in which meaningful debates over policy concerning resources, social justice, welfare and so on take place. If cultural studies does have a political project, then it is the misguided and impossible one of the take-over of the political by the cultural through claiming the cultural to be the political. In effect, this is to accuse cultural studies of allowing the concept of culture to exceed itself so that it comes to cover almost everything. More recent writers such as Tony Bennett have made similar arguments from a different perspective: they argue that cultural studies' political will can only be more than gestural if it begins to analyse and influence cultural policy (see pp. 73-7 for more on this).

We can accept that cultural studies is riddled with loose claims to political status and efficacy. Certainly the hopes that cultural studies academics would become organic intellectuals for new socio-political formations, claims expressed in the heady days of the discipline's emergence in Britain, have not been fulfilled (Hall 1996, 267–268). But critics fail sufficiently to acknowledge that the relationship between politics and culture has indeed changed over the last thirty years in most nations, and that their own scorn for cultural studies' politics of culture assumes a practice of politics that is increasingly rarefied.

In the West at least this shift in the relation between politics and public culture is extraordinarily complex, but it's enough to note that the old division between left and right, based both on a philosophy of history (history as liberation from inequity from the point of view of the left; history as maintenance of order and stability from the point of view of the right) and on a class base (the left as the party of the working classes and their liberal allies; the right as the party of employers and their traditionalist allies), has all but disappeared. So too has the situation which made Marxism seem persuasive to many. The key Marxist argument was that, under capitalism, social production is owned not by the people as a whole but by the bourgeoisie. However once a re-distributional tax system and the welfare state had redefined the economy as a public domain managed by the government, whose resources were to be allocated in the interests not just of property and capital but also of equity and welfare, then the force of Marxian analysis was much diminished. Of course the unwinding of welfarism and progressive tax regimes may revivify demands for equitable distribution of capital and social resources within mainstream politics.

As domestic mass consumption became a pivot of capitalist economies, worker/ owner conflict was also eroded by consumer/producer solidarity. Then much political argument really became a technical one about what kind of economic policies worked best in the interest of all in any particular situation, which means not much more than keeping unemployment and inflation/deflation within bounds, maintaining comparative growth of national output, and, more arguably, limiting internal national income inequities – the capability to manage the economy continuously and so to politicise it being enabled by increasingly speedy, computer-based means of collecting information about indicators and trends. Yet at the same time as politics became centred on economic management, national economies were more and more internally ungovernable, since they were increasingly determined by global finance flows ('flights of capital'), huge multinational corporations, job and commodities export markets and unforeseeable technological innovations.

The old left–right division has not been replaced by another strong, overarching political dualism. Indeed the right is marked off from the left as much by its 'family' cultural values as by differences on how to manage the economy – a culturalist turn within the very heartlands of politics. All this has meant that mass politics has been diminished. Party politics has ceased to matter as much to most people as it once did. Political parties increasingly communicate to and with the public through public relations, the media and polling. Campaigning requires more and more money, driving politicians and their parties closer to big money interests. Formal radical politics (that is, organised left politics outside party structures) exist further and further away from public recognition and acceptability, and their politics too is often driven by the necessity to attract media attention. Of course a less organised radical politics has emerged, mostly formed on the basis of what are ultimately cultural identities: the politics of feminism, ethnicity and race; the gay, lesbian, queer, transgender movement; multiculturalism; the green movement, the global justice movement. From the point of view of government, most of these function as relatively powerless if sporadically noisy interest groups.

In this situation it is unfair to complain that cultural studies has traversed politics; rather it is the political domain that has been emptied out by larger social forces. At any rate, it is within this diminished politics that cultural studies' political aspirations need to be viewed. And it is because politics is increasingly informed by culture that cultural studies can claim to be political. To insist that social and cultural hierarchies map onto one another and are mutually supportive; to remember that different social and cultural groupings bring different histories of domination and oppression into the present; to demonstrate that cultures are plural and partially incommensurable (cannot be translated into one another by a rational master code); to work for an education system which allows for critical analysis of (for instance) cultural nationalism and the driving force of enterprise culture; to affirm cultural difference; to examine the concept and history of 'terror' in light of the global 'war on terrorism'; and, in a more utopian spirit, to use cultural analysis to imagine new social relations – these are all political projects in the context of this emptying out of the political sphere.

At least on occasions, cultural studies can be political in a more practical sense: using the institution as a place where activists, academics and students can meet, and where a pedagogy based on self-reflective dialogue among students and between students and teachers provides an example of a well-functioning public sphere (this is the kind of pedagogy that Henry Giroux has theorised about at length: see, for instance, Giroux 1992). So far probably the most effective movement in this kind of cultural studies activism is the response to AIDS: the movement to banish the murk of homophobia which prevented those diagnosed positive from receiving the governmental and professional help they needed. Cultural studies and queer theorists played an important part in such activism, as we shall see later in Part 6 on sexuality.

We can put this case somewhat differently by stressing the political possibilities that open up from within the education system as a result of its central status in modern society. After all the education system remains a public institution (that is, organised and maintained in the public interest, and responsible to that interest, rather than simply as an assemblage of private businesses) and, in many countries, is part of the state itself. So it is from within the education system that culture and the public can be brought together. The political energy of, and possibilities for, cultural studies are a function of being situated at this key institutional site where culture and the public/the state meet. These days the academic humanities do not automatically grant cultural value to their objects of study, but they can provide a gateway to the schooled publics that the education system creates. They can preserve and give an official voice to the cultural formations that both the market and formal politics neglects, and that is a ground of their political force. Yet it is not as if the universities are universal in the old sense: as far as the humanities are concerned, scholarship and criticism now are compelled to articulate particular interests too. A claim to neutral, disinterested position is only possible in the most technical of work. As soon as interpretation and evaluation enter one is connected to interests that refer back to external cultural–political groupings (feminists, diasporic communities,

41

cultural conservatives, fan bases) as well as to divisions within the institution itself (particular disciplines or sub-disciplines) and the teachers who live by them.

Traditionally, of course, cultural studies aimed to 'democratise' culture. In his important book, *The Long Revolution* (1961), Raymond Williams argued for a 'participatory democracy' in which all individuals, as inherently creative and engaged, would play significant roles against the kind of formal democracies that actually exist (Williams 1961, 118). This has been taken up by those who see cultural studies as a fundamentally 'democratic' discipline (Couldry 2000, 26). One difficulty with this approach is that the language of 'democracy' has been co-opted by the American right, and has effectively come to mean the tyranny of majorities and the sovereignty of individual consumer choice. It is what George W. Bush fights for against the axis of evil, rather than what multiculturalists struggle for against the Christian or nationalist right, or what the labour movement urges against exploitative employers. Democracy is first and foremost a political concept but one which can cover a number of very different forms of organisation, so its use is limited as a description of a field of humanities such as cultural studies.

It is in these terms that it seems truer to state that the aim of cultural studies is not so much to democratise as to liberalise – to articulate an understanding of culture in the interests of the liberty of individuals and groups, their overcoming restrictions imposed by repressive prejudices, social hierarchies and economic inequities. Cultural studies has had trouble in taking one step past liberalism, that is in declaring that particular things and values are good in themselves. And it resists seeing itself as liberal not simply because liberalism connotes a failure to perceive individuals as socially and economically positioned but also because cultural studies retains a commitment to collectivisms of various kinds. Yet, as we have seen, its capacity to collectivise is limited. At best it can draw its practitioners into an institutionally and professionally based cadre, linked only indirectly to other social and cultural formations.

Cultural studies and political economy

Don't we now all accept that culture is shaped, indirectly or directly, by economic structures? But to what degree, and precisely how, do economic structures determine (or if that is too strong a word, 'shape') cultural formations? And if economic inequality remains the most important social issue, how can cultural studies affirm cultural forms without reference to their relation in maintaining such inequality?

Debates over such issues have helped form cultural studies. Nicholas Garnham in particular has argued that the discipline has been crippled by its failure to take political economy seriously (Garnham 1997 and 1999). What would a political economy analysis involve, according to Garnham? First, placing cultural production rather than consumption or reception at the discipline's centre; second, an acceptance of the class hierarchies embedded in capitalism as the ultimate horizon and target of cultural analysis; third, reinstating 'false consciousness' as a key category on the grounds that social and economic 'structures of domination' are veiled by popular culture, it being the task of cultural studies intellectuals to lift that veil and to disseminate the hidden truth. And, fourth, it would involve marginalising other, more or less emergent, social identities – feminist, ethnic, queer – on the grounds that they are insufficiently constituted in relation to the main game: class and capitalism.

Many would argue (myself included) that this is an 'old new left' line, which does not sufficiently take into account the shifts consequent upon globalising enterprise culture and the transformations of old-style politics. Thus, on the other side of the debate, Lawrence Grossberg points out that Garnham's concepts of capitalism, false consciousness and class are historically and spatially undifferentiated abstractions; that class, race and gender are articulated with one other, and that, for Garnham, the market, and its opening out of possibilities, is reduced to a classical antagonism between capital and labour (Grossberg 1998). One could add that Garnham is not at all clear about what his alternatives to capitalism are, or how the study of culture's political economy might help to produce them.

We should also note that in practical terms a great deal of cultural studies work does in fact consider how economic structures interact with cultural formations (Maxwell 2001a, 129–136). In light of this it seems as if debates over political economy continue to pursue a historical struggle between two old antagonists – liberalism (which foregrounds individual freedom and agency) and materialism (which regards cultural and social formations as epiphenomena of economic structures). Yet in these oversimplistic terms, as is noted above, it is clear that cultural studies belongs as much to liberalism as to materialism. After all, the field is grounded, first, on a rejection of vulgar Marxist dogma, by which 'the base determines the superstructure' and, second, in the understanding that the meaning and value of culture is to be located in the ways in which it is lived and used by individuals, rather than as the repository of particular values.

In fact the terms of this debate are reductive, since cultural studies tends to be a form of liberalism and of materialism simultaneously. Let's put it like this: at the level of theory, most forms of cultural studies are influenced by a concept articulated by Althusser and Foucault (and which we can think of as belonging to a tradition founded by the seventeenth-century philosopher Baruch Spinoza), namely that ideas and actions are forms of social energy and power too (see Althusser 1971, 168–169). As Raymond Williams phrased it, 'consciousness and its products are always, through variable forms, part of the social process itself' (Williams 1977, 60). If in political terms this means that not all forms of oppression and subordination are economic, in terms of cultural studies it means that the pleasures and uses of cultural production and reception need not be translated back into political–economic terms, and that economic and 'cultural' zones can be thought of as being relations of dynamic interrelation with one another, and not that the first simply determines the second.

Let's make this more concrete by imagining what a successful cultural studies analysis would look like, one based loosely on Janice Radway's exemplary analysis of the US Book-of-the-Month Club in *A Feeling for Books: The Book-of-the-Month Club, Literary Taste, and Middle-Class Desire* (1997). Such an account of the popularity of book clubs during the 1990s would note changes in the publishing industry in terms of ownership, amalgamation and marketing techniques, as well as shifts in the technology of book printing. It would explore the attitudes, motivations and intentions (not necessarily the same thing) of those working in, or on behalf of, book clubs, whether amateur organisers, marketing executives or the writers of critical and promotional material on or for book clubs. It would describe the cultural status of reading as a practice relative to, say, television viewing and web browsing so as to help convey what reading book-club books means as a leisure choice. At the same time it would offer some account of the economic and social situation of readers (their jobs, gender, income bracket). It might take cognisance of conditions in a world where books are produced as objects, and in which (I would guess) non-literary attitudes and low wages are endemic.

But this attention to business and socio-economic structures of book clubs and their readers would not function as an explanation for the clubs. No such explanation is being sought: the central section of a cultural studies approach to book clubs would likely report what participants themselves think and feel, whether these participants be industry types or readers. Readers would be encouraged to describe how their reading was absorbed into their lives. The point of a cultural studies approach would be to help one understand the book club world intellectually, critically and affectively. An intellectual understanding means to grasp the industrial and cultural conditions in which the clubs flourish; a critical understanding means to gain a sense of the social and cultural costs and exclusions of those conditions (and the conditions that enable these conditions), as well as the tensions and gaps – and continuities – between business values and readers' values; and an affective understanding means to empathise with readers and publishers, and perhaps to encourage one to join them oneself or to form new kinds of book clubs.

Individualism, subject positions and disciplinarity

The role of the individual (and the personal) in cultural studies is problematic too, as we are beginning to see. All interpretative disciplines tend to invoke personal and individualised understandings of their objects, even though the rhetoric of academic writing often figures the 'I' as a 'we' (in a figure of speech which allows us to imagine cultural studies as a political association). But to the degree that cultural studies refuses to accept cultural identities (the gay man, the American, the worker, the white) which override internal differences within the communities defined by these identities; to the degree that it refuses a psychoanalytic approach where individual psychic structures are organised by deep drives; and to the degree that it is interested in experience and life-practices, cultural studies is driven to find a basis in personal responses to cultural formations. So, increasingly, academics in the field find themselves writing essays in which they share their personal involvement with, and passions for, some or other cultural form (see Kipnis 1992 and Rapping 2002 for good examples).

The academic value of the personal response is always limited: academic writing is required to produce knowledge or theoretical interventions that are useful to and applicable by others, conditions which confessional writing often does not meet. Very few books manage to reconcile this tension. One of the few that does is Carolyn Steedman's *Landscape for a Good Woman* (1986), in which the author's own experiences are interwoven with descriptions of her working-class mother's life in a careful meditation on the history and society that shaped their very different careers. Here the personal casts new light on a larger history in ways that resonate with important ongoing academic debates and which also lie in the background of many, but by no means all, of Steedman's readers' lives. Yet, importantly, Steedman does not assume that she belongs to any coherent political collectivity: if she did her confessional approach would have much less point.

In general terms, cultural studies draws some of its energy from a systematic, long-term social turn to individualism across the West, which has been theorised by sociologists and cultural theorists from Foucault to Christopher Lasch (Foucault 1978; Lasch 1978). Few questions motivate students to join cultural studies more powerfully than: what are the external frameworks which have formed me and through which I might understand myself? However, when this question shifts enquiry from analysis of external structures towards the individual experience itself, we enter tricky territory. After all: what is individual experience? To the individual it may seem like, more or less, everything. In particular, experience is so much there for consciousness that it prevents us from recognising the complex grounds out of which we act. It is as if we, as a bounded interiority continually filled with sensations, memories, thoughts, feelings, are the originating agent in our lives. But the overwhelming interior plenitude that gives this sense looks very fragile under scrutiny. It is invisible; it is not as unique as it seems; it's fugitive. It is more as if subjectivity when thought of as a flow of unique interior psychological events is simultaneously a plenitude and a vanishing point. One further reason for this is that, in order for this subjectivity to be present for anyone else or, indeed, to matter to anyone else (and at least sometimes to oneself), it needs to be communicated. And communicative acts (when they happen in signs and conventions as they almost invariably do) compromise the individuality of the experience, or at least subordinate it to a mastery of communicative techniques, since individuality can only be expressed through such a mastery. (Of course we can communicate physically or emotionally too – a cry of pain, a touch – but, although these may compel empathy, they don't express much individuality.)

45

To approach the fragility of the subject from a different angle: to what degree is subjective reflection and experience structured and limited by larger historical processes embodied in social structures? One of the most influential interventions on this question claims that we are individuals through processes of individuation – to use a term associated with Michel Foucault. What the individual *is* differs across history and culture since individuals are produced through techniques of 'self-fashioning' of 'practices of self' as well as in particular theories. Thus, for instance, since the late nineteenth century (but not necessarily before) many Western individuals have possessed unconsciousness or subconsciousness, in which feelings and memories are 'repressed' and are likely to be expressed in displaced and unexpected acts or thoughts. It's a rich, historically specific kind of selfhood, heavily dependent on psychoanalytic theory, disseminated, for instance, in specific practices of child-rearing and therapy, which are themselves the product of complex social and institutional settings. Selves formed within such processes don't necessarily know themselves as such, believing that they are who they are as if by spontaneous nature. Indeed, coming to understand selfhood historically and socially (through academic study) may not be just to know something new; it may be to acquire a new form of self.

However, cultural studies has usually thought of individuality slightly differently: as a 'subject position' where, as we have seen, that phrase refers to the more or less fixed positions available to assign an individual with an identity inside particular social formations. Obviously queers or Iranian women or Bruce Springsteen fans utter certain kinds of statements and take certain kinds of attitudes which, in broad outline at least, come already prepared for them. That's what is meant by a 'subject position'. But this analysis is somewhat reductive since it is clear that we need not take up these 'positions' unthinkingly. Elements of them at least can be chosen quite consciously for tactical reasons or to make a statement. Why, for instance, might one be a conservative working-class woman or an Italian-opera-loving Parsi in Mumbai? Maybe to flag individuality; maybe to participate in that which excludes you; maybe to dis-identify with what you are marked out to be; or to identify with what you are not. Generally for cultural studies, inherited or imposed subject positions can be resisted, although one's power to escape them may be limited.

So when one examines how subject positioning works at the level of the everyday, it doesn't seem accurate to say that we inhabit established subject positions. Rather, we find ourselves in relation to them, sometimes taking the identities that they offer pretty much wholesale (whether knowingly or not), but just as often distancing ourselves from them by taking advantage of a whole range of tones and modes that allow this, including irony and camp (see pp. 145–52 for more on this topic).

At any rate individuality is not a category that can easily be used to save cultural analysis from abstraction and clumsy covering over of differences. But it is a category that can be used to draw cultural studies towards the artistic and literary. Since, for better or for worse, literature, art and performance are the cultural practices in which individuality is expressed and publicly cultivated most assiduously, as well as being, for that very reason, the cultural practices most open to impressionism and narcissism. Then too of course a strong emphasis on individuality runs the political risk of merging with that brand of popular liberal individualism whose conceptual basis is the uniqueness of every person, whose politics continually appeals to the rights of each individual to express and live out their specialness, and whose ethics is focussed on our responsibility to respect and listen to the uniqueness of others.

The difficulty for cultural studies is that it cannot assume a collectivity proper to itself, which it might set against individualism of this kind. In this regard, all it has is the professional teachers/academic writers who make their careers in the field and the generations of students whom they teach. And that institutional collectivity doesn't have the force or authority of an 'I' despite the fragility of the individuality which that particular pronoun marks.

Further reading

During 1999; Grossberg *et al.* 1992; Hall *et al.* 2000; Maxwell 2001a; Mulhern 2000.

Part 2

TIME

The past: cultural history/cultural memory

Cultural studies has an even more complicated relation to history than it does to literary studies, sociology or anthropology. Officially, it focusses on *contemporary* culture, unlike cultural history. Yet if that distinction were solid then it would limit cultural studies' interest in history to the way in which traces and representations of the past enter contemporary culture. Not an interest in witches as they *were* for instance, but in the way in which witchcraft circulates and is treated *today* and especially in today's popular culture. While cultural studies often does focus on the past in these terms, such an understanding is a little simplistic. After all, as soon as we want to explain the current state of things we are going to be tempted to tell stories about the past which might reveal how the contemporary came to be the way it is. Such stories (of which there are many in this book) promise more than they can deliver since history never does quite explain the contemporary: it is always too selective and partial for that. But historical narratives and explanations, however reductive, are much better than no sense of the past at all.

Then too, the 'contemporary' is not an unambiguous concept, as we shall see in more detail in section 2.2. Where precisely does the past (cultural history) end and the present (cultural studies) begin? That's a sneakily difficult question, which undoes cultural studies' borders. Furthermore, the various categories that we use to organise academic and non-academic thought about, and representations of, the past are always arbitrary, often implicitly political and cannot be taken as given for critical thought – least of all the concept of 'progress' which overhangs all modern thought about history. Thus this section is concerned to help clarify conceptualisations of the past as well as to provide a brief overview of the past's life in the present.

At one level the present is nothing except an expression of the past – nothing comes from nothing after all, and once we rule God and chance out of our conceptual frame-work, everything is enabled by, and a realisation of, past structures. Ordinary life is saturated in the past: to take an example, think of cooking and food and the ways they are entangled in memory. A recipe is handed down across generations, indelibly associated with a grandmother maybe; table manners structure intergenerational continuities too; a restaurant chain is associated with a particular phase of a life – a work lunch break at an old job say; a food you dislike recalls a time you were forced to eat it by your parents; an ex-lover's favourite food reminds you of him; a Smartie (or an M&M) takes you back to when you were a kid and it was your most favourite thing in the world; the chocolate in that sweet (or candy) is produced in a blood-soaked industry that has helped shape the world and in particular the history of colonisation. And so on.

Every action carries a trace of the past – an unconscious memory of it even. A great deal of contemporary theory analyses the way that the past is carried forward unknow-ingly into the present. With individuals, one word we use to talk about the unreflective determination of the present by the past is 'habit', and there exist embedded social habits as well. Sometimes too it seems as if old formations suddenly reappear, uncan-nily, the past flaring into life. Isn't contemporary anti-Islamic paranoia a strange repetition of medieval Christian prejudice, something that once seemed obsolete, and for that reason crammed with unconscious memories?

Yet at least for academic study, the past does not mainly exist as repetitions, social habits or unconscious causal chains, but precisely as history. It is important to under-stand from the first that 'history' is just one way of conceiving the past. As is often pointed out, the word itself is ambiguous: it refers both to knowledge about the past (and hence to an academic discipline) and to the past as such, and especially to the past as it continues to exist for the present. Indeed there is a sense in which all history belongs to the present. What has no presence in the present has no history; it has simply been forgotten. That ambiguity between history-as-knowledge and history-as-event is a sign that history is a *disciplined* way of figuring the past. And it is a relatively recent way of figuring the past – which is to say that while history is not a construct of European modernity, the kind of history that was constructed in European modernity has come to dominate our understanding of the past.

There is something paradoxical in saying this since modernity is itself a historical – and contested – notion. It usually names the transformation of society and ideology whose roots lie in the shrugging off of a primarily God-centred view of history during the Renaissance and the consequent embrace of commerce and technological develop-ment. Modernity emerged in full force around the time of the French Revolution when it became clear that, in certain regions of the West, the traditional society of 'time immemorial' was coming to an end (see Koselleck 1985). History constructed in the spirit of modernity was an enlightened history based on certain techniques (searching the archives) and certain ethics (aiming at truth and providing evidence for one's propositions, repudiating myths and legends). No less importantly it was based on a conceptual framework in which particular histories were narrated in relation to a temporal order in which human beings are gradually coming to order society and nature for their own benefit. That is: history as progress. Non-progressive views of history (for instance, that it is static and so best understood as supplying a stock of applicable lessons; that it is gradually undergoing degradation and will end eschatolog-ically in the Day of Judgement; that it moves in cycles comprising the rise and fall of empires) fell by the wayside. So did the 'providential' view of history in which God took an active interest in human affairs, constantly intervening in them. Although in the last decades (as we shall see in section 2.3 on the future) progressivism has come under considerable theoretical attack, modern academic knowledge remains under its spell in its future-directedness and its hope to contribute to social and cultural improvement.

The progressive understanding of history is itself rather ambiguous: it aggrandises humanity as the agent of historical change at the same time as it aggrandises history, which now becomes an ethical standard as well as the basis for social existence. It was by compar-ison with this kind of temporal order that other, colonisable societies were regarded as lacking 'history' and as belonging fundamentally to the past rather than to the present. History in this sense is haunted by that fundamental break between societies in which inherited models determine practices and those that improvise and invent their own futures. It was in relation to the temporal order of modernity that what (from the histo-rians' perspective) did not change in society, or what did not change in ways that could be related to progressive time, was 'timeless', 'traditional', unhistorical. And it was in relation to that temporal order that institutions and practices (such as hanging, drawing and quar-tering) which have ceased to exist in the modern world belonged to history in yet another sense: as the repository of dead things.

Societies that continually change, that make their own history, heap up history in this sense too: the ruined and the dated are as characteristic of modernity as the sheen of the new. Dead history creates a particular problem: the past becomes other – as other as other cultures. This poses a methodological challenge. How can we under-stand the past except in its own terms, terms which we moderns no longer share and which are more or less lost. This way of thinking about the past as fundamentally 'other' is called 'historicism' and is the intimate flip-side of progressivism.

In historicism the past helps us understand the present mainly through the seduc-tion of narrative and the pleasures of defamiliarisation since the forces which structure the present have only a tenuous relation to the past, even though they necessarily come out of it. The past can teach us most not because we share its world, but because it reminds us that there are other ways of doing things. Thus even where the past would seem to provide useful lessons (for instance, when it tells us of the repeated failures of orthodox economics that aim to extend market relations as widely as possible through society) those lessons are neglected. And an intimate knowledge of the past is no longer regarded as useful in helping us predict the future as it routinely was until the end of the eighteenth century when history was still more providential than secular. Rather, for modern thought, history can help account for the present, although these are explanations which lack the force either of scientific explanation or of explanations where for instance we make sense of a person's actions by reference to their intentions.

At the same time, because the past is thought of as other and vanishing, efforts to preserve it become more and more strenuous. It is museumified, the object of planned preservation and display. It is important to note that this mode of history, which monumentalises the past and which implies and carries with it the values and protocols of European modernity, has come under strong criticism from postcolonial critical historians, notably Dipesh Chakrabarty, determined to respect non-Occidental and non-historical ways of treating the past (see Chakrabarty 1992). In fact, although historicism and progressivism do dominate modern Western thought about the past and there is a sense in which secular and critical thought is centred on them, they by no means monopolise even Western culture. History retains very particular and close connections to conservatism, and that is one reason that the relation of cultural studies to history is problematic.

This connection first appeared in the anti-revolutionary writings of Edmund Burke (especially his *Reflections on the Revolution in France* [1790]) just after the French Revolution. Burke poses civilised national heritage (cultural history) against enlightened, radical social policy (reason), and views the latter not just as lacking reverence for the wisdom, chivalry and treasures that have been inherited from the past but as causing instability and fragmentation. Burke's intervention was especially important in that it helped define culture as a zone separated from politics, the economy and society, and it did so by thinking of culture as the site of national continuity and order which needed to be preserved from economic and egalitarian political forces. Burke's opposition may seem no longer to play a key role in Western politics but his logic remains fundamental to the linkages between nation and culture. The sense that national identity is intimately bound to a high cultural heritage still so important in Europe and increasingly taking hold in Asia is fundamentally Burkean. One of the important features of the USA is that – recognising itself as comprised of various diasporic groups and as founded by an enlightened revolution (with which a younger Burke had a great deal of sympathy admittedly) – it is post-Burkean. It has never tightly connected national identity to inherited culture.

Yet the political nature of history is clearest in debates over what in Australia is called 'black armband' history, that is to say the kind of history of contemporary society that emphasises the way in which the West's current prosperity and world dominance have been built on a history of inhumanity and violence, and particularly on the systematic slaughters of colonialism and the horrors of African slavery. Critical history of this kind was based on a new postcolonial understanding of imperialism that followed the break-up of the old formal empires in the fifties and sixties, but has also been popularised in the West, in particular as part of the 500-year anniversary of Christopher Columbus' so-called 'discovery' of America in books such as Kirkpatrick Sale's bestselling *The Conquest of Paradise* (whose title, interestingly, was mimicked in Ridley Scott's more ambiguously revisionary hit movie, *1492: the Conquest of Paradise*). In the USA the African American civil rights movement also played a key role in disseminating revisionary understandings of the role of slavery and racism in American history. Such critical histories stand in stark opposition to accounts that emphasised, for instance, the West's self-liberation from superstition and tyranny, its invention of a mode of production – capitalism – that allowed new levels of mass affluence or its global 'civilising mission'. Postcolonial histo-ries radically intensified self-doubt about the historical underpinnings of Occidental modernity already set in play by the Holocaust. The resistance to 'black armband' history was an important spur to the conservative attack on 'multiculturalism' after the eighties. At the time of writing it seems that the rift between academic understandings of the past which remain based on revisionary and critical accounts of imperialism and racism, and popular understandings which marginalise those formations, is if anything increasing, and not only in the West.

Let us turn to the ways in which the past is represented and used in contemporary leisure culture. We live in a society in which the present is said to dominate the past to an unprecedented degree, and yet in which the past is everywhere. At the most abstract level this turn to the past in everyday life can be read in two main ways: reac-tively, as a retreat from the difficult, uncertain present; or positively, as an investment of large resources of time and money in preserving the past, primarily in the interests of leisure culture. And, of course, the past often retains its presence in the contempo-rary without undergoing formal historicisation at all. One thinks of music sampling (and especially the citation of old songs in hip hop); golden-oldie stations; television reruns; and the presence of old movies on television. These kinds of objects exist in some ill-defined zone between the contemporary and the historical where the past (while marked as the past) is not museumified or academicised: it is simply made avail-able for consumption.

Whichever line one takes on all of this, it is clear that, at a more concrete level of analysis, history now fulfils a variety of overlapping and intersecting needs and inter-ests. For some it is a hobby defining something like a taste-community or subculture. Different groups of history fans, for instance, have commanding interests in different periods or genres (military history being especially popular, particularly among men, as is the history of Nazi Germany). Others become involved more actively and perfor-matively. They undertake forms of practical antiquarianism in local history societies or

55

help with archaeological digs. Or they play re-enactment games in the genre often called 'living history'. In the UK the fashion for re-enactment, for instance, can be dated to a 1968 event organised by a group of Civil War fans called the Sealed Knot, which today remains Britain's largest re-enactment society. In the USA the Civil War provides the most popular re-enactment events too, although these re-enactments have a conservative, not to say, racist edge since they tend to drip with nostalgia for the confederate (Southern slave-owning) side. And re-enactments have their hard-core fans who undergo amazing privations to live in the past just as it was, without any modern comforts at all.

For others history is a form of more passive entertainment, in particular as is provided by television documentaries. These have become increasingly commercialised – see the A&E cable network's History Channel which (like the similar Biography Channel) is disseminated internationally and which is able to produce what the company itself markets as 'global programming events' such as 2000's pathbreaking *Modern Marvels Boy Toys Week,* a ten-hour programme on the history of gadgets and toys designed specifically for men who are still boys at heart. History and especially historical biography is a core genre for the publishing industry too, books on such topics being especially popular as gifts for men who aren't really 'book people'. In Britain the periodical *History Today* has been a surprising success. As entertainment, history is of course often fictionalised: the era of historical fiction, which was inaugurated by the Scottish novelist Walter Scott at the beginning of the nineteenth century, is by no means over (Scott's project was to reconcile progressive historicism with Burkean conservatism by developing fiction's capacity for rewarding characters, shaped by historical forces, who reconciled themselves to the *slow* onset of modernity).

Nowadays historical fictions, whether in print or as audio-visual media, rarely have such focussed ideological objectives. They tend to circulate received ideas about particular epochs within fine-tuned generic conventions: let Barbara Cartland's bestselling romances, which have contributed massively to the image of the dashing, rakish English Regency period (the very period during which Sir Walter Scott wrote), stand as one such example. Recently, however, a new kind of writing, which indeterminately mingles history and fiction, has emerged within art literature. Such writing resurrects streams of underground history that are deemed valuable because they fall outside widely disseminated public memories, and which, for that very reason, cannot be referenced without being placed at risk. In two of the most noted practitioners of this genre, the English writer Iain Sinclair and the German W.G. Sebald, the mood is melancholic. Horror of the present is only warded off by a virtuoso literary style. In Sebald especially an older sense of temporality seems to be reappearing: the Baroque sense of history as graveyard.

Despite historicism and progressivism, the past also continues to function as a ground of identity at various levels. At the level of the family, genealogy began its rise to popularity in the late seventies, on the threshold of the 'postmodern' moment. These days, in the West, many libraries and archives seem to be dedicated primarily to helping people uncover their family lines – a sign less of a seismic shift in the culture's relation to the past, I suspect, than of an ageing and dislocated population with time and money on their hands.

At a more social level, historical narratives continue to form a basis of identity for ethnicities and nations. This can take the form of a straightforward identification of certain events (generally traumatic ones) as defining current ways of life and structures of feeling: slavery for African Americans, colonisation for many colonised communities or even the Blitz for Londoners. French identity is still articulated around its sense that France brought modern civility and rationality to the world, a piece of ideology that is much more powerful than foreigners recognise (they tend to see France through other historical moments, especially the late nineteenth-century *belle epoch*). In the People's Republic of China, the Communist Party has attempted to deflect the socially unsettling consequences of its turn to state capitalism by encouraging pride in China's ancient civilisation. The feminist movement of the late sixties and early seventies gained a great deal of its energy from its highly successful efforts at historical retrieval, rescuing women's contributions from abysmal forgetfulness to create a transhistorical gendered community under new terms.

Identity through history can also take a weaker form, through the deployment of nostalgia, as in nostalgia for imperial and traditional class-based society so apparent in middle-class Britain today, which, for many, seems to represent an essential tradition which defines Britishness. Critics such as Fredric Jameson theorise current 'nostalgia' as a sign of the lack of real History in the present (that is, a materialist History which will ground revolutionary action). But it makes more sense to see such nostalgia (like the fad for genealogy) as a consequence of the weakening of the role of the past and of inheritance in the construction of social identities. Nostalgia and genealogy are the weak histories of a post-historical age, which means not just an age that knows history increasingly as entertainment, but also an age that is decreasingly burdened by the past.

Amateur relations to history merge into what is often called at the level of official institutions 'the heritage industry' and, at the level of the community itself, 'cultural memory'. These terms are linked because they both refer to those elements of the past that remain current beyond formal and specialised scholarship. Furthermore, cultural memories have become increasingly bureaucratised and commercialised, that is drawn into the heritage industry. After all, the past that we remember is, to a large degree, the past that organised, and mainly commercial, interests present to us to be remembered. Indeed history as taught in non-research educational institutions is entering into increasingly close relations with the heritage industry too, as schools in particular seek to interest students in history via its commercialised modes of presentation. The

57

heritage industry covers those forms of historical entertainment that we have just been discussing but extends into a wider range of practices and institutions, including museums, urban planning and industry self-memorialisation (such as the USA's non-profit Steel Industry Heritage Corporation committed to conserving remnants of old steel technologies and sites) as well as tourism.

Within cultural studies, debates about the meaning and effects of the heritage industry continue. From one point of view, the emphasis on heritage as it emerged in the UK during the eighties, for instance, can be interpreted as part of an effort to deflect attention from current social difficulties, in particular the increase in economic inequity which followed Thatcherite neo-liberalism (Hewison 1987). From another, the heritage industry has a popular (albeit mainly middle-class) base, and is much less elitist than older forms of cultural memory and historiography (Samuel 1994). The passions around this debate probably assume that the past is more important than it really is. It is incontrovertible that many heritage industry attractions simplify the past, often into the most stripped-back and sentimental of stereotypes; it is also incontro-vertible however that many such attractions do in fact inform visitors about the past. During a visit to Sovereign Hill, near Ballarat, Victoria, Australia, a re-creation of a gold-mining village circa 1865, I learned more about the actual techniques involved in extracting gold ore than would have been possible, I suspect, by any other means. At the same time, the thickness of history had evaporated: the violence, the deceits, the fantasies, the disappointments, the hardships, the anti-Chinese racism involved in the Gold Rush were either ignored or converted into nostalgic, visitor-friendly images.

Similar tensions exist when the category 'heritage' becomes regulative, as it so often does. Laws against the demolition or even the alteration of old buildings are passed in its name, sometimes in the interests of preserving important and attractive constructions, but other times as the expression of anti-contemporary philistinism. Here the tension is, once again, between conservatism as resistance to change and historical continuity as a ground of (in this case, aesthetic) value.

Not all cultural memory is subsumed into institutionalised heritage however. One particularly important and interesting form of popular cultural memory, which has resisted what we might clumsily call 'heritagisation', is generational memory organ-ised around decades. Each decade has its own set of images, moods, mix of nostalgia and counter-nostalgia (the feeling of relief at having managed to get past that) – the twenties, the thirties, the forties, the fifties, the sixties, the seventies, the eighties, the nineties. At a certain point these popular memories fade and a decade dissolves into amnesia: take for instance the 1880s, which once had its own unique identity but which now no one except a few professional historians knows about. Some decades have stronger personalities than others: in the early (nineteen) eighties it looked as though the seventies were without style, a merely transitional decade (Hunt 1998, 5–6). How that has changed! These memories often express anxieties and self-understandings of the present: the notion of the conformist fifties (a particularly grotesque simplification albeit one based on the popular sociology of the time) allows later generations to congratulate themselves on their liberation and sense of adventure; the affectionately presented figure of priapic masculinity during the seventies *à la* Austin Powers, although (like the seventies *tout court*) a joke, expresses a certain resentment against the feminism that also emerged during that decade.

Another set of public–cultural memories able to resist the heritage industry are those firmly based in the local, and especially in communities with a strong sense of unity and roots. Such memories can become historicised through oral histories, memoirs, hobbyist 'local history' research and writing. Upon occasion cultural studies academics have helped to historicise and preserve cultural memories of beleaguered communities. The Butetown History and Arts Centre, founded by Glenn Jordan in Cardiff, for instance, organised a museum and archives, and published oral histories of the old multicultural, working-class port community of Cardiff's Tiger Bay which had often been demonised, or, in complete contrast, romantically praised, by outsiders (see Jordan and Wheedon 2000). This kind of history has various functions and effects: it provides a resource for the children and the children's children of community members, those who feel attached to the community for familial reasons but who may no longer retain any lived connection to it. It confers a certain visibility, status and solidity on a community. It becomes, in sum, a ground of identity. In cases such as Tiger Bay, organised cultural memories may help resist and correct the false representations of outsiders, and in communities of the poor and marginalised, the formalisation of cultural memory may have political resonances. This is especially true for communities that remain the object of prejudice and oppression, and truest of all in colonial contexts, where memories and myths of a pre-colonial past may be the most valuable asset of indigenous peoples.

During the nineties the relation between history-as-injury and contemporary life underwent something of a shift. It did so along two interconnected fronts: one public, one private. In the public arena it became increasingly possible for victims of past injustices to call for reparations now, in the present; in the private sphere, historical horrors were increasingly diagnosed as traumatic, in a semi-psychoanalytic sense, for those who lived through them. At the heart of this new relation between the past and the present lay the Holocaust, which became a defining event for European modernity, symbolising Enlightenment's supposed failure, man's inhumanity to man and the ferocity of European anti-Semitism all at once. By the same stroke efforts to repair the Holocaust's horror become representative of current society's claim to civility. The concept of trauma both recognises the Holocaust's damage but also contains the promise of a certain recuperation from it.

Although historical trauma was focussed on the Holocaust, it is worth noting that the uncovering of history as trauma occurred at the same time that child abuse and other forms of familial and social persecution were becoming increasingly open to media discussion and drawn into the ambit of the juridical and therapeutic professions. Trauma became a popular paradigm for thinking about the past after US military personnel returning from Vietnam and suffering flashbacks, hallucinations, rage and depression were diagnosed with a new syndrome – Post-Traumatic Stress Disorder (PTSD). Somewhat later, organised collective injustices such as the 'stolen generation' among Australian Aborigines (the governmentally sanctioned uprooting of children born into Aboriginal communities) or the enforced prostitution of Korean women by the Japanese during World War II were also recognised as traumatic and simultaneously received increased publicity and demands for apology and reparation (see Frow 2001).

Trauma is a contested concept (see Leys 2000), but at its heart lies the notion that some events are too damaging to be able to be dealt with consciously. Trauma victims repress their pain and displace it into symptoms, many of which involve more or less distorted repetitions of the traumatic events themselves. In them the past lives on, but not in the form of conscious, or at least controlled, memory or representation. The crucial question that confronts thinking about trauma psychologically is: to what degree is it a performance in which strategy and suggestion mingle with pain and pathology? Can, for instance, the Holocaust be regarded as a trauma for modernity or just for (some) survivors? Is Australian cultural identity in part a collectivising response to the trauma of Gallipoli, the disastrous World War I campaign that cost over 8000 lives for almost no military gain and which has become an official icon of Australian (Anglo) character. The problem with trauma theory once it is applied to groups rather than individuals is that it tends to overemphasise the unity and shared experience of groups and, indeed, to grant past experience too great an influence on present realities. After all, if there is one thing that sustained reflection on the past from a cultural studies perspective teaches us it is that the past we have today is not, in any clear way, the past as it was once variously experienced. Which nonetheless does not mean that it is, as historicism supposes, simply other.

Further reading

Connerton 1989; Hewison 1987; Leys 2000; Morris 1998; Nora and Kritzman 1996; Samuel 1994; Williams 1961.

The present

The contemporary

As we have seen, cultural studies is marked off from disciplines such as literary studies, film studies and art history partly through its focus on the *contemporary*. In this section I want to examine what the contemporary means, first by analysing it as a concept and then by offering a summary of postmodernism, which has been the most influential category used to theorise it. And we should remind ourselves at once that the contemporary looms larger in the West today than it has ever done. After all, it seems as if we are today more interested in time now than in time past compared to earlier generations – the emergence of cultural studies being itself an expression of that. Cultural studies' commitment to the contemporary orientates it towards what in critical terms is called 'presentism', which means both seeing the past through the light of the present in ways that lose sight of the past's otherness and being narcissistic historically speaking, that is, being overconfident that historical trends are reaching their apogee now (even though, as we know from section 2.1, anti-presentism also has its costs).

So what is the contemporary? At one level, it connotes the present. But to say that is to say very little since the present is an elusive category: simultaneously, the zero, through which the future becomes the past, and the plenitude in which our lives occur. As semiotics teaches us, the present acquires meaning only by virtue of its place in an ordered array which contains elements different to itself, that is, in relation to the past and, though much less so, to the future. The present means something in terms of its perceived differences and similarities to the past, where the past is figured as a jumble of (debates over) events, images, tendencies, thresholds, repetitions and dead ends. Thus (in the West) the present means what it means in relation to events such as the

French Revolution and the Holocaust, which define it as a moment in modernity, or for instance in relation to a supposedly more tranquil past as imaged by a more or less mythical traditional English village without media or consumerism and with an unspoiled environment. Or, alternatively, the present means something in terms of its relation to the future, to predictions of an era when China will become more powerful than the USA, or when human beings will be synthesised with machines, say. The present is strictly meaningless without imagined and narrativised pasts and futures, images and narratives constituted by tropes of events and processes. And the greater the will to make the present meaningful (perhaps because we are losing our confidence in history as a meta-concept), the more likely that the pasts and futures which grant it meaning will be represented over-simplistically. It follows from this that academic historiography, which sets itself against the past's over-simplification, is, to the degree that it is successful, robbing the present of meaning.

But the contemporary is not simply the present. Some of what is happening now seems more contemporary than other things that are also happening now. The contemporary is that parcel of past time that we recognise as belonging to us now, that which seems not to have reached closure in a narrative sense. Raymond Williams famously divided the present into three: the residual (current formations which were inherited from the past but had little future); the dominant (formations that control the present); and the emergent (those which had not yet attained their full development and influence). However it is not easy to categorise social formations in these terms today: where does religious fundamentalism belong for instance? And in its unremitting progressivism, Williams' schema does not really address the category of the 'contemporary' since what is most contemporary at a particular historical moment need not be 'dominant' at all. Indeed there is a sense in which commitment to the contemporary is a commitment to the ephemeral (in the sense that the latest movie hit for instance is an ephemeral phenomenon), even if cultural studies makes the ephemeral less ephemeral by bringing it into a disciplinary archive, and, in some instances, by allowing ephemeral cases to become reference points for future analysis and case studies. Let us not forget that academic disciplines and institutions play an important part in bringing pasts into presents and presents into futures. They are also memory banks – cultural studies included, and especially as it ages.

There is also an important set of relationships between the concept of the contemporary, youth, fashion and cultural studies. Youth culture seems more contemporary than the other cultural niches. And cultural studies has a particularly strong connection to the young (a certain sector of youth at any rate) since it's they who mainly crowd the classrooms which remain its most important institutional site. Because it is a discipline that does not take its own authority or the authority of those who belong to it for granted, it has a different relation to its students than had older disciplines. Ideally at least, it listens to its students; it takes on board their interests and knowledge. The student is figured not as an empty subject to be filled with scholarship, a capability to be trained, but as an interlocutor with whom certain modes of thought and perspectives on the world are to be presented and with whom teachers are in dialogue. Because of this, generational differences between students and teachers loom large: after all, and especially in Anglophone cultures, the interest of the middle-aged in the young is often considered voyeuristic, slightly improper. Furthermore the logic by which styles pass from cool to boring and uncool to half-forgotten and laughable to cool and retro is inexorable. Which in the classroom means that the teacher who remains true to the cultural loves of his or her youth (stereotypically, the Clash circa 1977) and the teacher who valiantly tries to keep up year after year with what's latest risk looking equally ridiculous to their students. And in the parade of generationally inflected styles the contemporary lapses into the fashion; the present into the 'trend'.

At a more abstract level, the contemporary is often said to be particularly difficult to grasp, and not for philosophical reasons. One argument that moves in this direction contends that the contemporary is changing faster than it used to, so fast in fact that it is difficult for intellectual analysis to grasp it (see Grossberg 2000, 149). But it is difficult to know whether history is moving faster now than previously since there are no clear criteria by which to make such a comparison and, at the level of perceptions, it seems pretty unlikely. To take a couple of admittedly extreme examples, what would the British in 1939 have thought of such an assertion, or the Americans in 1862 in the midst of the Civil War? And, on the other hand, didn't we hear, only a few years ago, a great deal about the end of history (meaning that democratic capitalism had triumphed as a global system and no alternatives looked plausible)?

The contemporary is also said to be difficult to grasp because we no longer have a unified and generally agreed set of terms by which to analyse it. Knowledge and value have fragmented, so the argument goes, and the 'master narratives' of human progress and liberation have lost credibility (see Lyotard 1984). In a word, as Fredric Jameson (1991) puts it, the contemporary is 'unmappable'. Whether or not this is the case, there has never been a society that has possessed more detailed information about itself than ours today. To take just some examples: market research companies have rich and detailed descriptions of how consumption patterns spread across space, 'social maps of desire' as Dick Hebdige (1989, 53) has called them, which regulate marketing campaigns, product launches, the establishment of retail outlets. Law enforcement agencies have rich descriptions of the geography of crime; economic geographies have an extremely detailed sense of the spread of economic activity across space; politicians and or bureaucrats draw up electoral boundaries pretty much to the street on history of voting patterns; plant and animal habitats (although much less well mapped than human society and culture) are better and better described and known – for some very endangered species every surviving individual has a name. In fact, in a networked consumer society, to act is to be mapped: a purchase on a credit card leaves a trace on a

63

map of consumption immediately. The problem is not that contemporary societies and cultures aren't mapped, but that there is an increasing discrepancy between the amount of information we have about them and the normative frameworks we have to evaluate and 'make sense of' that information.

One thing is clear: we tend to see the contemporary more in terms of processes and tendencies than in terms of fixed traits. It is mobile in this as well as in other senses. How then do we periodise it?

The postmodern

Future cultural historians will, no doubt, think of the eighties and nineties as the age of postmodernism. Postmodernism, that is, belongs to that specific moment – the last decades of the twentieth century. It then emerges as a concept after some intellectuals (the most influential being the Marxist literary critic Fredric Jameson) concluded that it was no longer possible to tell coherent stories about society. That conclusion was entwined into a complex diagnosis of the contemporary, including the judgement that emotional life was being deadened (in a so-called 'waning of affect'); that the past was being endlessly and meaninglessly recycled; that more and more everyday life was being experienced ironically, as if in quotation marks, and more and more superficially (in so-called 'depthlessness'); that secular faith in progress was evaporating; and that reality itself was vanishing as it became more and more intertwined with the imaginary and the actual disappeared into its own reproduction (or 'simulacrum') (Jameson 1991).

Yet in the new century, 'postmodernism' looks less and less like a convincing diagnosis of an epoch or a cultural totality than like the name of a style that covered a number of genres at a particular moment. It may seem as if postmodernism has been replaced by globalisation as a diagnosis of the contemporary, yet, finally, globalisation is not the name of a cultural mode but of a set of economic, social and political processes. So we are in the rather strange situation in which culture has an unprecedented presence but lacks a generally agreed conceptual and critical framework. This is not to say that the insights articulated within postmodern theory and criticism are all obsolete. What, then, if anything, remains useful in postmodernism? To answer that we need to delve more deeply into the reasoning that produced postmodernism as a concept.

Virginia Woolf famously remarked that human nature changed on or around 1910. Today this may seem puzzling – were people in 1900 really so different to those in 1920? How many people did this difference really affect? If we try to understand what made Woolf's exaggeration possible, then some quite profound shifts occurring around the turn of the nineteenth century do come into view. These we now group together under the name 'modernism'. They include, in the arts, a break with realism towards utopian experimentation; in the domain of social values, a markedly less moralistic attitude towards sexuality – especially non-heterosexual sexuality – as well as a new relation between the classes in which the workers ceased to be absolutely different from the bourgeoisie; a new mode of economic production and consumption in which consumer durables flooded a marketplace which was less and less confined to the rich; and an increasing tolerance for state intervention in the welfare of the people.

Those who use the word 'postmodernism' (as in 'we now live in the postmodern era') are staking a big claim which updates that of Woolf. Around 1980, or so the argument goes, society changed again, in the terms I have begun to outline. Can we locate a set of social conditions underpinning postmodernism similar to those that underpinned the diagnosis of modernism? The answer to this is a qualified 'yes' – qualified because, in the end, postmodernism is not just a break with modernism but also represents its intensification. Many (but not all) of the processes at work during the early twentieth century were still operating in the seventies and eighties, although their cultural effects may have been different.

Still, it is clear that some important social settings have changed. Among the various events that underlie postmodernism we can identify: the rise of neo-liberalism and image politics, especially but not only in the West; the amazing (if not total) success of the women's movement, again mainly in the West; the 1989 end of the Cold War and the effective collapse of socialist ideals globally; the further decline of class as a marker of identity and cultural difference; the emergence of television as a core media; the extension of tertiary education into the population in many developed states; and the acceleration of migrant flows around the world, leading to pressures for the implementation of multiculturalist policies.

And I would draw especial attention to a couple of other factors: postmodernism seems to be intimately related to the collapse of the utopian ideals of the sixties. The critical account of contemporary life as 'postmodern' has strange affinities with a bad acid trip (all that incoherence, repetition, affectlessness, schizophrenia [another word much used by postmodernising theorists]), and that is no accident. It is as if once the revolutionary hopes of that decade turned sour, modern normality had been destroyed and nothing remained to take its place. At a more 'world historical' level, I also would point to the withdrawal of Western powers from their old colonies, or what can be called the triumph of formal decolonisation ('formal' because the decolonisation of the period involved giving up governmental and legal control but not necessarily economic and cultural domination). The reason why this was so important was that the West's sense of itself as a world-historical agent of progress and enlightenment was so deeply entwined with its belief in its colonial 'civilising mission'. Once the old colonies became (in theory at least) equal nation-states, and enlightened civilisation was not confined to the West, then everything changed. It is hard not to resist the conclusion that behind postmodernist theorists' sense that modern progressivism and rationality are in jeopardy lies a concealed (and unthought) response to the passing away of official Western – white male – global hegemony (see Morley and Robins 1995). And once

65

that hegemony ended, 'relativism' became a standard world view – that is the notion that all cultures, peoples, faiths are equal, none being more advanced than others – or at least standard for the liberal rich.

And yet these shifts can also be interpreted differently: not in terms of a sense of jeopardy and threat but of overweening confidence. Perhaps most of all, postmodernism represents that shift in our understanding of the past that I have already gestured at in section 2.1. Instead of history appearing to be the story of progress – the long, painful struggle towards increased social justice and prosperity – it came to seem a parade of variations of social structures and ways of living. That way of thinking is associated with relativism, since, if no mode of life is more advanced than any other, how can history be told as progress? And paradoxically it appears as if the capacity to think in those terms is a sign of the first world's immense sense of security and finality, that is to say of its confidence that history will not move past democratic capitalism, the form of social organisation nurtured in the West that is now, nominally at least, in force in most of the world. We can state that thought like this: the idea of progress can at last be jettisoned because progress has reached its apogee.

Modern democratic capitalism's legitimacy and aura, in turn, largely rely on its capacity to co-opt all resistance to it. In broad terms, democracy and the market's joint power of co-option can also be interpreted in two ways. One can either say that democratic capitalism provides its victims and dissidents with no effective language or power base with which to contest it. And one crucial reason for this is that today the media – especially television – can influence values, provide beliefs, cause pleasures and limit representation and even wants to such a degree that those who lose out under the current system cannot express or represent their loss. Today democratic capitalism is also a postmodern image capitalism: as I say, it looks more as if the media constructs and constrains as opposed to reflecting our reality.

From the other side, one can say that mediatised democratic capitalism has reached the point at which it can play host to an extraordinary and positive proliferation of identities: by enabling empowerment it has enabled people to live as 'gays', 'feminist separatists', 'new agers', 'greenies', 'right to lifers', 'Jesus people', even radical Muslims. Such groups belong less to a public sphere in which national communities or indeed other geographically defined communities are involved than to de-spatialised communication and consumer networks of an economic system increasingly directed at increasing consumption and networks above material production.

In this situation – and this is also a defining feature of the postmodern – politics, as we saw in Part 1, becomes a scene of debates over economic management played out within an amazingly sophisticated technology of information retrieval and image construction; it is no longer the contest of the left, the party of equality and social justice, against the right, the party of individual freedom. In postmodern formal politics one does not vote for what is just or for what represents one's interests. For those interests can barely be represented politically in a conventional sense at all (gay or feminist interests for instance). But the most characteristic postmodern effects of all emerge from the way in which the choices available within representative democracy are designed to appeal to desires and needs that are themselves largely media constructs. Pollsters reveal that voters often vote for candidates who stand against the legislation that they would most like to see enacted. An ex-actor whose fictional roles in war movies are recycled as part of his own biography was elected as President of the USA. And when these lies are pointed out, no one really cares. It doesn't really matter. More than anything, it was the shock of this that allowed postmodernists to claim that there was no reality any longer, and that affectlessness reigned. Where communities or nations resist democratic capitalism the persuasiveness of the postmodern diagnosis breaks down. If one thing has been responsible for postmodernism losing its viability as a concept it has been 9/11 – which forced democratic capitalism to confront its enemies.

But, you might object, isn't postmodernism a cultural rather than a political or economic phenomena? It is true that the term first became popular in the arts (and in architectural criticism in particular), yet the cultural aspects of postmodernism have increasingly come to look like the manifestation of the kinds of transformations and events described above. Take architecture as an example. In this context, once again, 'postmodernism' means two things. First, it can refer to the movement famously represented in Britain by Prince Charles. This movement rejects modernisms in the name of local communities and identities. Old-style modernist architecture, associated with large-scale, high-rise housing blocks, represented a utopian vision and confidence in social planning. Such architecture emerged from a vision of an urban, classless, anonymous, comfortable citizenry, brought into being by a benevolent state and made concrete by designers whose taste would have no truck with popular kitsch or any kind of ornamentation. Architectural postmodernism (of this kind) rejects modernist hopes and the designs that expressed those hopes, at best aiming to provide environments for a proliferation of identities. But, in the end, it seems to restrict architectural styles to those inherited from the past.

The second type of architectural postmodernism would replace the modernist vision with buildings that express no grand social or aesthetic programme. Externally, such buildings characteristically 'quote' previous styles without regard for hallowed notions of harmony or coherence, or they express a zaniness marked by a disjuncture between interiors and exteriors. Internally, they provide spaces which offer as little guidance for activities as possible. And their exteriors symbolise non-progressive liberation by imitating or riffing on pretty much anything at all. This kind of postmodernism has its analogues in other arts, literature and painting in particular. There the notion that art should reflect some stable reality or express a set of stable values (beauty, harmony), or strive for a radically different mode of reading, seeing or being, is considered, if not impossible, at least utopian. Instead, such cultural postmodernisms deal in 'pastiche' –

the arbitrary borrowing of old codes and styles. And, for them, the difference between high culture and mass or popular culture no longer works – that is to say, high cultural forms cannot be considered to have any more worth (more 'profundity' or 'maturity') than popular cultural forms. (In this sense, cultural studies is itself a form of postmodern knowledge.) This is partly because features such as self-referentiality and ironic intertextuality, which were once confined mainly to experimental and high art, have become commonplace in commercial culture also (Collins 1995, 2–3). And, finally, postmodern art and literature has come to terms with the market. The idea that great artworks can be something more than commodities has become difficult to sustain – and, again from the point of view of affirmative postmodernism, this is to be construed more as a gain than as a loss.

To draw together the threads of this discussion: postmodernism's power as a concept is that it compels us to pay attention to the ways in which the contemporary world has changed, maybe beginning in the eighties, maybe earlier. But we also need to recognise that postmodern theory only uncertainly grasped these changes. Some particularly urgent questions and doubts remain unanswered. For instance, not everyone lives under postmodern conditions: not an Indonesian making clothes for the US market at 70 cents an hour for instance. Basically, postmodernity only covered the world's urbanised rich, wherever they may live. And that was why the world it described was unprepared for the geopolitics of the war on terror.

However the greatest intellectual difficulty with the idea of postmodernity is that it is internally incoherent. If postmodernity did dominate our society in the terms that its critics claimed, we would never really know it. For the idea of the postmodern is put forward not just as another marketed image of society but as an objective description of what society really and truly is. Yet, to put it very bluntly, there is supposed to be no space for truth and reality in postmodernity. Perhaps in the end the category finds its strength in this contradiction. At least 'postmodernity' indicates that the present is to be thought of historically – that 'post' is a temporal notion after all, which allows for the likelihood that the social-economic regime it described belonged only to late twentieth-century history. To put this critique of postmodernism somewhat differently: the self-contradictory image of a postmodern world presented by progressive critics expressed their various fears at least as much as it formed an accurate picture of the world. Yet it may be that the expression of those fears can help us commit to an order where they are indeed baseless – and therein might lie the very usefulness of the diagnosis.

Further reading

Grossberg 2000; Latour 1993; Lyotard 1984; Morris 1990.

The future: policies and prophesies

For all their progressivism, the humanities have always, at least consciously, been more past- than future-directed. When they have been orientated towards what is to come, they have mainly been driven by a philosophy of abstract humanism. Theoretically at least, there has been the idealist project of developing the full and balanced potentialities of individuals so as to help secure a more civilised and unified society for the next generation. Nineteenth-century cultural critics such as Matthew Arnold added to this traditional humanism the notion that culture could be a seedbed for social change. And around the same time, idealist thinkers such as T.H. Green argued that culture was where our 'best selves' could be imagined, if not actually lived out. Culture acquired a utopian dimension. For Raymond Williams, as we have seen, ordinary culture could provide a space for forms of collective experience capable of undoing the social status quo. In this context the critic's role was to nurture such a culture.

For Raymond Williams cultural studies can be understood as the last gasp of a traditional progressive socialist view of the future – the future offers the promise of the community taking control of its conditions of production. Since his time, of course, that view of the future, and indeed any linearly progressive view on the grand scale, has become all but impossible. As has the notion that the humanities are important agents in shaping the future. Contemporary academic knowledge in the liberal arts, as I have suggested above, remains progressive in its hopes for improvement, but it does not hold widely acknowledged hopes for new forms of society and culture, and it is increasingly unconfident about its own role in helping prepare for the future. Leaving the postmodern theorists aside, Michel Foucault's work has been especially influential in this downgrading of progressivism. For Foucault, history is a passage of punctures and abrupt transitions, rather than a continuous flow (see Foucault 1972). His contribution was liberating insofar as progressivist theories of history were profoundly judgmental. As we have seen, they approved of what was on the side of progress (as they conceived of it), but everything else, it is no exaggeration to say, was on the side of death. Moreover, Foucault argued that social policies based on a progressivist theory of history (such as the replacement of old forms of cruel punishment by imprisonment) could increase the regulation of social and individual action in ways that did not so much lead to liberation as to the increased docility of populations. But his dismantling of linear history also helped undercut a primary legitimation of his own institutional site: the academic humanities.

Perhaps most powerfully of all – although this is not a line of thought that Foucault himself pursued – it has become clear that the harnessing of a rhetoric of progress by authorities, especially in so-called 'undeveloped' regions, may encourage projects that are often not in the best interests of the environment or of the poor. A classic case of this is dam-building in China and South Asia, which has been the object of devastating critique by activists, the most famous of whom is the novelist Arundhati Roy (see Roy 1999 and also Sen 2001 for a strong liberal defence of developmentalism). In these cases, in a profound inversion of values, progressive politics becomes an insistence on sustainability or conservation. The critique of developmentalism resonates with a wider unease, tinged with guilt, that today's population is consuming more than its fair share of finite resources and is jeopardising the responsibility of the present generation to deliver a safe and sustainable future to its heirs. (See p. 211–2 for Andrew Ross's rather different approach to this topic.)

The question is: what is the place of the future in cultural studies (which to some degree means 'in the culture') after progressivism? As was the case for the past, this question leads in two broad directions: the future exists in representations or images of the future (images which may contain an element of prophecy of course); it also exists in the planning which attempts to prepare for this future. Most of this section will deal with the latter instance, since cultural studies has become deeply involved with planning processes under the rubric 'cultural policy', but it is important to have a broad understanding of how the future is imagined today.

We know that the faltering of progressivism has not led to a return to the old views of history as cyclical, providential, as awaiting messianic redemption or as undergoing continual degradation, at least in any sustained form. And even though clairvoyance, palmistry, tarot card reading and so on have had a 'new age' revival since the seventies, the faltering of progressivism has not led, in the West, to a major revivification of the magical forms of prediction that characterised pre-Enlightenment epochs. In fact the decline of the concept of progress seems linked to an increase in confidence in rational prediction (based in part on probability calculations). Prediction has become what in the fifties came to be called forecasting, which thought of the future not as a domain to be imagined or to be speculated about but as the result of present actions, whether intended or unintended (Bindé 2001, 94). Forecasting is not just an expression of a confidence that we can, to some degree, control the future and calculate the probabilities, but that knowing the future first (whether we can control or not) accrues material advantage. At any rate, it relies on a confidence that we have enough information about both past and present to extrapolate beyond them. The extraordinary panic in the USA about an event such as 9/11 can also be understood as a response to the disruption of forecasts and forecasted risks. It was unforeseen in an epoch when more and more is, at least officially, foreseen, at least at the 'macro' (large-scale) level. (This, of course, goes right against the grain of postmodernist thought.) And the foreseeability of the future means that the future is increasingly an object for political and managerial processes. Global warming, for instance, is not just one of the most urgent challenges to internationalism, but is also an important if not (yet?) overwhelming political and technical issue on the basis of the predicted future.

The forecasted future takes cultural shape and splits off from the experts to join the world of entertainment and culture in representations that have become a genre all of their own. We can call these images 'futuristic' with an especial relation to science fiction, itself the genre of imaginable futures and at its beginning closely allied to new technologies: for instance, Hugo Gernsback, generally regarded as the founder of modern science fiction, was the producer of the first radio magazine and a pioneer retailer of electronics. (The term 'futurist' itself begins its history in another cultural realm, as a name for those who believed that the divine coming would occur in foreseeable human history.) Futuristic narratives and images are divided internally into utopian and dystopian visions – the futuristic has a deep historical relation to utopianism but nonetheless, of the two, the dystopian becomes more powerful when the future seems to be wholly under the control of the forces of managerialism and social planning. After all, where in today's popular culture are the utopian alternatives to, say, *Blade Runner*, *The Truman Show* or *Minority Report*?

Futuristic images of the future are of course projections of the present in which they were created. Watching fifties sci-fi movies, for instance, can be an uncanny experience as, on the one hand, now outdated technologies (the rotary dial telephone, the reel-to-reel computer) exist as the latest thing in the future, while, on the other, that future seems to share little with where we seem actually to be going (skyscrapers towering into outer space, linked by shiny, highly organised, mass transport systems) (Gleik 1997). But despite this, and more interestingly, the faltering of progressivism has led to an often implicit, somewhat unsettling and certainly not literally logical, sense that *we are living in the future now*. This is in part a result of major publicity campaigns for new technologies. Since the twenties technologies such as electricity, television, radio and personal computers have been sold as the future: let the 1939 'City of the Future' exhibition at New York's World Fair stand as an example of this – it presented an imaginary twenty-first century megapolis, a city of 'science, of atomic power, of space travel and of high culture' as the journal *Amazing Stories* put it. How

71

wrong can you get? But, in the last instance, understanding the present as the future here today needs to be understood as an effect of the long history of Western utilitarianism by which present situations and policies have been abstracted out of the continuum of traditions and life-ways in order to be assessed in terms of their future effects. For to judge the present by its future effects is already, in an important sense, to be living in that future.

The present's appropriation of the future can be felt in many cultural zones. It is felt, for instance, in the *Back to the Future* sub-genre of science-fiction films in which time travel takes not just the form of exploration but (whatever the contradictions involved) of rescue of the present – that is, travelling into the future allows an intervention in the present (as a future past) that will change the future. In this genre, relations between the past and present are dynamised; no deep difference between the two is conceded. It is also felt in those fictions where present-day everyday life, proceeding ordinarily enough, suddenly opens up to the unexpected and new: cloned dinosaurs on a holiday island in *Jurassic Park*, or the visit of a spaceship to the American suburbs in *ET*. Here the future is not some other thing: it's a little twist in the way things are.

For all that, the intersection between the present and the future is also often spoken of through a trope of radical newness. In the words of Thomas Homer-Dixon, an influential futurologist: 'The past century's countless incremental changes in our societies around the planet, in our technologies and our interactions with our surrounding natural environments, have accumulated to create a qualitatively new world' (Homer-Dixon 2000, 3). Paradoxically, this new world is the world of a future that is happening now. It's a newness that is not essentially political or cultural, since at least the formal structures of politics and culture have not changed radically, even if their relations to social formations have indeed changed. There is a strange disjunction between newness as theorised by figures such as Homer-Dixon and the innocuous futures of Steven Spielberg, or the gloomy futurism of the Hollywood imaginary, or indeed of mid-twentieth century dystopian classics such as Aldous Huxley's *Brave New World* and George Orwell's *1984*. Perhaps one can say that, in general, today's sense of the future tends towards mild utopianism when it concentrates on communications and social connectivity, and to dystopianism when it concentrates on social control and nature (these are topics which will be explored further in the sections on digitisation and nature below). What seems most of all to ground our sense of the future is the notion that human biological existence is leaving the order of nature and entering the order of technique and science. Otherwise put, the old distinction between the organic and inorganic is crumbling, which places us already inside a post-human future whose larger possibilities and threats we cannot envisage. And that is a world in which totality (the drawing together into a single system) extends into nature itself, so that the agent of this appropriation – which in the final analysis can be nothing but capitalism – is seen both as more powerful and secure than ever before but also as exposed to massive risks and total disasters simply because the system is both so complex and so unified.

Cultural policy

As we have begun to see, cultural critique within the humanities has not felt the responsibility to spell out, in any detail, the means by which contemporary conditions might be changed. It was the social sciences, born in the age of planning, which contributed concrete attempts to order the future ever since early sociologists such as Auguste Comte and Henri de Saint-Simon developed detailed blueprints for future societies and, in doing so, provided the ethos for French state governance. (In Britain a somewhat similar, if much less statist, role was played by the followers of Jeremy Bentham.) But a branch of cultural studies has developed a planning rather than a humanist relation to the future through embracing the study of the processes and norms of policy making.

Cultural policy itself has a history. Jim McGuigan has sketched various moments in its development in Britain since the mid-nineteenth century, a scheme that (albeit with some important variations) is applicable to other Western European nations. He singles out four moments, each dominated by a particular paradigm legitimating state support for cultural activities: social control (in which culture was supported to counter the supposed levelling and anarchical tendencies of democracy from about 1850 to 1940); national prestige (from the early forties to the early sixties); social access, which emphasised the need for neglected communities to participate in the wider culture (from the mid sixties to the late seventies); and the market-orientated policies of the present (McGuigan 1996, 54–60).

As a branch of cultural studies, however, cultural policy studies has a narrower range and a narrower history. It began as a strand of analysis, again dependent on Michel Foucault, that questioned whether cultural studies was an effective critical practice. It made the point that cultural studies did not spell out how critique might lead to practical outcomes (see Bennett 1998a). From the cultural policy point of view, in order to achieve practical outcomes one needs to influence the actual governance and organisation of culture, and that is only possible, first, by having a secure place within the social system (i.e. as a discrete, transparent and principled academic discipline), and then by engaging the institutions which do govern 'culture' – which means in effect by becoming involved in the policy-making process.

This means giving up on the scorn of bureaucracy and the idealisation of the intellectual as remote from the messy, corrupting world. At the level of theory, this move was backed by an interpretation of Foucault's theory of modern power, in which flows of power are not to be regarded as instruments of repression or control, but, in principle, as empowering and forming their subjects, typically by processes of government (which is when power becomes so-called 'governmentality'). And importantly, these governmental flows of power are also characteristically open to reflection and negotiation. It was in these terms that cultural studies also turned to the German sociologist, Max Weber's concept of 'value-rationality', which sanctioned the bureaucratic implementation of values – Weber here drew upon a long Prussian history in which German philosophers and theorists such as Johann Fichte and Wilhelm von Humboldt were involved in policy making and administration circa 1800 (see Hunter 1994, a key document in this line of thought). At any rate this strand of cultural studies has had the effect of making co-operation between culture, theory and government respectable, if not uncontroversial. And it has been encouraged by pressure on academics to produce work with practical outcomes.

From a different perspective, a widespread acknowledgement of culture's economic and hence national value has encouraged governments to develop cultural policies. Four particular, if very various, forces have led governments in this direction. First, the growing sense of the economic importance and potential of cultural industries, and in particular of cultural tourism; second, the perceived threats to national culture under neo-liberal international trade policies and the financial and distributive might and reach of Hollywood and US brands; third, the backlash against subsidised high/avant-garde art which offends so-called community values (a term which means, in this context, the views of cultural conservatives and in some cases of 'silent' majorities); and finally, the emergence of governmentally endorsed and managed multiculturalism. There are at least four different frameworks, then, within which national cultural policy tends to be articulated: that centred on the cultural industries or arts organisations themselves; that centred on the national economy; that centred on cultural nationalism and self-promotion; and that centred on local cultural communities.

The impulsion towards cultural policy studies is less powerful in the USA, which does not have a co-ordinated cultural policy framework, than it is in the rest of the developed world. In Canada, the UK and Australia – to mention only Anglophone nations – the old neo-Foucauldian form of cultural policy has been transmuted into support for 'creative industries' and 'cultural development'. The term 'creative industries' is relatively recent, having emerged in the seventies with the English regional councils (especially the Greater London Council) and then the 1994 Australian Commonwealth cultural policy document, *Creative Nation*, leading the way. The concept of creativity implicit in the term is much older: the notion that ordinary cultural activities are creative and cannot be seconded to high culture on this ground goes back in cultural studies to the first chapter of Raymond Williams' *The Long Revolution*. Creativity for Williams is not a high romantic concept that points to a creator's God-like imaginative powers, but a general human capacity. Today, however, it is used more in the sense that advertising agencies have 'creative directors'. This involves a glossing over of important – arguably crucial – nuances and distinctions:

while few would mourn the end of the old idea of privileged aesthetic creative imagination, there remain real differences in the kinds of skills and talents required to write a script for *The Simpsons*, say, and copy for a marketing catalogue.

The concept of 'cultural development' was originally articulated by French foreign policy bureaucrats and UNESCO during the 1960s. As Lisanne Gibson and Tom O'Regan put it in a definition that begs a large question: 'cultural development gives priority to the building and enhancing of cultural capacity for the twin purposes of both social and cultural inclusion *and* industry development' (Gibson and O'Regan 2002, 5). (The question this begs is, of course, do industry development and cultural inclusion routinely work in the same direction?) On the other hand, creative-industries discourse emphasises cultural activities, based on individual talent with market potential, paying special attention to cultural forms that can produce intellectual property (in US economic circles, where the term 'creative industries' is barely less used, such industries are sometimes known simply as the 'copyright industries'). The notion of the creative industry thus draws energy from the sense that contemporary economies are increasingly based on intangibles, including design, style and imagination. It often seems, however, that 'creative industries' has become a term used mainly by those with a vested interest in talking up the contribution of their particular sector to national economies. At one level, creative industry policy is a form of industrial policy like any other, concentrating on matters such as tax concessions and incubation schemes.

More particularly, the aim of much creative industries and cultural development work is to develop synergies and partnerships between the public and private sectors for a wide variety of leisure and cultural interests and enterprises in specific locations (O'Regan 2002, 18–20) These might include, to conjure a list at random: swimming pools, art centres, Internet cafes, comedy festivals, walking trails, libraries (although public libraries are probably the most popular and least commercialised of publicly subsidised cultural institutions), fashion shows, dance companies and public artworks. As such, cultural development policy needs to work with town planning, industry-facilitation programmes and the marketing departments of governments at various levels. When we reach this degree of concreteness, that question as to the status of the creative industries returns: to what degree do they have their own particular status and economic structure; to what degree are they really a form of service industry? Some proponents of the term argue for the latter, although in doing so they risk expressing a bias against the aesthetic as such since art and creativity of course have not traditionally seen themselves or been seen as *services* (Cunningham 2002, 59–60).

So cultural planning remains primarily focussed on the development of specific places (usually nations or cities) and characteristically works hand in hand with other policies designed to encourage local growth, and which are responsive to global flows and the neo-liberal political–economic environment. This is so even though the evidence for the argument that cultural development in cities leads to economic

75

expansion is ambiguous. Partly because of this, there have been various attempts to present cases for cultural development of urban areas in terms which include concepts such as 'cultural rights' in addition to more narrowly economic ones (see Landry and Bianchini, 1995). 'Cultural rights' traditionally means an individual's right to partici-pate in and express themself through a culture of their own choosing, but it can be extended to include the right to cultural respect from others, and cultural policy inter-sects with cultural rights at the point where one of the objectives of the first is to ensure the second (see http://www.unescobkk.org/culture). Cultural studies of course is well placed to demonstrate the importance of cultural rights and the politics of difference to which they belong.

To summarise a large debate, we can itemise the most often discussed problems with the creative industry approach in relation to cultural studies, taking artists', politicians' and academics' perspectives in turn. From the point of view of producers, policy makers tend to underplay the importance of their participation in the process, as well as paying insufficient attention to the logics of prestige and innovation which order their activities, especially in the high arts. (What tends to really matter to artists and producers is the quality of their contribution to the genre and recognition of that by peers.) Under cultural policy 'culture' risks becoming official and bland. It has after all been approved and planned for. A form of censorship may also enter in which art must either respect not so much democratic as majoritarian values and interests (in particular as mediated through the market) or become part of official cultural diversity policies. A great deal of strong and/or radical culture cannot survive the politician and bureaucrat's blessing.

The differences between different arts and cultural fields also tend to be lost sight of in cultural policy formation. The old high arts especially tend to be individualistic and governed by ideals that stand outside or even resist bourgeois and economistic values (even if they regularly feed techniques and styles into more commercial modes). Paradoxes abound here since the more programmatically non-commercial the artist the more subsidy, usually from government, he or she requires to fulfil large-scale projects – as policymakers are likely to point out. The rationalism and commitment to the equiva-lence of cultural forms that most cultural policy thinking requires means that the question of quality is marginalised. Although arguments about the allocation of funds for highly subsidised, high-status arts such as opera as against more popular forms are endemic, and help show why cultural policy is necessary, that argument is not itself an argument about quality, since, as we shall see in more detail in Part 7, it is tendentious to assume that any form of culture is of itself of higher quality than another.

From the point of view of the politicians, cultural policy creates problems also. They become vulnerable to the question, for instance, of why public money is being spent on any specific project, particularly avant-garde ones whose acceptance is weak in the wider community. And they may be compelled to confront the real tensions between the emphasis on multiculturalism (thought of as the encouragement of different cultures within one nation-state) or cultural diversity (thought of as the openness to different cultural global flows) on the one side, and the perceived demand for cultural cohesion within nation-states on the other. In most Western states majorities support the latter, whereas cultural policy analysts and cultural studies academics alongside minority communities themselves support the former.

From the academic point of view, it is probably the case that cultural policy studies tend to reduce independence. Many cultural policy academics work in centres that are dependent on contracts from governments and large cultural businesses, and have foregone the traditional autonomy of academic research. There are dangers in this move since academic independence also provides space for scholarship extending beyond the realm of the practically useful: for example detailed research into historical backgrounds or careful reading of texts, films, images and so on which are critical in the sense that they uncover the value assumptions, rhetorical moves, contextual references, etc. of their objects. Certainly cultural policy itself cannot help articulate an analysis of society and culture that will actually inspire, or at any rate provide a point of reference for, artists, writers and other cultural workers.

Given all these difficulties, it is still the case that it is important for cultural studies to demonstrate that particular cultural landscapes are not natural or inevitable but are instead shaped by particular policies and modes of production. The study of cultural policy is a powerful aid to such a pedagogy. More than that, as long as resources for cultural production are limited and ordered by some kind of public administration then cultural policy will be necessary, and sensitive cultural policy important. More than that, cultural policy study is also an offspring of cultural studies, the main purpose of which is to contribute towards the training of would-be arts administrators, policy consultants and project managers – it is vocational, which is to its great advantage. Cultural policy's dependence on others (politicians, private-sector patronage, economic planners, philanthropists) may mean that its academic branch will continue to lack status in relation to more autonomous, idealist and critical fields, but I can foresee a future in which cultural studies academics increasingly seek out possibilities of exchange with cultural policy professionals and in which (given the university system's entrepreneurial turn) academics will increasingly need to moonlight as consultants anyway. So for all the difficulties and limits that a cultural policy approach poses for cultural studies, it is clearly one of the discipline's more stable elements. The crucial question that this picture of the future makes us confront is: how precisely should we balance cultural policy against the less instrumental engagements of critique, celebration and scholarship?

Further reading

Barr 2003; Bennett 1998a; Crane 2002; Cunningham 1992b; Miller 1993; Ross 1991.

Part 3

SPACE

Thinking globalisation

As we've begun to see, since the nineties, globalisation, a word with multiple meanings, has replaced 'postmodernism' as a master term used to name, interpret and direct the social and technological transformations of the contemporary era. Among its various meanings, two stand out. It refers to the colonisation of more and more areas of life with market forces in more and more places. As such, it overlaps with neo-liberalism, since neo-liberalism names the doctrine and policies that most consciously promote this colonisation. It overlaps with capitalism as well, since capitalism is the mode of production by which contemporary markets are supported. Globalisation, then, names the global dissemination of capitalism, especially in its more market-orientated forms.

Globalisation also refers to the process by which planetary distance is being overcome. As the theory has it: a new 'borderless world' is appearing, freed from the tyranny of distance. At the very least this transformation means that local acts increasingly have consequences or objectives across a distance – which is Anthony Giddens' influential definition of globalisation (Giddens 1990, 64).

These two meanings of 'globalisation' seem to point in slightly different directions: one social, the other spatial, although in fact, and as will become apparent, there are many points at which they merge. The merging of the social and the spatial means that it is easy to over-emphasise the degree to which market forces and capitalism are extending into all corners of the world. In particular, it is easy from the fastness of middle class life in the world's 'metropolitan' regions to forget that, for instance, much production in sub-Saharan Africa is not capitalist at all. Or that about 2 billion of the world's population are not on the electricity grid while 4.5 billion have no access to telecommunications. And, finally, the notion of globalisation encourages the processes it describes: Paul du Gay, for instance, argues that the discourse of globalisation allows various kinds of authorities to intervene 'to shape, normalise and instrumentalise' institutions 'in the name of making "globalisation" more manageable' (du Gay 2000a, 116).

Space

At any rate, to think through the concept of the 'global' is – or seems to be – to think more in terms of space than of time. This in itself is a sign of a shift in our analytic habits. Over the past thirty or years or so (not coincidentally the time frame of contemporary globalisation), thinking about space has changed. It used to be that time was the dimension granted primary agency by social and cultural theory. Space had little or no agency. That is to say, history changed society while geography provided the ground upon which history worked. This way of conceiving the time–space relation was a heritage of that progressive temporality developed during the West's modernising era in which history promised much. Conversely, identities and societies that had not yet entered the processes of modernisation (and were thus placed outside history) were defined in spatial terms. Such societies were, so to say, trapped in sheer locality.

But today geography has been transformed. Its object is now what Doreen Massey has called 'the stretching of social relations over space' (Massey 1994, 23), or, otherwise put, the way that the geography orders and enables (particular forms of) society and culture. In the academy, this means that, disciplines such as sociology and anthropology, geography jostles for space with cultural studies. More concretely, at the intersection of cultural geography and cultural studies, the older, modernist notion of 'space' (an abstract grid detached from the human world) is replaced by notions of 'place' (space broken down into localities and regions as experienced, valued and conceived of by individuals and groups). (See de Certeau 1984, 91–130, for the classic definition of the space/place opposition.) This leads to a problem for the category of the 'global': it cannot be experienced in the ways that, say, a town or even a country can be. And yet it is not an abstract grid either: it has a real presence in everyday life. Furthermore, it soon becomes obvious that articulations of space (and time) differ within and across cultures, and articulations of space (and time) are at stake in the struggles around how to organise and plan for the future. Indeed it becomes apparent that space and time are not easy to pull apart. For instance, at the moment there are few hotter political issues than whether one is for or against globalisation – and the terms of that debate make it clear that globalisation is a temporal, social and political concept as well as a spatial one. They address divisions about what future society should be like in the same breath that they deal with questions about how we might manage to defeat the tyranny of distance.

A brief history of globalisation

Given globalisation's complexity, it is useful to have a sense of its history, which in part duplicates the underlying conditions of 'postmodernity' discussed above. Popular understandings of globalisation seem to regard it as a more or less continuous (if uneven) process leading to a contemporary borderless world as its more or less inevitable endpoint. This has become a contested topic among historians and sociologists with, for instance, fierce debates about whether national economies are more globalised today than they were around 1900, or whether national governments play a greater or lesser part in ordering their citizens' lives than they did in the past (for a good introduction into one 'global history' school, see Hopkins 2002; for the argument that the late nineteenth century saw more globalised economies than today, see Hirst and Thompson 2000). And because globalisation by definition is not simply a Western process, the history of globalisation, like the history of modernisation (a topic to which it is intimately related), leads to the question: what are the non-Western trajectories towards globalisation?

Historians today speak of 'archaic globalisation' – exchanges between regions, and especially non-European regions, which existed outside modern states and economies (Bayley 2002). However, the 1648 Peace of Westphalia stands as a key moment in the emergence of modern globalisation since it was then that the modern idea of the sovereign state first gained wide recognition. This paved the way for all regions of the globe to share a single political structure (i.e. the state) and for international relations to take shape as relations between nation-states who, between themselves, possess sovereignty over the total land mass.

At another level globalisation needs to be regarded as the outcome of a history of Western expansionism, which began in 1492, and which reached its apogee in the late nineteenth century when the major European powers (along with the USA) drew the rest of the world into their economic and/or political spheres. Nineteenth-century imperialism was driven not just by military power but by a set of communication technologies of which the most important were the railway, refrigeration, steam shipping and the telegraph (which first freed communication across a distance from transportation: see Carey 1989). These modes of transportation and communication necessitated the division of the globe into a universally accepted grid of latitudes and longitudes, as well as the establishment universally of Greenwich Mean Time in 1884. Abstract global space as understood in our terms comes into existence at this point.

During the imperialist epoch some Western nations became affluent to a hitherto unimaginable degree. (Historians have contested the actual economic benefits of imperialism for European states, but the weight of evidence is that empire played a crucial role in their wealth production (see Arrighi, Silver and Ahmad *et al.* 1999, 37–97). Partly as a result of this affluence, their political systems were slowly democratised, and they began to fund social agencies aimed at improving (or, depending on your point of view, managing) the education, culture and health of their populations. Indeed around 1900 many socialists were also imperialist because the money to implement social policies was thought to require imperial profits. After the Great Depression of the 1930s which intensified working-class activism, and, even more, once World War II had demonstrated the productive power of state-managed economies (not least in Germany and the Soviet Union), Western states developed large welfare apparatuses and tax regimes aimed at the redistribution of wealth. By that time these policies were funded mainly by the remarkable growth in trade and output between Europe, Japan and the USA – the precondition of late twentieth-century globalisation. In the ex-colonies, programmes of industrialisation and import-substitution were encouraged but, despite this, immigration from poor to rich nations boomed during the post-war years, feeding funds and cultural changes back into undeveloped regions and accelerating transnational mobility generally.

As we have seen, after World War II European imperial states gradually divested themselves of direct control of their colonies (the British had drawn back from governance of white settler-colonies from the second half of the nineteenth century). The main impetus behind the withdrawal was the resistance to colonialism and will to nationalism by the subject peoples themselves, but there can be no doubt that the widespread revulsion towards racism which followed the revelations of the Nazi genocides, and the example of the Japanese (who fought their war in part under a banner of anti-European colonialism, although that is often forgotten), also played an important role. In the early years of decolonisation, most ex-colonies followed policies of development that involved close state management of economies and a relative lack of exposure to market forces.

There remains considerable debate as to why the Western regime of welfarism began to lose ideological steam, and why neo-liberalism and entrepreneurialism replaced it as orthodoxy. It is probably best to regard the transformation as the result of a confluence of more or less contingent factors, some economic, some technological, some political and some cultural. Among the most important of the underpinnings of contemporary globalisation was the spread of industrialisation throughout the decolonised world, under the ideology of development and the guidance of transnational agencies. This process was spurred on by the felt vulnerability of the Western economies to the Arab oil states after the OPEC cartel engineered price rises in 1974. This (along with, in the USA, the Vietnam War) triggered inflation and accelerated declines in profitability in first-world manufacturing and primary commodity sectors and thus intensified demands for economic restructuring aimed at increased competitiveness. Economic restructuring meant directing investment into sectors where return on capital and productivity rates were comparatively high. The constraints that fixed-currency and financial regulation imposed upon national competitiveness became more and more apparent as flights of capital punished relative losses of national productivity more and more immediately. Nation-states pursued policies that would encourage foreign investment and trade, deregulating their economies, offering tax breaks and so on as they jockeyed for advantage.

Simultaneously, relatively undeveloped countries were positioned as attractive sources for labour and attractive options for investment. Japan and Europe in partic-ular increased their share of international direct investment, clawing back US dominance in this area. Particularly in Anglophone countries, privatisation of state enterprises accelerated. Offshore manufacturing and first-world de-industrialisation meant that fewer workers in first-world economies worked as industrial (and espe-cially skilled) labourers. Unemployment grew (partly too because it was used by economic policy managers as a brake on inflation and partly because women's partici-pation in the workforce increased from a low base in the post-war period) so that it now tends to float between 6 and 15 per cent of those in the labour market. These tendencies had profound cultural and political effects, including the loss of union influ-ence, the decline of the old left socialist parties based on labour solidarity and the downgrading of class as a category for social and cultural analysis — all of which, of course, helped cultural studies itself to emerge.

Another crucial moment for globalisation was the fall of communism in 1989, which meant the end of the Cold War and the disappearance of socialism as a legitimate political system and idea. The USA now became the sole world military superpower (which meant that more than ever it dominated economic policy through its control of transnational agencies such as the IMF and the World Bank who actively pursued neo-liberal policies). The opening up of the Eastern bloc hastened the process by which more and more corporations were becoming involved in transnational trade of one kind or other. Some firms outsourced their manufacturing, without attempting to invest in or control the overseas plants, merely globalising their marketing strategies and distribution chains. Some franchised their brand and organisational expertise across nations. Others merely sought to increase the importance of export markets to their trading. The political and cultural influence of those corporations that had full-scale operations in many countries (multinational companies) increased as they took a bigger and bigger share of the global economy. But such companies differ widely in how much control is exerted by the head office over its branches.

Technological factors in the process of globalisation include the development of new communications technologies, especially the Internet, but also the application of computing to the financial system. The latter enabled the internationalisation of finance capital and services spurred on by the deregulation of banks and the floating of currencies. New financial instruments (warrants, options) became possible as computing power grew. And fast, cheap, transcontinental air travel underpinned a vast extension of global business exchange, as well as positioning tourism as a key global industry.

Vernacular globalisations

Globalisation as a concept in journalism, politics and everyday life refers to something rather different than this historical trajectory. Let's look a little more closely at how the term seems to work in the ordinary life of the middle-class Westerner – these observations being impressionistic since there is little work on how globalisation is conceptualised and perceived on the street. It can mean simply the shrinking of the world (the theoretical term is 'time–space compression') as instantiated in what have become a bunch of truisms. Our clothing is most likely made in China or some other 'third-world' country. Communicative distance is being destroyed by the Web, cheap telephony and so on. Jet travel is the bus service of the global era. This shrinking leads to sameness: the sense that national and local differences are being erased as import/export trade grows and brands are globalised. Shopping in Singapore is like shopping in Vancouver, which is like shopping in Berlin. Less commonly globalisation is understood to mean that nation-states are becoming less powerful – the populist right-wing attack on the United Nations in the USA is just one expression of this. Globalisation is also often connected to large-scale movements of labour and the politics of immigration and multiculturalism as they have taken shape since the 1970s.

Vernacular globalisation can also imply what we might call either a transnational multiculturalism or a popular cosmopolitanism, which probably does carry beyond the rich West. I mean by this the transnational 'we are all one' feeling, promoted by Benetton, the Olympics, the various World Cups and satellite television charity events such as 1985's 'Live Aid' concert. Such popular cosmopolitanism is also triggered by geography itself, and, historically, can be seen in the popularisation of globes, which allow people to imagine the world as a planet they share with others. Nowadays geographical globality is probably communicated most effectively through ventures into space. The globe is a smallish image when beamed back from a spacecraft – as, for instance, seen on satellite weather maps. Our identification with the spatial view of the planet 'from above' allows us more easily to imagine a global community.

Popular cosmopolitanism can also mean the kind of transnational or cross-cultural sensibility and competence that are required by diasporic peoples, who often have to live within two cultures. Filipino maids in Kuwait; Sudanese taxi-drivers in Australia; Maori building labourers in Chicago; Mexican car-washers on the US eastern seaboard; Pakistani shopkeepers in Britain; Iraqi traders in Indonesia; Australian teachers in Papua New Guinea; Turkish piece-workers in Germany; even middle-class South Asian IT workers in Vancouver – all these folk need a capacity to work and think across cultures if they are to survive. But such capacities are not limited to those who travel: in Southern Africa most people (except for the whites) have, for decades, spoken more than one language and dealt intimately with more than one culture as they negotiate with their employers and their neighbours from other tribes. A South

Asian working for a US bank's phone help-line in Mumbai needs to be able to inhabit (and impersonate) a certain Americanness daily. It's likely that globalisation will disseminate such cosmopolitanisms much more widely.

A further sense of vernacular globalisation is much more negative. Globalisation in this sense means the increasing control of local and national economies by big capitalism and neo-liberal policies so as to reduce local autonomy and rights and increase insecurity of employment and a wider sense of dislocation. Globalisation here is regarded as being to blame for continuing and increasing economic inequities across nations and regions. This sense of globalisation merges into another: globalisation as the Americanisation of the world, sometimes for good, mainly for ill.

Global sameness

The key propositions of vernacular globalisation, then, are that distance and difference are both being reduced. It shares this interpretation with the mode of globalisation theory, which argues that the processes of globalisation lead to a global uniformity. Key theorists of totalising globalism such as David Harvey and Immanuel Wallerstein, who take what is often called 'the global-systemic approach', come out of Marxism, and their understanding of globalisation is a version of the Hegelian–Marxist understanding of capitalism. For them globalism is capitalism, and capitalism is a mode of production that swallows up all the alternative modes of production and radically constrains the lives of those who live inside it (see Wallerstein 1999; Harvey 1990). Globalisation is particularly dangerous from this point of view because it places democratic structures at risk. Strong democratic governance is local, so the argument goes, since the larger the territory under political control the more faint the local voices heard at the centre.

Global systems theory belongs with another post-Hegelian school, this time those who connect the *global* to the *universal*. (The difference between these concepts is crucial: what is universal is true everywhere and forever whereas what is global is merely a feature of the planet here and now.) Public intellectuals such as Francis Fukuyama have pictured globalisation precisely as the realisation of universals. As we know, Fukuyama has urged the 'end of history' argument by claiming that all societies are tending towards democratic capitalism, as if it were a universal and basic truth that democratic capitalism is the most just and efficient mode of social organisation (see Fukuyama 1992).

One risk in all such accounts is that they lead us to underestimate how differently processes of globalisation work in different places. Indeed there are some places where globalisation locally causes something like the opposite of what 'globalisation' is generally assumed to mean: increases in unionism among Hollywood writers, or the increasing isolation of island communities (such as Pitcairn Island) which are not part of global travel networks, especially since the decline of shipping (Massey 1994, 148), or indeed (with qualifications since it is itself a global movement), political resistance to globalisation itself. Certainly in ways that matter a great deal there is no globalism conceived of as an overarching world community. Nothing better indicates the strength of a shared sense of global collectivity than international aid figures, which are depressing. In 1974 OECD nations promised to allocate 0.7 per cent of their GDP to aid; in 1997 the actual figure devoted to overseas aid was about 0.22 per cent (Development Aid Committee 1998). At the time of writing the USA gives 0.13 per cent of its GDP in aid. Indeed US hegemony itself works against the global community in important ways: this is the reason why co-operative action on global warming and a host of other transnational issues has stalled.

Another related risk with these Hegelian accounts is that they overestimate the decline of difference as such, even in spaces which are well covered by the social and political processes of globalisation. Indeed there is a case to be made that differences across the world may well not be decreasing, even though of course there are now things (technologies, cultural references, some social and economic organisation elements) that more societies share than they used to. But this in itself does not make these societies less different in any absolute sense; that depends on what else is happening in those societies, and some globalising technologies (the tape recorder, the Web) can actually intensify local differences by helping to maintain and disseminate local cultures.

In the final analysis, there is a conceptual problem in the argument about decreasing differences. How can one tell if the world contains less local differences now than it once did, since these differences are based in experiences, which are, strictly speaking, incomparable? The spread of baseball to Japan seems to create a 'sameness' between it and the USA, and yet the experience of watching a Japanese baseball match is very different from that of watching a US game (and both may differ widely among themselves). Are they more the same than the experiences of a US baseball game and a Japanese sumo-wrestling match? At one level, obviously yes, but then the sharing of a national game across two nations and two cultures allows all kinds of new differences, maybe in a more minor key, to be apparent to more sports fans. There is a sense that the convergence of games creates more difference as well as less.

To put this abstractly, to the degree that we share overarching measures of comparison and cultural references then differences increase since we have common means of, and occasions for, recognising and perceiving them. Maybe it is best to conceive of the problem like this: as communications across the world improve and as cultural forms are increasingly shared, the world is moving into a network of differences rather than of what we might call othernesses. Is what is *different* from us less different than what is *other* to us? It's a complex question and one which totalising arguments about the globalising effects of cultural homogeneity tend to overlook. (For an excellent discussion of the problems of the 'end of difference' thesis in relation to 'cultural imperialism' see Tomlinson 1991.)

Global justice

In September 1999, about 40,000 demonstrators gathered in Seattle to protest against a World Trade Organisation meeting which was to discuss the further promotion of transnational free trade. Drawn together from many parts of the world and from disparate political groups, and organised largely through e-mail and web sites, demonstrators came together to protest, in particular, job losses in industries under attack from foreign competition; the downward pressure on the wage rates of unskilled workers; child labour; the rights of indigenous peoples; environmental degradation; and what was often called the cultural imperialism of a US-dominated global media. The protest garnered enormous publicity worldwide and was seen (probably falsely) as contributing to the failure of the WTO meeting. After Seattle a number of similar protests took place in different places, including an especially violent one in Genoa in July 2001 during which a protester was shot by police.

These protests were a public face of what quickly became called the anti-globalisation movement – a name many in the movement resisted, preferring to be called the 'global justice' movement. The movement was also helped by Naomi Klein's bestselling book, *No Logo* (2000), which some regarded as its manifesto and which certainly provided it with a genealogy, including Ken Saro-Wiwa's fatal struggle against Shell oil in Nigeria. In *No Logo*, Klein combines two separate if interrelated critiques. The first is a cultural critique of the dominance of branding and marketing in contemporary capitalism – she cavils against image capitalism in the name of the relative innocence, spontaneity and authenticity of unbranded consumption and experience (seemingly under the influence of the sixties French avant-garde theorist and filmmaker Guy Debord and his early version of postmodernism known as 'situationism'). The second is an economic argument against the effects of offshore manufacturing by first-world and multinational corporations.

The events of 9/11 and the consequent 'war on terrorism' have set the global justice movement back partly because the anti-war protests absorbed and displaced its programme, and partly because the politics of anti-globalisation shifted after Al-Qaeda's attack on US interests. After all, Islamic fundamentalism is itself a form of anti-globalisation. Yet the movement has by no means lost its energy – let the widespread interest in the campaign against the mega-dams in the Indian sub-continent stand as one instance of this. Another is the continuing vitality of Europe's Association for the Taxation of Financial Transactions to Aid Citizens (ATTAC), which, among other things, urges the so-called Tobin Tax, the proposed small tax on international currency transactions. It is fairly safe to predict that in the future such agendas will be more apparent in mainstream politics.

At the heart of the appeal of the global justice movement is the fact that globalisation has increased rather than decreased global inequities. Today the richest fifth of the world's population in North America, the EU and Japan consume about 90 per cent of world's output. The combined assets of the world's three richest men are greater than those of the population of all least developed nations and their 600 million people (United Nations Development Programme 1999, 3; for a perhaps rather exaggerated account of inequality and globalisation see Greider 1997). These are traditionally 'internationalist' concerns, the solution to which would seem to require a centralisation of world governance.

But the movement also reacts to newer formations, that is to the way in which, because the world is increasingly interconnected, actions in one place have consequences elsewhere. Hence massive over-consumption in first-world countries (especially the USA) shapes economies and environments around the world. Choosing a teak outdoor table helps destroy wilderness in a country such as Indonesia; driving a car rather than taking public transport not only worsens the environment for everyone but weakens public transport industries nationally and internationally. The global justice movement, then, is consistently concerned to bring home the effects of first-world consumption on the larger world.

The difficulty that the movement faces, however, is that these arguments have an economic dimension, and the measurement of the costs and benefits of even neo-liberal economic policies is difficult. Take for instance the issue of offshore manufacturing: if the loss of manufacturing jobs in the USA leads to more such jobs in China isn't that to be welcomed, given that it tends to international economic equity and given that job substitution is much easier in the USA than in China? And won't increases in Chinese wages to some degree balance out decreases in US wages? Freedom of trade, increased communications and mobility of capital all help this to happen. The problem seems not so much that market liberalisation policies are wrong in grand terms but that they are deeply connected to other social transformations: in particular the urbanisation of underdeveloped nations and the increased ease of finance-capital transactions across borders. As a result, local insecurities and divisions between winners and losers increase, and so too does the urgency of the need to compensate or protect against damage. These are issues that need to be addressed on a case-by-case basis. Indeed anti-globalisation critique often leads to technical and tactical debates about the size of state welfare in particular circumstances, about efficient, equitable loan mechanisms for raising public funds, about legal regimes protecting landlords, about means for providing cheap money to landless peasants, about providing for urban infrastructure and housing and so on. Behind such issues, however, lies a larger one: what kind of government (protected by what kind of legislation and constitution) is likely to enact good policy while remaining sensitive to popular will?

More abstractly, the anti-globalisation movement is also a form of resistance to the process of 'de-socialisation' by which, under increasing global competitive pressures, nation-states tend to manage all institutions in terms of their relation to economic productivity, so as to increase efficiency and accessibility to market forces and a consumerist ethic. This form of state management positions each individual as a human resource, one who needs continually to increase his or her value as a resource – that is, to deliver themself to their employers as a set of energies, skills and knowledges.

The 'global justice' movement ambiguously sets itself apart from forms of progressive global politics which embrace universalisms. Among these are the human rights movement, which is open to charges of cultural imperialism since rights are historically a Western liberal notion, and which does indeed bear an uncomfortable similarity to those forms of imperialism that promised to liberate non-liberal societies (see Supiot 2003 for an excellent account of the difficult politics of globalised human rights). By the same token, it sets itself apart from the movement towards what is sometimes called 'international civil society', that is, towards a global framework for mutual deliberation over public issues aimed at achieving a common and democratic understanding and equity whose institutional bases are the liberal internationalist non-governmental organisations and think tanks rather than the more provisional and underground bases of the global justice movement itself. It is in this context that the movement returns to a humanism that insists on the dignity of the powerless – a theme that is powerfully expressed in Roy's novel, *God of Small Things*.

A third formation that needs to be distinguished from the global justice movement, and that is less institutionalised than either the international civil society or the human rights movement, is contemporary intellectual cosmopolitanism. In the West, antagonism towards localism has long been named 'cosmopolitanism', and for this reason its history too deserves briefly to be recalled. Its roots lie in ancient Greek Stoicism and, during the European Enlightenment, it was allied to the concept of 'world citizen'. During the period of imperialist, anti-Semitic nationalism, cosmopolitanism acquired largely negative overtones, often then specifically denoting 'rootless' Jews. Since the nineties it has made a recovery at least among academics as a way of negotiating between universalisms and globalisation. It has defined itself against cultural nationalism, neo-liberal globalisation and (more cautiously) against the politics of identity and postcolonialism. It has made this move by affirming border-crossing cultural flows, transnational organisations such as the progressive non-governmental organisations, and in ideological terms, doctrines of human rights that respect cultural differences. A great deal of work has gone in to arguing that cosmopolitanism need not stand in opposition to localism or 'rootedness' (see Cheah and Robbins 1998).

One limit to cosmopolitanism is that it too seems too closely allied to the intellectual framework of Western liberalism. It carries with it a specifically European and elite history remote from the actual flows of contemporary global culture. But more importantly it does not of itself bring any analytic power to bear on the conceptual/political difficulties that beset the analysis of global culture. As an expression of the embarrassed politics of Western liberalism in a global epoch, it does not itself provide a banner for cultural production. In fact its chief value would seem to be as a mode of critique of first-world cultural nationalisms and identity politics.

We have yet to see what, if any, academic concepts and cultural maps will cover the various spheres of globalised culture as older terms such as postmodernism (and post-colonialism) fade. Cultural studies itself, as I have suggested, is likely to satisfy itself with more modest projects which accept the power of global flows and technology to energise in all directions, along with an acknowledgment of the costs and risks involved in the world order which produces that energy.

Globalisation and culture

It should be clear by now that globalisation's rather abstract emphasis on large-scale, multifaceted processes, based on political economy, is rather foreign to cultural studies. Likewise, while the global justice movement is in part driven by cultural concerns, it does not chime easily with cultural studies because it tends to be suspicious of cultural commodification as such. A cultural studies approach to globalisation needs to resist the various rhetorics through which the concept is disseminated in order to remain sensitive to how local differences are both metamorphosed and maintained through the contemporary world system (Clifford 2000; Friedman 1994).

But there are a number of further cultural outcomes of globalisation to which the discipline is turning. These can be listed as follows:

1   There exists very little popular culture on a genuinely global scale (During 1997) even though globalisation has led to an increase in transnational cultural exchange and to the increased importance of export markets. What stars and products really are recognisable everywhere? Very few: maybe just one – Coca-Cola. In complex, high-investment cultural industries such as film (and to a lesser extent television), globalisation means pretty much the same as it does to, for instance, the car industry. Product is developed for various national or regional markets, tweaking marketing (and in television franchises the product itself) to take account of local differences.

2   Globalisation of cultural production restructures cultural industries. Take film: as producers sell into world markets (and Hollywood's overseas revenues are now bigger than its domestic ones), budgets for individual films increase so risks have to be minimised, leading to tighter control of the creative side of the production

by market research and stars, since these are the lynchpins of marketing campaigns. Finance and insurance are solicited from international investors to spread risk. Labour-intensive elements of production are sent offshore where costs are cheaper while intellectual rights, star power and overall project management usually remain domesticated in the USA. Certain styles seep from import back to export markets, the kung-fu-isation of Hollywood action blockbusters being an obvious example. Furthermore, global film profitability is increasingly dependent on the games, books, CDs and (in the case of children's films) toys that can be franchised from them. And on the other side, magazines and advertisers thrive on the star power that they help sustain again across national/regional boundaries. In a word, globalisation gigantises and binds some cultural niches.

3   Globalisation increases the importance of national cultural and media policies and fuels debates between cultural trade deregulators (mainly the USA and Japan, which is also a major cultural exporter) and those who want to protect local industries and cultural formations. The most famous instance was the breakdown of negotiations in the 1993 Uruguay Round of the General Agreement on Trade in Services (GATS) when the USA and EU could not agree that culture should be treated differently from other forms of production. Here the specific issue at stake was Europe's desire to preserve quotas for local television programming, but the larger issue was the right of particular nations to cultural sovereignty – to protect their cultural industries in the name of national traditions and global cultural diversity. These concerns are largely a result of US dominance of broadcast TV and film exports worldwide: The USA accounts for about 75 per cent of television exports globally. But Japanese exports into Asia, and even the Middle East, have also caused concern among nations worried about losing their cultures.

4   Local culture is certainly not preferred to import cultures across the board. To take just one instance: Marie Gillespie studied consumption among young Punjabi Londoners during the early nineties. She discovered that they responded very well to Coke advertising on television because, on the one hand, it was not English and they connected Englishness with racism, and, on the other, it was not South Asian, which they associated with the restrictions that parents implied and imposed upon them. For them, being American and young was cool, liberating – although this may be less the case since the 2003–2004 Iraq war (Gillespie 1995).

5   The increased flows between regions are intensifying the position of English as a world language. This accrues economic power to English speakers and is leading to Anglophone formations whose frame of reference is not the old Anglo-American world. Indian fiction in English is a harbinger of these.

6   Global cities have emerged as places that exercise cultural and economic sway (as against governmental or managerial control) not just nationally but regionally, either as centres of financial industries or culturally or both. They have an

extraordinary high cultural profile themselves (as 'must-see' tourist destinations). They are domiciles simultaneously of the mega-rich and of large, poor, migrant communities. It is in world cities that the infrastructure and regulatory frameworks that hyper-mobile global exchanges require are managed (Sassen 2001). Hence they are key markets for advanced architecture and design. They are also trendsetters for urbanisation, urban renewal, multiculturalism and heritage consciousness. There exist only three clear *global* cities in this sense: London, New York and Tokyo. Other large cities function as 'regional world cities'. At the time of writing these are usually considered to be Hong Kong, Mexico City, Sydney, Buenos Aires, Milan, Los Angeles, Paris, Frankfurt, Toronto, Bombay, São Paulo, Bangkok, Tapei, Johannesburg and Shanghai.

7 Globalisation intensifies the crisis over diaspora. At one level, immigration is a response to two consequences of modernisation in underdeveloped nations. State centralisation allows the increasingly effective repression of minority or unfavoured communities, sometimes causing civil wars and sometimes simply giving members of these communities strong motives to flee. And industrialisation and urbanisation cause labour surpluses and uncertainty over employment, again providing motives for immigration. At another level, immigration is enabled by the increased cultural contacts between nations: television shows, military bases, tourism, the presence of multinational corporations, all channel knowledge about rich countries to poor countries making immigration seem all the more possible and attractive. And migration feeds upon itself: once some family members are established abroad it is easier for others to follow. The cultural face of immigration is of course multiculturalism, which is discussed below.

8 Globalisation does demand new forms of mental connection across a distance. Arjun Appadurai has argued that globalisation has increased the role of imagination in everyday life. He writes:

> The imagination is no longer a matter of individual genius, escapism from ordinary life, or just a dimension of aesthetics. It is a faculty that informs the daily lives of ordinary people in myriad ways: It allows people to consider migration, resist state violence, seek social redress, and design new forms of civic association and collaboration, often across national boundaries. This view of the role of the imagination as a popular, social, collective fact in the era of globalisation recognizes its split character. On the one hand, it is in and through the imagination that modern citizens are disciplined and controlled – by states, markets, and other powerful interests. But it is also the faculty through which collective patterns of dissent and new designs for collective life emerge. As the imagination as a social

force itself works across national lines to produce locality as a spatial fact and as a sensibility, we see the beginnings of social forms without either the predatory mobility of unregulated capital or the predatory stability of many states.

(Appadurai 2001, 6)

It would be wonderful if this were true. But how are we to match this invocation of the extension of the imagination into everyday life with imagination's retreat in more formal settings? For instance, hasn't the political role of the sympathetic imagination – empathy with the suffering of other peoples – declined under the rise of identity politics and globalisation? Isn't religion historically the grandest expression of imagination, which globalisation-as-secularisation minimises? Hasn't globalisation so far led, if anything, to a narrowing of Hollywood product for instance? Doesn't it produce as much fear and paranoia as 'new forms of civic association' – just think of the war on terror? Nonetheless perhaps a case can be made that globalisation, by increasing cultural choices and forms of expression, and by drawing together less predictable audiences and collectivities, can enable experimentalism and intellectual adventure. Cultural studies needs to be a testing ground for this hope.

Further reading

Appadurai 1996; Held and McGrew 2000; Robbins 1999; Roy 1999; Sassen 1998; Tomlinson 1991.

The regional, national and local

Regions

The medium-sized units of socially organised space – and especially nations and regions – have been relatively neglected in cultural studies. They have organised divisions within cultural studies more than they have been objects of its study. For that reason, this section seeks to introduce a sense of how regions and nations work culturally rather than to provide an overview of work in the field.

One effect of globalisation which has real implications for culture is the way that increased global economic competition is dividing the world in new ways. In particular, since the late eighties there has been an increasing emphasis on 'regions', especially in Europe, North America, East Asia and South East Asia. For the most part these regions do not have fixed political borders. They exist primarily as ideas or images or inspirations (and often loose and shifting ones at that), although they can also exist as alliances designed to promote regional economic activity or security. Particular nation-states may exist in quite different regions: the USA belongs to The Americas but also (or at least its western seaboard) to the 'Pacific Rim'. A nation such as Turkey, which borders Europe and the Near East, and which once from the European point of view was regarded as simply part of the East, is now generally considered to belong to both regions, and is currently a candidate for joining the EU.

At one level, this tendency towards regionalism is usually regarded as a fall-out of the Cold War's termination and the consequent need to restructure defence alliances and to regroup into co-operative economic blocs able to stand against other larger national or regional formations, especially the USA and Japan. Regionalism is also however, to some degree at least, a cultural phenomenon. Some regions at least are thought of as the transhistorical bearers of specific and hallowed cultures. Europe and Asia in particular are reinventing themselves as cultural unities, each based on their antiquity. As Tani Barlow has argued, the East Asian Chinese diaspora has come together through a new notion of Chinese culture (*wenhua*) which involves an appropriation of Western racial thought even while focussing on Confucianism as an antidote to Westernisation (see Ong 1999, 59). Movies and television shows are produced to express (and to take advantage of) this regional identity: MTV Asia and Star TV have been at the forefront of this move. Perhaps the most famous example of Asianisation in Asia is the Japanese daytime TV drama *Oshin*, produced by NHK (Japanese Broadcasting Corporation), which has become a hit across much of Asia by appealing self-consciously to East Asian experiences and values (see Takahiko 1997). Nonetheless, anxieties about domination and submission, exclusion and inclusion lie near the surface. Japanese popular culture is saturating South Korean and Taiwanese markets, creating cultural-nationalist backlashes against their old colonial masters, especially in Korea. And the sense that Japan and China will one day struggle for cultural as well as for economic hegemony in the region problematises efforts to imagine Asia as a unity – as does the ambiguous status of the South Asian sub-continent in a larger 'Asia'.

Similarly Europe is becoming a more self-conscious cultural unity as nations create tighter and tighter links economically and politically. It may be that 'European' cultural products are still rare, and tend to be confined to the high end of the spectrum – movie co-productions between France, Germany and the UK say, or cultural histories that look for the origins of a European sensibility (most of which are produced in France). And yet in sports, tourism and holiday industries a popular Europeanism is emerging: a familiarity with and acceptance of differences within a region that is understood as shared. European football competitions have a broad fan base. The Brits holiday in Spain; Germans in Greece and Italy; Italians seem to love London. Europop is a recognisable genre.

It is noteworthy that the Americas barely exist as a cultural entity – this despite work by the Cuban anti-Spanish revolutionary José Martí for instance, circa 1890, to imagine ways that the hemisphere might 'become America' (see the essays in Fernández and Belnap 1998 for more on Martí). Which is not to say that regionalisation is not occurring there, merely that it is happening outside or in opposition to the hegemony of Anglo North America. It exists mainly in flows between Latin America and the US Chicano/a and Latino/a communities (which have a population of about 33 million, having recently overtaken African Americans in number). Yet this is a very complex phenomenon. On one level, the Spanish-language media that binds this regionalism together is increasingly visible in the USA, and Spanish television, a feast of imported *novellas* (soap operas), talk shows and music videos, creates strong transnational imaginaries and bonds. Yet on the other hand, only about half of the US Latino/a population regularly tune into the Spanish media, and the second generation, born in the USA, all speak English. What the future would seem to hold in the USA itself, then, is an Anglophone hybridised Latino/a culture, probably with little regional reach, leaving American regionalisms to flourish only south of the border.

In Africa, efforts to create a Pan-African sensibility and politics date back at least a century and have left a legacy whose failed hopes have yet to be overcome. Pan-Africanism, which derived a great deal of energy from African diasporic intellectuals such as W.E.B. Du Bois and Marcus Garvey, who hoped to establish return emigrant communities away from the ruins of slavery, remains alive as an intellectual and a political movement. Today it draws sustenance both from the concept of (non-regionalist) Africana Studies, which is becoming a standard programme of studies in the US university system, and from the failure of so many of the region's nation-states. However, it remains an open question as to whether Pan-Africanism will be able not just to overcome past disappointments but to detach itself from the abstract 'Africanism' (the stereotypes of African being) in which black affirmation and white racism exist in a tangle (Ackah 1999). A post-Pan-African African-ness, focussed on the region, is struggling to be born.

In sum then: cultures based on transnational regionalism remain underdeveloped, caught between localisms and globalism.

Nations and nationalism

Regions may remain under-examined within cultural studies but nations and nationalism have received a great deal of attention, since they are, of course, much more substantial political, economic and cultural units. Nonetheless globalisation theorists have argued at length that the nation is an obsolete or 'residual' formation (see Ohmae 1996 for an articulation of this point of view). But the groundswell of opinion and the evidence points the other way, since, after all, capitalism requires and augments regulatory and infrastructure frameworks that remain under state control (see Hirst and Thompson 1996). Most developed nations have actively promoted policies that have accelerated globalisation (albeit some more keenly and thoroughly than others) in their own interests. And it is no accident that states and nations are weakest where globalisation is weakest – that is, in Africa.

Certainly it remains one of modernity's core features that the world is divided into sovereign nation-states with no remainder. Almost everyone is born a citizen of a particular nation-state. This does not mean that everyone lives in nation-states: people can be stuck, sometimes for generations, in refugee camps in Africa, the Gaza Strip and West Bank, Pakistan and Indonesia. And certain areas of the world – the border area between Pakistan and Afghanistan for instance – are not actually under state control. But these are the exceptions rather than the rule, and indeed refugee life often generates utopian ideas of a homeland and can lead to hyper-nationalism (see Nyers 1999).

Once, nations were analysed primarily as political and economic units, but since the eighties they have been understood as much as cultural units. The most important contribution to this shift was doubtless Benedict Anderson's notion of the nation as 'imagined community' in his book of that name, a notion which has been extrapolated onto the global level, as we have seen, by Arjun Appadurai (Anderson 1991; Appadurai 1996). Anderson, an expert on Indonesian politics and history, developed the concept of the 'imagined community' in his thinking about Indonesian decolonisation. He argued that individuals who had never thought of themselves as members of a national community in the pre-colonial era came to do so as readers of newspapers and participants of print culture distributed across many local (and tribal) territories. Print media invited culturally, and indeed linguistically, disparate readers to imagine themselves as citizens of a single nation, all reading about the world at the same time. Before nationalism, to quote Achille Mbembe on Africa, 'in some cases, political entities were not delimited by boundaries in the classical sense of the term, but rather by an imbrication of multiple spaces constantly joined, disjoined, and recombined through wars, conquest, and the mobility of goods and persons' (Mbembe 2001, 27). After nationalism, individuals recognised themselves as belonging to a community of reading citizens. At the same stroke, they accepted new notions of time (time as bringing forth news and information at regular intervals; time as the measurement of national progress) and space (the borders of the nation coinciding with the reach of shared communication networks and collective interests).

Anderson's imagined community was the result of bottom-up nationalism, the popular affirmation of the political geography devised by the decolonisers, who had divided the world up into discrete nation-states. In this context, it is important to recall that, in the colonial world, national identities were simultaneously modern and anti-colonial identities. To be an Indonesian was to join the modern world – but not as a subject of the European colonial powers. The impetus to become a citizen of a sovereign nation was finally to be located in resistance to the colonisers, and in this sense it was more political than cultural. Indonesia itself had little substance: it was indeed an 'imagined' concept. Perhaps this helps explain why it could call upon extraordinary self-sacrificial passions very quickly: people were almost as willing to die for their country as they were for their religion (another ideological formation based on the organised imagination).

But it also helps explain why in many postcolonial states, including Indonesia, national unity has been so hard to sustain. Once the colonisers depart, national unity is jeopardised and communities imagine themselves once again in religious or culturalist terms, that is, as sharing their own traditional inherited culture rather than a national culture. Because most national borders the world over have been set in Europe during the imperialist era (which is one way that history passes through Europe, as Dipesh Chakrabarty reminds us), tensions between cultural units and postcolonial nations are endemic (Chakrabarty 1992). This is especially the case because the geography of the nation tends to overlook internal regional inequities and to focus on administrative and commercial urban centres. After a certain point, being a member of a national state cannot compensate for living in poor, neglected provinces.

The idea of an 'imagined community' works even less well in the metropolis than in the recent colonies. The general consensus of scholarship is that European nationalism emerges around 1800 when the political and economic will to autonomy is linked to demands for cultural self-expression. By this account, the invention of 'culture' as a concept by Herder and his romantic progeny is intimately linked to European nation-alisms. For the cultural nationalists circa 1800, collective values are stored in languages, myths, folk stories and so on – that is, in culture. This notion of culture, and the nationalism it grounds, is only very indirectly linked to the media in the terms that Anderson supposes. For this Herderian line of thought, cultures, being inherently *expressive*, require freedom to fulfil themselves. They ought not to be governed from afar, by members of other cultures: each demands its own nation and its own state.

The new national–cultural identities were often almost indistinguishable from ethno-racial ones: as we shall see in more detail below, culturalism and racism are closely connected. In this context, Etienne Balibar has argued, in a post-Marxist mode, that nationalism is a formation that allows for a sense of a community which transcends real social divisions, namely the divisions between classes (Balibar 1994). But, for him, nationalism can never quite offer the unity and satisfaction that it promises. This means that it needs to be supplemented by racism and xenophobia. His is a structural argument that is worth attending to since it does help explain nationalism's appeal, but it provides little help in accounting for the ways that relations between racism, culturalism and nationalism differ in different regions and at different times. And it does not sufficiently acknowledge that nationalism is strongest when it becomes a spur for liberation.

Today, for instance, irredentist nationalism is to be found around the globe, including of course in Indonesia, and is most powerful among communities that share a language, a tradition, a religion and an ethnic identity. Yet characteristically in such cases, nationalism from the very beginning is articulated in opposition to, and to the exclusion of, other cultural identities, especially that of the oppressor. Here xeno-phobia is not a consequence of nationalism's emptiness as much as it is part of the armoury by which the nation is achieved.

If Balibar's notion that nationalism turns to racism because of a structural inability of the nation to supply its citizens' emotional needs has its limits, there can be little doubt that his logic does seem to cover other aspects of capitalist nationalism. As we shall see, one basis of nationalism is individual attachment to the economic benefits that the state provides, but, under capitalism, these benefits are ambiguous since the economic system through which individual interests are pursued causes constant instabilities. Capitalism, after all, is committed to change, to competition, to insecurity. As such, it also and reac-tively encourages passionate attachment to ideological counter-forces, of which 'traditional' national identity is one. So modern nationalism is characteristically both an attachment to an economic structure in which markets and states combine and, to some degree, a passion running counter to market forces. There is a sense in which globalisation intensifies this dialectic. National identities are energised in resistance to the perceived groundlessness, first of transnational capital and then of the postmodernisms and cosmopolitanisms which that capital brings in its wake.

Tourism

Cultural nationalism has another more direct and more powerful, if no less complex, relation to globalisation – tourism. Certain nations market themselves as national cultures in order to attract both tourists and business investment, drawing upon the whole armoury of modern communications technology to do so. This is especially apparent in countries such as Thailand but also, for instance, in Australia and the UK. Tourism has largely been theorised in cultural studies through the sociologist John Urry's concept of the 'tourist gaze', itself an application of the theories of the 'gaze' as developed in film theory (Urry 2002). For Urry this is a historical notion, which emphasises how the emergence of tourism during the eighteenth century focussed on one particular sense – vision – and required both a material and an ideological infrastructure.

Tourists, so the argument goes, travelled – and still travel – primarily for visual pleasures which involve both the pleasures of recognition (seeing sites whose value and meaning are known in advance) and of the exotic (what they could not see at home). The tourist gaze, although pleasurable, is detached and superficial, missing the deeper meanings and experiences of the sites and lands that are toured. Following this line of thought, tourism is primarily conceived as a business enterprise whose gradual industrialisation through the nineteenth and twentieth centuries matches the processes by which cultural consumption has become massified after it became an important aspect of developed national economies – first from about 1760 in Britain.

Yet to think of tourism in this way is to cast too rigid a distinction between what tourist sites mean for visitors and what they mean for locals. After all, tourism has been an important element in the development of many local cultures, and not just under the banner of inauthenticity. Let me give two very different historical examples, the first concerning the New Zealand/Aotearoa Maori.

It is widely acknowledged that Maori culture, and in particular Maori carving, survived the impact of colonisation to the degree that it did because from the mid-nineteenth century (when the colonial wars were still raging) it was involved with the tourist industry. The state supported the New Zealand Maori Arts and Crafts Institute in which the craft was kept alive largely because it helped Rotorua (a North Island village) to maintain its already strong position as a tourist attraction (centred on its hot

101

springs and geysers) and enabled the Te Arawa *iwi* (tribe) to take advantage of that. Around 1890 the Rotorua tourist industry also produced what is today widely accepted as Maori music, although it is in fact a grafting of Maori lyrics onto versions of Western melodies. And to take a more recent example, the *whare runanga* (meeting house) at Waitangi in the Bay of Islands, which was completed in 1940, was built partly as a visitor's attraction (it is on one of New Zealand's premier tourist sites) but is also widely acknowledged as a masterpiece of Maori carving (its twenty-eight panels represent each of the Maori *iwi*) and has become a powerful symbol of New Zealand's official 'bi-culturalism'.

The second example is the development of Stratford-upon-Avon as a tourist site in central England. In this case, unusually, the beginnings of a formalised tourism industry can be located with a great deal of specificity. Stratford's position as a formal tourist destination begins in 1769 when David Garrick, the actor-manager who dominated the London theatre world of that time, organised a 'Jubilee' there to commemorate Shakespeare. He did so in response to pleas from locals who were worried that visitors' interests in the area would decline after the man who owned Shakespeare's old house cut down an oak tree said to have been planted there by Shakespeare himself. The Jubilee is important to English nationalism since it helped channel Shakespeare fandom into site-based commercial tourism, and because Shakespeare worship (so-called 'bardolatry') has been an important component of English cultural nationalism since Garrick's Jubilee. Shakespeare became an icon of English nationalism by symbolising a character type with which the English identified: he represented the naturalness and lack of hierarchy that was supposed to distinguish the English personality from its main rivals of the period – the French (see Deelman 1964).

The point of these examples is, first, that tourism is not adequately accounted for by notions such as the tourist gaze since tourism helps produce and maintain national and local cultures themselves. And, second, that in the interactions between tourism and culture it is not always easy to distinguish the authentic from the inauthentic since attractions designed for tourism may also belong to, and indeed be crucial to, local and national cultures and identities. And, third, that nationalism is not just a desire or identification: it is also a business, namely tourism. (Not all tourism is available to nationalist marketing of course: sex tourism for instance; and equally obviously not all leisure travel is tourism – the resort holiday for example.) At any rate, in the contemporary world of mass tourism, being a tourist and being a local anywhere at all become increasingly less distinct as all localities begin to present themselves as travel industry attractions. Nations such as Thailand, which can seem like giant themeparks to visitors – the theme being 'Thailandness' – are probably not harbingers of what is to come, but they do point to a future in which travellers' interests, pleasures and knowledges increasingly govern those of the locals.

And yet of course, at the same time first-world tourism of third-world nations can be profoundly challenging for the tourist because it often enjoins encounters between the rich and the poor that are much more confrontational than any back home. I'd suggest that for the rich to withdraw from such encounters is to enter the narcissism of privilege, a blocking out of the real. It is important to know, to see, to feel, all the more so because these encounters often carry with them risk and the challenge of the unexpected. What may be another matter are tourisms of melancholia (aka 'dark tourism') – niche tours of economic devastation, genocide memorials, natural disasters, urban chaos, war zones and so on – since they can involve not so much a confrontation with the realities of global inequity as a refinement by which the touristic attention is intentionally and safely directed at cruelty and destruction (Lennon and Foley 2000).

Patriotism and cultural nationalism

Returning now to other formations of nationalism, it is important to remember that nationalism is powerful where it is politically and economically most viable. Indeed there are cases – Scottish nationalism for example – where rather minute distinctions can motivate nationalist partition. The Scottish and the English share a language (although they speak slightly different dialects); they have been politically unified for almost three centuries; their basic values and cultural references are more or less identical (although it does not always look that way in Scotland); migration and exchange between the two territories has been intense for centuries. What stands between them are mainly political–economic concerns: the (well-founded) anxiety that, as a region governed from London, Scotland did not have enough autonomy to secure its own interests – an anxiety which magnified as the oil revenues began to flow in the 1970s. And that anxiety plugged into public memories of England's past annexation of Scotland.

In general then, the cultural analysis of nationalism tends to downplay nationalism's political and social impulses. It is no accident that cultural nationalism has increased in equal step to the increase of the extent and power of the state and to democratisation. Indeed nationalism carries with it a democratic charge in that it gives status to all citizens merely by virtue of their belonging to the nation-state, and conversely democracy gives nationalism a charge by endowing each citizen with a share of sovereignty. One reason, for instance, that China does not have a standard form of nationalism is that the Han – China's dominant ethnic community – have not granted equal social rights to minorities, Han identity remaining civilisational rather than national or racial–ethnic. The rational sub-stratum of nationalism is that all citizens have a stake in the nation-state, in the final instance, to the degree that they would suffer – individually and / or collectively – if the state were taken over by groups that did not represent their interests.

This is the lesson of American patriotism which, unlike most European and post-colonial nationalisms, is not based on cultural or ethnic identities but instead on a commitment to democracy on the one hand and, on the other, economic self-interest (where the self may be an individual or a family or a larger grouping still). Self-interest provides a key to the intimate relation between welfarism and nationalism: strong support for nationalism among the working classes has relied historically (at least in part) upon the sense that a strong nation is necessary if welfarist policies are to be implemented. Bruce Robbins, who argues from a basically cosmopolitan or what he calls 'internationalist' point of view, believes that it is important to negotiate between internationalism and nationalism for that very reason (Robbins 1999, 34–36).

Other voices from the left have reconciled themselves to patriotism on somewhat similar grounds. Jürgen Habermas, for instance, has argued for a 'constitutional patriotism'. For him the old kind of 'organic' nationalism based on an ethnic identity can be substituted by a shared commitment to a set of political principles and institutions, to a 'democratic citizenship' (Habermas 1998). But such thinking tends to underplay the continuing culturalist, xenophobic, and indeed militarist, history of nationalism. One should not forget, for instance, that current Hindu radicalism in India which connects being Indian to being a Hindu, in opposition to official secularism and protection of the Islamic minority, is encouraged by loops between the electoral process, the mass media and economic interests. Nor that English imperialism in the late nineteenth century was intensified by processes of democratisation just as much as nationalism. As the political franchise reached the working classes for the first time, 'jingoism' (aggressive and mass-mediated patriotism based on a sense of imperial destiny and racial superiority) became a dominant cultural formation in Britain.

These ways of thinking of nationalism politically also need to be able to accept groups who understand themselves as belonging to a nation separate from that of the state in which they live. The classic example of this historically is the Jews, but indigenous peoples can also regard themselves as belonging to nations other than the ones of which they are citizens. It is probably enough to say that, typically, such groups have historically been identified as 'other' to the norm, and have been disallowed full access to social and economic goods inside their state. This has certainly been true of most indigenous peoples in settler–colonial states. The identity of the 'native' is characteristically grounded in ethnicity and culture, and the prejudice and exclusion that they encounter can lead to an overestimation of the purity and traditionalism of 'their' culture. But the failure of subaltern groups to be co-opted into nationalism does not spoil the wider argument that cultural factors are less important to nationalism than most accounts suppose. As we shall see, one corollary of that argument is that multiculturalism is much less of a threat to nationalism than the conservatives pretend.

The local

The discourse of globalisation has had the rather paradoxical effect of highlighting the concept of the 'local' just because the global has influentially (if simplistically) been conceptualised as the local's dangerous other. This has led to arguments such as that here – that, in fact, globalisation takes many local forms and can empower as well as weaken local formations. At a certain level of abstraction, the distinction itself is tendentious since, as Bruno Latour argues, the words 'local' and 'global' offer points of view on networks that are by nature neither local nor global, but are 'more or less long and more or less connected' (Latour 1993, 122). Nonetheless, in the world in which we actually live it is often not hard to distinguish what is local from what is not, and that distinction can be extremely important both politically and culturally.

Indeed just as the power of nations is under challenge from transnational forces, it is also under challenge from sub-national forces. In many places in the world, as we have begun to see, there are pressures from communities and regions within nations to acquire some of the rights and cultural visibility more traditionally located in the nation-states themselves – consider the 'break-up' of Britain; the pressures for decentralisation in France; the localisation of political culture in South Asia. Ironically, at least in developed nations, technologies and the political economy of globalisation coupled with US domination help enable this since together they have reduced the cost of state administration and the provision of security. Like many contemporary cultural–political formations this push to de-nationalise does not conform to the logic of the old left–right opposition. Neo-liberals tend to applaud decentralisation on the grounds that it weakens the power of the national state; local culturalists demand the capacity to express their traditions against what are often seen as colonialist or neo-colonialist regimes in power in national capitals.

The local, like the national and the global, has a different force and direction in different places. Certain communities remain much more closed in their local ways of life than others; certain communities, however mobile and wired, remain more attached to locality than others. Mexican migrants in southern California for instance remain more involved with the life of the villages from which they came than do Kenyan immigrants to Germany. And certain aspects of all communities remain much more localised than other aspects: the weather, for instance, not unimportant to culture and economies, is historically local even if it is influenced by *global* warming.

One key to the power and attraction of local culture is the way in which individual wealth, identity, leisure interests and public memory come together locally. Let me give a personal example. The suburb I lived in for several years – Clifton Hill in Melbourne, Australia – was rocked by the building of a freeway between it and its close neighbour Collingwood in the seventies. This was seen to divide Collingwood – a working-class, migrant suburb with a long history of struggle, labourism and fanatical devotion to the local Australian Rules football team – from the somewhat more affluent Clifton Hill. Many in both neighbourhoods opposed the motorway, not least because it enabled them negatively to compare the outer dormitory suburbs (whose commuting cars were breaking apart their neighbourhoods) with their own 'inner-city' lifestyles.

The losing fight against the motorway has not been forgotten, and Clifton Hill's sense of itself as an unwillingly yuppie suburb is still experienced around that moment in the now not so recent past. But this memory is fading, and the more that house prices rise, and older residents sell out to richer and younger incomers, the more local history and memory decline as supports for local identity. Indeed, during a period of rising property values, the primary relation between Clifton Hill residents and their locality seemed to be a shared interest in what prices houses were fetching, and discussions about this topic competed with discussions about the weather in neighbourly conversations. In this case locality is not an important component of culture: apart from the Collingwood Football Club (which is of less interest to many migrants who are more attuned to soccer or to the professional middle classes many of whom have few sporting interests) and the locally funded and widely used public libraries, locality barely competes with the media and other cultural forms (including travel), which are national or global in their provenance and financing. In Collingwood itself, however, local attachments remain stronger and the old proletarian sense of autonomy and rebelliousness has been imaginatively absorbed by some members of the middle classes (mainly bohemians or starter professionals) who have moved into the area.

Of course there are many other ways of living in local culture, but from a cultural studies perspective the point of this example is that it helps show that the local–national–global triangle of differences is not always the best grid through which 'local' cultures are lived or should be analysed. Localities differ in their capacity to take charge of their own cultural trajectories and, as this anecdote shows, history and political economy remain essential if one is to gain a strong sense of such differences. In thinking about Clifton Hill, space quickly gives way to social processes and economic relations, since memory and money together shape the geography of social and cultural organisation.

In general, cultural studies' relation to space requires further thinking through. If the discipline is deeply connected to mobility, as I argued in Part 1 of this book, and is ultimately positioned against those kinds of identities and cultural formations defined in restricted spatial terms, it still needs to consider space as a primary co-ordinate of cultural formations. In particular it needs to consider, without losing sight of either, how power and the capacity for networking into global flows are spread unevenly across space and yet how the increased mobility of culture can intensify 'local imaginaries' also.

Further reading

Anderson 1991; Bhabha 1990; Massey 1994; Morley 2000; Nairn 1981.

Part 4

MEDIA AND THE PUBLIC SPHERE

Television

In 1964, when British cultural studies was getting underway, a new medium – television – was showing signs of its extraordinary capacity to shape culture. At that time and place, TV was still relatively tame: the pictures were black and white, the public broadcaster, the BBC, was just opening its second 'quality' channel which gave the British public all of three channels to watch, and posh announcers introduced an evening's entertainment as if they were presenting a variety show in the living room. Nonetheless, the new media was already fanning the flames for a new kind of cultural event – Beatlemania – which not only put Britain into the rock'n'roll age, transnationalising its pop culture for the first time, but opened the way for a revolutionary decade – the sixties – defined by a new kind of youth power. In the USA, TV had made Elvis a national sensation almost a decade earlier, and a 1961 Disney broadcast had persuaded consumers that colour sets were worth buying. In 1964 in the States, CBS turned to videotape, marking the end of an era when most television was broadcast live. This was when Lyndon Johnson used the first 'negative' political TV ad against his republican rival. Two devices designed to transform the medium were introduced – the instant replay, which gave TV an edge in sports broadcasting (and led to US pro football realising that the real money was in television), and the wireless remote control which dissolved the formality of TV viewing. Television as it would exist in its greatest moment was being born. (Check http://www.museum.TV/ archives/eTV/ index.html, an online source for television history.)

Closer to home, television, as the dominant medium of the period, has a unique relation to cultural studies which, it's clear, has been formed around its encounter with TV. The discipline's turn to populism and devaluation of high culture; its emphasis on cultural reception as a life practice rather than on interpretation or production; its sense of cultural consumers as segmented, all owe much to its contiguity to television and to a TV-centred understanding of the 'media' (a word that, revealingly, only came into common usage at the end of the sixties). Of course, in being shaped by TV, cultural studies is by no means unique: it is just about impossible to imagine contemporary party politics, sport, music, film, and indeed consumer culture generally outside of their complex interactions with the box .

But an important qualification is necessary at once. Different nations have different television industries and, once again, transnational generalisation is just about impossible. Once again, the USA stands out in this regard. Because the medium first took off there (although it was a British invention), because technological and, usually, programming innovations tend to happen there first and because its products dominate world export markets, it is easy to believe that the medium exists there in its purest form, and that it is where the future happens first for other nations too. This is a misconception, and yet it is impossible to treat other national television systems except in comparison with the USA and, for better or for worse, much of what I have to say below has a US focus.

What kind of medium is it that has achieved such power? It is useful to see it as containing four different elements: the broadcast content; the set on which the content is watched; the means of distribution of that content; and the industry which produces the content. And the medium's development since the sixties can be summed up like this: sets in both private and public spaces have proliferated; after the popularisation of satellite and cable, channels have proliferated also, and programming has become routinely 24-hour. As part of this process, TV has become less and less dominated by scripted shows and especially by fiction. In many countries, the industry has been deregulated and has been more and more closely integrated with other leisure and media forms, notably sport and newspapers. All this can be summed up more abstractly: during its relatively short history television's interactions with everyday life have been radically intensified.

The set

Among the rich (globally speaking), the TV set exists primarily in domestic space and for that reason television's content and regulations have always had to address family values and lifestyle patterns (see Morley 1995). The marketing of the new media in the fifties placed a great deal of emphasis on positioning the set in the main family room (Spigel 1992) and the question of where the television set should be placed still has lifestyle and self-presentation consequences. One TV set in a family household tends to mean disputes about programme selection; several sets tend to isolate family members from one another. The set, like everything else about television, has evolved and since the mid-nineties has metamorphosed into the 'home entertainment system' which further appropriates public forms (the movie theatre, the concert) for domestic space, subtly eroding public culture in the process. It has also increasingly been used as a visual display unit for computer games and video and DVD viewing. Insofar as cultural studies has come to concern itself with the 'sociality of television use' (Lembo 2000, 29), the materiality of the TV set becomes of primary concern. And by concentrating on the set it is easier to understand the precise social frameworks in which television is figured, in the West, primarily as a domestic medium. It is easy to forget that in many parts of the world television is watched mainly in public, in cafes or bars, and that alters its impact considerably. And in nations for which domestic space has a different function and significance than it does in the West, as for instance in many Hindu and Muslim regions where the domestic realm is sanctified, is dedicated to purity, and is under the control of women, then the positioning of a TV set there can cause tensions with Western-style programming where it tends to the erotic, the counter-cultural or the profane.

The industry: funding and regulation

When it comes to the industry, one question dominates: how to fund it. After all, TV, like any broadcast medium, does not offer commodities in the traditional sense, able to be presented in a marketplace, priced via the play of supply and demand. At least when broadcast by radio waves, broadcast media can be picked up for free by anyone who owns a receiver (which is why, during the early days of radio, programming was provided by receiver manufacturers, which is what the pathbreaking broadcasting company RCA was in its first incarnation). Furthermore television is an expensive medium in relation to print or even film, partly because of what is sometimes called 'content exhaustion': the way in which content has constantly to be replenished. This commits the medium to novelty and, as technology and deregulation have increased the numbers of channels, increasingly to competitive novelty (Corner 2001). One of the reasons that fiction and scripted shows are under pressure in the industry today is that novelty comes easier in live shows which are also considerably cheaper to produce.

Funding models differ widely across different nations: television may be funded either by government, by advertising or (in the case of cable and satellite) by periodic fees, or by a mix of these. Governments tend to pay for television programming either through the tax system (as in Australia), by selling off the right to use frequencies or by charging licences for set ownership (as in the UK). The USA is unusual in having almost no wholly government-funded television: there, 'public television' generally means television broadcast on frequencies reserved for non-profit stations who typically receive less than half their funds from public sources, yet who may broadcast commercials only if they are disguised as non-commercial adjuncts.

Funding through advertising turns the medium into a system whose primary economic function is to sell potential consumers to advertisers, via the buyers of advertising time, set at prices determined by ratings whose measurement worldwide is dominated by A.C. Nielsen and, increasingly, its controversial 'Peoplemeters'. In the USA, audiences are now sold to advertisers every six or seven minutes by the major networks. Yet, as competition in the industry has grown and as the technology has permitted increased numbers of channels largely by lowering the costs of studio production, the television audience has been divided into various taste-cultures or niches of very different economic power. Advertisers chase young adult audiences for the rather counter-intuitive reason that the young spend less time in front of the TV set than do either children or their elders. As its audiences segment, television mutates in form. Families no longer watch a night's programme obediently, and fewer programmes grab national attention. Rather the medium offers up a kind of background chatter against which attention drifts in and out. New taste-cultures proliferate: some based on ethnicity (black TV in the USA); some on age; some on level of education; some on gender; some on rhythms of a working week (i.e. the time of day TV is watched); some on political orientation; some on less material differences – daytime soaps or talk shows? Yet it is not as if national or transnational audiences for a single event or show never happen. On 11 September 2001 the whole (rich, urban) world watched those jets smash into those towers *on TV*.

Perhaps surprisingly, cultural studies has been more interested in industry regulation than in its actual organisation. Why is regulation important to television in a way that it isn't, for instance, to print publishing? Partly because the most common mode of delivery – through radio frequencies – enabled the state to take responsibility for the allocation of the spectrum. Furthermore, regulations are constantly open to renegotiation since media technology changes so quickly that a particular technological regime cannot be assumed to maintain its place for more than about five years. But, most of all, television is a policy issue because of its social power.

The principle issues at stake in industry regulation differ according to how programming is funded, but in general they concern the balance of market and non-market funding of programming and the safeguards, first, to maintain diversity (through limiting the market share of any one broadcasting company); second, to ensure the right of the media to 'free speech' without which, as traditionally has been argued, democracy withers; and, third, for civic decorum, through censorship. In the West neo-liberal regimes have consistently supported market solutions to issues of balance, quality and diversity – that is, deregulation. Cultural studies has a stake in this through cultural policy studies, but its response has been muted, because (to speak very generally) its liberalism and populism provide few strong, critical arguments for maintaining a strong regulatory environment.

But the question of how restricted media ownership should be in any particular market remains a vital one. It's a question that is all the more acute since many of the biggest transnational media companies – Time Warner and News Corp in particular – own newspapers, publishing houses, sports teams, film studios, tourist attractions, national periodicals and so on, globally. Recently the emergence of the Internet has been used to downgrade concerns about the narrowness of media ownership and to justify further relaxation of regulations (see Streeter 1996 for an excellent contribution to cultural policy studies of television in this regard). In general we can say that arguments about ownership break down to industry issues on the one side (concentrated ownership threatens free markets, not least because the barriers to entry into television broadcasting remain high) and into public service issues on the other (limited ownership puts at risk the principles of balance, diversity and quality). These too are probably not debates to which cultural studies intellectuals as such can contribute a great deal, even if cultural populists in particular need to recognise the constraints that ownership regimes place on content.

When it is state-funded television that is in question, however, the situation changes. Then the most important policy topic becomes the degree to which programmers need to chase ratings (so as to legitimate their public funding) and, conversely, the degree to which they should provide quality programming of interest only to a minority of viewers. It's a much contested issue since 'quality programming' generally means programming watched mainly by educated liberal professionals. And it's an issue that divides cultural studies which (speaking very generally) finds it hard to belong to either party, since the go-with-the-ratings argument links public television to populist majoritarianism while the quality argument links it to elitism.

Television regulation also involves questions of censorship and self-censorship, which is a particularly highly charged issue because television is so attractive to children. And the issue of television and children which touches upon debates about the medium's relation to violence, sex and family values, is one that is itself debated in the public sphere as well as being the object of considerable academic research. Again, cultural studies has tended to stay away from these debates, especially where they broach the dreaded question – To what degree does television encourage violence among children? – a question which attracts numbers of positivist media researchers, many of whom hope to show once and for all a causal relation between television viewing and 'anti-social' behaviour, or what is often called in the literature 'proven harm' (Gauntlett 1995). One can be fairly confident that that relation will never be demonstrated satisfactorily, since connections between social action and television viewing are too mediated and dispersed and too based on difficult historical comparisons for models appealing to a unidirectional causality to be proven. And cultural studies research so far tends to picture children as surprisingly discriminating viewers, with television reinforcing rather than transforming their values and understanding of the world (Gunter and McAleer 1997).

While Stuart Cunningham has reminded us that cultural studies academics risk irrelevance in avoiding these debates (which are of genuine concern to parents as well as to media companies), it is probably as important to think about what is at stake in the debates themselves as it is to engage in the kind of research which contributes to them (Cunningham 1992b). In these terms, Lauren Berlant has persuasively taken up the argument that putting the protection of children at the centre of social policy normally serves the interests of authoritarian and retrograde political groupings by reducing the richness and freedom of adult product (Berlant 1997). The fuss over children's television viewing, with its polemicising for formal or informal censorship, is in part another instance of this. Yet, in debates over children and their relation to television, what also seems to be at stake is a struggle between two centres which are simultaneously ethical and social, one based in the family, the other in the media, and beyond the media, in the consumer marketplace.

As we know, television, and not least children's television, belongs to the consumer marketplace. It delivers the attention of children (and their parents) to toy manufacturers, confectioners and drink marketeers, fast-food outlets, the recorded music and film industries and so on. Whatever its other effects on children, it seems clear that it socialises them towards consumption, and thus towards the social apparatuses upon which the market is built (Kline 1993, 349–350). It takes them away from more physical play, including, it needs to be said, bullying and violence. At this level, it stands at some distance from the more ascetic, generationally interactive, socially and educationally aspiring values and clusters of family memories and styles which are habitually clumped together as family values. And yet, however discriminating they may be, children love TV as they love little else. Let us recall that in the USA at least there is a television set in over half of all children's bedrooms, providing parents with welcome (possibly necessary) space and time by monopolising their children's attention for hours (the equivalent figure in the UK is less than 10 per cent [Gauntlett and Hill 1999, 35]). Furthermore, television provides children with an imaginative world and its own form of far from negligible ethical and affective instruction. And as children grow up their memories of a childhood watching TV are often invested with a deep nostalgia that nurtures intergenerational bonding – each generation, after all, has its own TV memories. In this light it may seem as if television is a site for intergenerational struggles over style and autonomy, but I'd suggest that in the last instance the debate over children's television can be regarded as an expression of anxieties concerning the usefulness of television as a substitute for parenting.

The audience

Traditionally at least, most cultural studies work on television has concentrated on audience reception – which is a sign of the medium's lack of cultural value. It is as if the programmes themselves aren't worth taking as seriously as their impact on viewers. So it has been impossible to concentrate on close readings of TV texts or to construct a TV canon. And partly for that reason, the study of reception has undergone almost constant transformation as it has tried to figure out exactly the value and impact of television. Various stages in this history can be isolated:

The *'uses and gratifications' approach* was pioneered by Paul Lazarsfeld during the forties and used statistical analysis of data retrieved through quantitative ethnographic studies to show that, in the USA at least, television viewing integrated viewers into capitalist society by reinforcing its norms and marginalising deliberative analysis. For this approach, television is supposed primarily to satisfy specific needs that exist outside the viewing situation. Lazarsfeld's work headed an avalanche of 'mass communications' research that linked patterns of television viewing to gender, education, age and economics and tried to view the impact of such viewing on 'behaviours' in terms of these variables (see Schramm 1961 for a classic book in this tradition).

The *'critical theory' school*'s most famous representative was Theodor Adorno who, like Lazarsfeld and at around the same time, argued that television reduced its audience's capacities to reflect on and critique society and culture. For Adorno it did so by providing powerful forms of 'distraction' which transformed 'modern mass culture into a medium of undreamed of psychological control' (Adorno 1991, 138). TV de-individuates people; it offers them a profoundly standardised image world; it reinforces the false domination of private life over the public sphere; it creates fantasies and false satisfactions that allow capitalism to maintain itself. Television possesses so great a power of seduction that the distinction between its 'dream world' and reality becomes confused. Adorno is often (and rightly in my view) accused of not understanding TV's manifold pleasures, and at the same time of taking it too seriously. Yet for the first time he brought to the field a complex theory of subjectivity, based in part on Freudian notions of the unconscious, as well as a clear idea of the limits of capitalism and the deliberative value of high culture. And he was one of the first social theorists willing to think about television genres in some specificity (see Adorno 1991).

The *'encoding/decoding' model* was the first influential intervention in the field from within cultural studies proper. In an important essay of that name, Stuart Hall suggested a four-stage theory of communication: production, circulation, use and reproduction. For him each stage is 'relatively autonomous' from the others (see Hall in During 1999). This means that the coding of a message *does* control its reception but not transparently – each stage has its own determining limits and possibilities. The concept of relative autonomy allows Hall to argue that polysemy is not the same as pluralism: messages are not open to any interpretation or use whatsoever simply because each stage in the circuit limits possibilities in the next. In actual social existence, Hall goes on to argue, messages have a 'complex structure of dominance' because at each stage they are 'imprinted' by institutional power relations. Furthermore, a message can only be received at a particular stage if it is recognisable or appropriate – although there is space for a message to be used or understood at least somewhat against the grain. This means that power relations at the point of production, for example, will loosely fit those at the point of consumption. In this way the communication circuit is also a circuit that reproduces a pattern of domination, and it thus belongs to 'ideology' thought of as the system of meanings through which social structures are regarded as natural or commonsensical rather than a means by which capitalism (and its class hierarchies) reproduces itself (Hall in During 1999).

Hall loosened the tie between the text's meaning and its reception. For him, dominant meaning was only received under certain circumstances. And in the late seventies and early eighties cultural studies expanded the gap between meaning and reception by accepting that audiences could actually resist a programme's values (Morley 1980), and then by showing that television flow did not have a single meaning but rather contained a number of meanings or that it primarily communicated not meaning at all but emotion or pleasure (Fiske 1987). From this perspective popular television could embody forms of critique or transgression too. It could undo as well as embody ideology.

The emphasis on the polysemy of television and the variety of modes and moods in which it was viewed led cultural studies in the late seventies to pay increasing attention to television viewers not as members of a massified audience but as (socio-culturally formed) individuals, not as 'cultural dupes' with limited powers to accept or reject television's meanings but as people living more or less attentively around the television set.

This move, which was so important to the discipline's sense of itself, was also inspired by Roland Barthes' concept of the 'pleasure of the text'; by feminist work on women watching television in which researchers and viewers were allied in a new kind of solidarity; by Michel Foucault's critique of ideology as too totalising and coherent a concept; and by the emergence of a generation who could actually confess to liking television and who were familiar with its history.

It's no accident I think that this shift occurred at the same time as, first, in the USA programmers began to pay attention to viewer demographics and 'quality' shows began to be produced for particular audiences, and, second, cable television, with its promise (not kept) to usher in an epoch of commercial-free choice and variety, took off. The consequence of all this was that cultural studies work on television became committed to a particular kind of empirical research on media audiences: qualitative research, often involving participatory observation (i.e. the researcher joining with his or her subjects in their activities), aimed not at studying how shows were understood but at understanding the role of television in everyday life, and most of all among fans of particular genres or shows. Such work has often pictured TV fans in romantic, sixties-idealist terms: for instance, they are conceived of as being engaged in upsetting received norms of good taste and aesthetic culture by 'poaching' particular elements from shows and using them as a basis for their own creative expression (see Jenkins 1992). As cultural studies researchers examined viewers more and more closely they also began to analyse the criteria that viewers use to judge programmes (with 'realistic' turning out to be key). And they paid attention to how television was infused into 'practices of self' (the techniques that people use to construct their character and life) – for instance by inserting memories of watching old shows into life stories.

Once television viewers became the object of research so too did TV sociability – the way TV draws people together or isolates them, the way it reinforces family authority structures or undoes them, and so on. It is in this context too that one branch of cultural studies has become increasingly interested in the impact of TV (and the media generally) on the 'public sphere'. The 'public sphere' as a concept remains tied to Jürgen Habermas' analysis of the civic institutions which underpinned European Enlightenment. For Habermas, famously, a 'bourgeois public sphere' emerged in the salons and coffee houses of late seventeenth-century Europe (especially in England), marked out from commercial and domestic life on the one side and the apparatuses of state on the other. It was not dominated by the court, and was dedicated to discussion and the circulation of ideas through which rational reflection and reform could gradually be applied to social institutions. For Habermas, this public sphere (which exists more as a theoretical construct than as a historical reality) was under threat by the nineteenth century. High capitalism 're-feudalised' it; and, or so the argument goes, the modern public sphere is under the sway of commercial interests, mass entertainment and technocrats (Habermas 1989).

This argument has been reconceptualised by John Hartley, who has put forward an alternative notion of the 'mediasphere'. For him the media connect together different 'cultural domains' for audiences (the media is a bridge rather than a field), as well as creating a sense of the audience itself as community. This is in opposition to Habermas' notion of a public sphere shared by a politically delimited national community (Hartley 1996, 28). For Hartley, the media become the primary means through which a community not only knows itself to be a community but also makes the internal connections required to become a community. This is an important notion because it helps us see the productive role of television, which lies outside both the model of representation (since television connects social and cultural fields rather than represents society) and the Habermasian model of discursive rationality in which television was seen as failing to provide for rational and civic public debate.

However Hartley's concept risks overestimating the degree to which the media and television in particular has subsumed older concepts of society. If you are immersed in the media, either as a cultural studies academic or as a viewer, then the media seems to be the stage on which social reality presents itself. But to whatever degree society has absorbed television into itself, most everyday lives are lived at a certain distance from television, even in the West. It is important not to forget that most information and orientation about the world comes from elsewhere: from friends, from schools or workplaces, churches, etc., or indeed from books. What is the public sphere for young urban blacks in the USA for instance? It exists in the basketball courts, swap meets, local stores, schools, clubs, street hangouts and parties as much as if not more than in the media (which, of course, almost uniformly represents them negatively). What is the public sphere for the educated upper middle class? For the born-again Christian? For the recent Ethiopian migrant? To repeat: especially for those who do not recognise their lives in TV representations, the media forms a kind of background hum to the rhythms of ordinary existence, the occasional distraction or amusement rather than the framework of life itself. What we need to acknowledge is that while TV and the media do systematically structure society and culture and have had an especially profound impact on certain of their audiences, nonetheless, in everyday life they remain at the sidelines for many, probably most, people (see Hermes 1993).

Content

It is, of course, impossible to do any justice to TV content in the context of an introduction to cultural studies, and my aim in this section is simply to sketch some parameters for a cultural studies account. This aim would be even more laughably reductive than it is, if it were not the case that cultural studies, especially in its early days, rarely concentrated on individual programmes or 'texts' as they are often called. Rather it dealt with media content at a more abstract level – in terms both of scheduling and of genre – and I will follow it in this.

The cultural studies approach to the medium generally began when Raymond Williams developed the concept of 'flow'. On his first visit to the USA in 1974 he turned on a TV in his hotel room only to discover that what he was looking at had a completely different feel than he was used to back home. An evening's viewing consisted of an uninterrupted, unpunctuated stream of programmes, advertisements, announcements and logos. Unlike in Britain, no presenter announced the evening's entertainment (Williams 1975, 91–92). For him this was a eureka moment: in its essence, he realised, television was 'flow'! Williams was certainly on to something since, from the perspective of the programmer, what is at stake in an evening's line-up is not the individual show but the 'architecture' of the schedule, which as relations between ratings and programming have become more and more finely tuned, have been more and more carefully considered (Ellis 1992). Shows deliver particular sectors of the audience ('demographics') to advertisers, and prime time is scheduled in 'strips' in which a sequence of shows is designed to keep particular demographics viewing one programme after another, with careful consideration given to audience changes determined by real-life events – domestic meal- and bed-times (in the USA, for much of TV history special regulations have ordered 'prime-time' TV towards family viewing). Within the strips it is important that commercials retain viewers' attention so they merge more and more seamlessly into programming in order to prevent the channel skipping and muting enabled by the remote. In a sense, TV is a battleground between the 'strips' designed by the programmers and the 'skid' enabled by the remote.

Cultural studies has also paid sustained attention to genres. There are, of course, various approaches to the generic television text, and three in particular need pointing out. First, we can analyse the constitutive features (textual and/or institutional) of a particular genre, e.g. news programmes, soap operas, nature documentaries. Thus, for instance, a large generic distinction, unique to broadcast media, has been made between 'series' (in which each episode, while sharing characters, has a distinct narrative) and 'serials' (in which the narrative unfolds from episode to episode). And serials themselves come in different genres, of which, in the seventies and eighties, by far the most analysed was the soap opera. Feminist theorists recuperated soaps, showing that their focus on dialogue (gossip) and the personal, along with their melodrama and endlessness, enabled female viewers to find value in their own everyday lives. Such theories provided a way of positively acknowledging lives lived around relationships and emotional responses rather than work and the public sphere. Or, in another formulation, soaps can present an imaginary world in which the male-dominated public side of life is judged by feminised and more private values (Rapping 2002). And soap opera was especially meaningful since it valued survival above all things (Ang 1985, 51–85; Brunsdon 2000).

The concept of the TV genre has its limits however. For instance, the 1990 ABC hit 'America's Funniest Home Videos' is sometimes regarded as inventing a global genre. But should it rather be regarded as a version of earlier voyeuristic, comic reality shows such as 'Candid Camera' and 'Life's Most Embarrassing Moments'? Or, more particularly, of the hit Japanese show 'Fun with Ken and Kato', produced by the Tokyo Broadcasting Company, in which viewers were invited to send in their amusing videos, if in a rather different spirit and with a different kind of presenter than the ABC's bland Bob Saget (genres of presenter-style exist too). And leaving this kind of ambiguity aside, what seems most interesting about 'America's Funniest Home Videos' is the way in which it draws material from the real world, leaving behind all dramatic and fictional framing. In this it gave a signal of what was to come – reality TV.

Reality TV has its own genres, of which maybe the most popular has been the 'competitive reality show' (whose first big hit was 'Big Brother', an idea imported into the USA from Europe). These shows often use viewer feedback via the phone and Internet and elements of the game show as well as of soap opera. It's a technically and formally sophisticated – and gripping – generic hybrid but, again, what seems fascinating about it is not its generic make-up as such, but its innovative use of the possibilities of the medium's interactivity with both viewers and participants. And in terms of genre: is a reality show fiction or not? Obviously programmes such as 'Cops' and those shown on 'Court TV', with their roots in the traditional documentary or news report, are non-fictional. And yet … if one takes into consideration the amount of control that producers exercise over the production of apparent slices of 'real life' in the competitive reality show especially, the question of their fictionality does not easily disappear. Control is exercised not just in the editing but in the set-up: to take one example, the 2004 Donald Trump hit show 'The Apprentice' received 250,000 applications from would-be contestants, who were whittled down to sixteen by a casting agency after a demanding vetting process which involved full-scale rehearsals in mock shows. During that process, contestants were not only being selected they were being trained to perform.

Putting aside the question of fictionality, the first 'dramatic reality show' in the USA was MTV's 'Real World'. It was pitched to the channel by a production team including Mary-Ellis Bunim, a long-time producer of daytime soaps including 'Santa Barbara'. She understood that MTV was used to airing videos it didn't pay for and would not risk investing in an expensive production. She was also fascinated by arty fly-on-the-wall documentaries such as PBS' legendary, twelve-hour 'American Family', first aired in 1973 and now often cited as the beginning of 'reality TV'. ('American Family' eavesdrops on the life of an unhappy American family, the Louds, and produced the first reality show celebrity – Lance Loud, the gay son, whose coming out seemed to have helped trigger his parents' divorce in what turned out to be a deeply involving drama.) So 'Real World' put a bunch of adolescents in a fancy Manhattan loft and watched (the highly controlled) consequences. It worked – somewhat to MTV's surprise. And its success produced a spin-off genre, the competitive reality show, whose first example 'Road Rules' (1994) was also produced by Bunim, although it took the success of Europe's 'Big Brother' and then 'Survivor' for the genre to dominate Anglophone television from the mid-nineties, partly as we have seen for economic reasons.

This is to talk about content at the level of genre. What about at the level of the text itself? Analysis of programmes has also often taken the form of showing how programmes produce their meaning through the use of signs. This method is used mainly for advertisements because, although (or because) they're short, they can be so complex and dense at this level. One might analyse, for example, the way in which an instant coffee commercial uses exotic and sexual images to link drinking coffee to sensual mystery. The classic work in this area is Judith Williamson's *Decoding Advertisements* (1978), which remains a standard text in the teaching of what is called the 'semiotic' approach to media texts, i.e. an approach that breaks texts down into their constitutive signs. The problem with semiotics in this mode is that it tends to neglect 'polysemy' (that is, it tends to claim that signs have one meaning rather than various meanings, especially across different communities). Semiotics, by its very nature, also tends to pay relatively little attention to the actual way that texts are received by viewers. For that reason, in cultural studies, it tends to survive only in introductory courses.

Individual programmes can also be read closely and subtly in a way habitual to literary, art or film criticism, even though, as I have said, it is a sign of television's degraded place in academic culture that there is remarkably little of this kind of criticism. The lack of easy access to many old shows is also a problem here, and the question of television preservation is an urgent one: it's a materially ephemeral medium, which also puts its long-term cultural value at risk. Nonetheless, television has been praised because it has a positive political and sociological function, as when feminism recuperated soap opera, but only rarely in terms that relate specifically to the creativities demanded by the medium itself. There is a rich future for this kind of criticism since it allows cultural studies to transmute TV fandom into established academic modes. And it promises opportunities for changing these modes too: what kind of criticism might a serious and detailed appreciation of the competitive reality show create for instance?

Finally, television can also be understood in terms of its relations to other cultural and social institutions. In particular, television is in competition with a wide variety of other institutions that fulfil similar functions or offer similar pleasures. One of contemporary TV's most remarkable features, I have suggested, is how keyed in it is to other media, especially the Web. Not just in terms of industry synergies either – information, gossip about plot lines, stars and so on often circulates on the Web before productions are aired, giving producers headaches.

But TV competes with certain other institutions at a deeper level too. TV is in competition, for instance, with the education system as a purveyor of information, knowledge and comment about the world; it is in competition with live sports events as a leisure choice; it is in competition with literature again as a leisure choice but also (sometimes) in a struggle over lifestyles and cultural values; it is in competition with the Internet, not just at the level of information about shows but as a technology of communication, and one which will probably swallow TV. Of course it is not *just* in competition with other social or cultural institutions; it enables and shapes them too, perhaps most notably formal politics (see Part 1). And TV is itself represented in other technologies of representation: in film, in literature, in the print media, in the classroom – representations in which it is consistently, but by no means completely, demonised, partly because it is in a competitive relation to other institutions and partly because its unparalleled power to be absorbed into, and thus shape, the culture is feared. The academic study of television needs to be understood in these terms also. Here the higher reaches of the education apparatus are concerned with a (in most ways more powerful) rival. This helps us to understand why the most negative and paranoid academic representations of television shows, such as that articulated by Joshua Meyrowitz (1985), regard it as overriding all boundaries, blurring distinctions between the public and the private, between masculinity and femininity, childhood and adulthood, politicians and their electors.

Conclusion

The sense that television is creating a culture without shape or order is, in the end, untenable because it fails to appreciate the actual ways that TV is used and enjoyed. That kind of complaint is a version of the reactive cultural criticism on the rejection of which Raymond Williams founded British cultural studies. Nonetheless it does point to something important: television, and the media generally, is not a site of authority, standards and hierarchy. Ultimately this is because it is so interfused with everyday life itself. To take just one further example: TV produces reality as well as representing it. One way it does so is by generating celebrities who are often now famous not for any accomplishment but just (as they say) for being famous (see Rojek 2001). These celebrities exist in a weird cultural zone: they have real existences in a world we share with them but they are also imaginary creatures – imaged on the screen, in print and on the Web in all kinds of complex collusions and synergies. It is their ambiguous condition of being that makes them so fascinating. Finally, their lives can be understood as real-time, lived experiments on the power of the media to shape a life as spectacle: think most of all of Michael Jackson (although of course he did bring serious talent to his fame). Or think of the Olsen twins: media figures since they were nine months old (when they began appearing in the prime time sitcom 'Full House'); stars of computer games and animated TV series; media moguls (executive producers at the age of seven of a video series that has grossed over US$500 million); brand names for a 'tween' orientated line of clothes, cosmetics, home furnishings, books and CDs; and web site and movie stars as well. The countdown to their eighteenth birthday was a minor-league major media event in the USA. In living in and through the media network (which remains centred around TV) celebrities of this kind acquire a symbolic function: they become metaphors of the way in which sections of the community also live in interaction with the TV/media imaginary, not as celebrities themselves but as consumers, obsessionals, dreamers, lovers, gossips, who are in the end the masters of the celebrities whom they anoint.

The old understanding of the media – that it represents or comments on the world and that it exists on a different plane than life itself – has been completely undone by the broadcast media over the past century. And, as we shall see, it has been further undone by the Web. In that sense Hartley's mediasphere does not really exist. Rather the media *folds* into everyday life; it *transverses* it; it fuses into it and *deterritorialises* it; it forms *blocks* of emotion in the real world or grounds social activities there which appear and disappear in their own opaque rhythms. The italicised words in this sentence are borrowed from the French philosopher Gilles Deleuze, whose theoretical concepts work exceptionally well when deployed to describe relations between contemporary life and the media (see Rajchman 2000 for an excellent introduction to Deleuze). It says something about how complex and vital that relation is that it helps to have a recondite philosophical vocabulary to describe it.

Further reading

Ang 1991; Boddy 1990; Brunsdon 1997; Ellis 1992; Hartley 1996; Jenkins 1992; Lembo 2000; Press 1991; Spigel 1992.

Popular music

Television is a 'top-down' institution in that TV broadcasts are comparatively expensive and require considerable technical expertise and its channels of dissemination are relatively finite and highly regulated. Nor has the move from analogue to digital technologies (as yet) empowered TV viewers or radically changed the industry's business model. All this is less true of popular music, which remains, at least to some degree, a spontaneous product of individuals (both musicians and fans) who come to it outside the highly capitalised recording industry itself, and have poached new technologies to make and listen to topics on their own terms. Music isn't just records and marketing. That's why, for instance, although it rarely makes much sense to ask of television or even specific television genres how authentic they are, that question remains powerful when it comes to music. Likewise it rarely makes much sense to ask of TV shows how oppositional they are. But cultural studies has consistently posed that question of popular music, partly because rock'n'roll has connoted rebellion from its very beginnings. In fact cultural studies' claim to a politics of resistance has been deeply inflected by rock's rebellion.

Although popular music is genuinely popular, it is also divisive, segmenting communities by generation, class, race, ethnicity, tastes and, if less so, gender. Music quickly germinates something larger than itself – micro-communities and lived styles, each tied to a genre or sub-genre or set of genres. The big multinational corporations that dominate the music industry themselves organise their music divisions into units each concentrating on a different genre and audience. Black audiences are marked out from white, and certain genres (notably so-called 'modern rock') are given more attention because of their history of profitability (Negus 1999, 496). It's because of music's capacity to segment and germinate that, for instance, the concept of the 'subculture', appropriated from sociology, has been developed in cultural studies terms largely via work on popular music. And it's because of that capacity that cultural studies' work on African diaspora cultures and drug cultures also tends to be mediated through music – even if this emphasis exposes the study of music to certain distortions.

Of course rock music in particular has also become hegemonic. Even 'authentic' rock stars can belong to the establishment, if, in general to the liberal establishment. Over the years they have acquired significant political clout, of which there are few better instances than Bono of U2's role in increasing US aid to the world's poorest nations. At the UN Conference on Development in Monterey, Mexico in March 2002, the USA increased its aid budget for the first time in twenty years by $5 billion. The White House confirmed that lobbying from the rock star was significant in the USA's unexpected change of direction (which led to the European Union increasing its aid budget also). In the light of this clout and respectability, rock's history of, and carefully maintained image of, rebelliousness begins to fall apart, as we shall soon see in more detail. What, for instance, happened to 'alternative rock' which can now be used to hook youngish viewers into a truly mainstream product such as Fox's *Dallas* revamp *The O.C.*? But the mainstreaming of rock generates new internal divisions, as musicians invent modes to counter its influence.

Punk and reggae

The first popular music genres to come under the examination of British cultural studies were reggae and punk, the street music of the disaffected young in the late seventies when the discipline was young. British punk was a reaction against its various predecessors, namely: (1) the highly industrialised and show-biz music that heavy metal and other rock genres had by this time become; (2) the faded utopianisms of the hippie movement with their middle-class overtones; and (3) the foppishness and perceived pretentiousness of 'glam rock' whose biggest stars were David Bowie and Roxy Music. Punk was urban, working-class, young and aggressively anti-establishment. Some of its elements (including the name and its revisionist 'back to real rock'n'roll' music credo) had been imported from avant-garde New York art-school scenes (and in particular ripped off the New York Dolls) by Malcolm McLaren, the Sex Pistols' manager. Nonetheless, British punk was a whole new thing.

As to reggae: this was the time that reggae was exploring studio-based techniques such as dub and perfecting the technique of 'toasting' which had developed in the early fifties in Kingston's sound systems. (A sound system is a portable record deck, amplifiers and speakers used for street and other parties and was mainly popular in the poorer neighbourhoods.) Toasting DJs, working for and individuating the sound systems, improvised slang lyrics and interjections on top of records, a tradition which began to fade among the Jamaican systems in the late eighties at a point when hip hop, which can partly be regarded as an offshoot of toasting, was already a major genre in the USA. (In Jamaica it transformed into 'dancehall' or 'ragga', one of the most innovative, technologised music genres of the nineties.)

In the seventies too, 'roots reggae', as produced by stars such as Bob Marley, Burning Spear and Culture, had incorporated Rastafarianism, a Jamaican religious cult much influenced by Marcus Garvey who preached a 'Back to Africa' doctrine in the first decades of the twentieth century. Rastas reject the white man's materialist world and believe Haile Selassie, the last Ethiopian monarch, to be divine. Their religion is also a style: dreadlocks, ganja-smoking, patois-speaking. During the seventies Rastafarianism began to spread beyond the working-class Jamaican men who had formed its base since the thirties. Simultaneously, in London, reggae began to enter into complex interactions with punk, most obviously in the music of groups such as the Clash and the Slits as well as in the lyrics of tracks such as Marley's 1977 'Punky Reggae Party'. (Marley's sense of where popular music could go was influenced by hearing the Clash.)

In his book *Subculture: The Meaning of Style* (1979), which did much to popularise cultural studies in the Anglophone world, Dick Hebdige theorised punk as a transgressive 'signifying practice'. According to him, punk 'cut up' and recombined various working-class styles, past and present, in a 'phantom history' motivated by parody. Its safety pins, bondage trousers, S&M paraphernalia, ripped clothing – a radicalised 'ragamuffin' look – are interpreted as imitations of impoverished British working-class styles, worn brazenly and out of context to express the emptiness and meaninglessness of the social situation in which British working-class youth found themselves under Thatcherism, i.e. under first-wave neo-liberalism. Punk's appropriation of nationalist signifiers, especially the Union Jack, was, likewise, in-your-face ironical. But, for Hebdige, the most important function of the punk style was to form the punk community: punk identity and collectivity was articulated in and through its signifying practices.

Hebdige's account of reggae in *Subculture* was somewhat more straightforward: dub, toasting, roots reggae and the culture of the sound systems provided an alternative to white hegemony for its fans. In the music they found an alternative Africanist identity, 'a black heart beating back to Africa on a steady pulse of dub' (Hebdige 1979, 38). Rastafarianism deepened a long-standing ethos of rebellion and disaffection among Jamaican youth, providing it with an everyday life ethic that (like punk style) wore its difference and refusals on the body, but it also, in the case of roots reggae, offered it a spiritual and historicised self-understanding. Aspects of the rasta style were disseminated globally: after Marley's trip to New Zealand in the eighties (during which he was welcomed as a hero by Maori youth) dreadlocks, rasta colours, dope-smoking and so on became common marks of resistance for young Maori, and successful Maori reggae bands appeared. These days, sound clashes (competitions between sound systems) have gone global: the World Clash, normally held in Queens, New York involves sounds from as far afield (and far from Africa) as Japan and Italy.

For punk the attractions of reggae were clear enough. Punks could identify with reggae's refusals and otherness, especially as these took musical form. And yet, Hebdige argues, punk music was formed as much in opposition as in alliance with reggae. Musically punk favoured the treble not the bass, and it preferred a rhetoric of abuse rather than of allusion. Punk drew some of its energy to resist white rock from reggae, but reggae's turn to ethnicity froze punk out so, Hebdige contends, 'at the heart of the punk sub-culture, forever arrested, lies this frozen dialectic between black and white cultures – a dialectic which beyond a certain point (i.e. ethnicity) is incapable of renewal, trapped, as it is, within its own history, imprisoned within its own antinomies' (Hebdige 1979, 69–70). Here Hebdige's own notion of punk as a signifying practice in process – capable of constant mutations and negotiation with external cultural forces – reaches its limits.

It is possible to cavil with some of Hebdige's findings: his analysis is too London-based and it romanticises punk culture by over-emphasising its working-class nature. Important figures such as the Clash's Joe Strummer were in fact upper-middle class, and, as we've seen, punk had art-school and commercial genealogies too – let's not forget that its style began in a King's Road boutique and, as Greil Marcus has pointed out, had links to Guy Debord's 1960s French avant-garde art world/cultural theory movement known as 'situationism' (Marcus 1989). Like all theorists determined to find socio-political significance in cultural formations, Hebdige neglects the role that entertainment, pleasure and sheer blankness play among fans. As far as reggae goes, he doesn't fully articulate the associations between modernity and technology that constituted some of dub's appeal to its Jamaican fans. Black music of various kinds has a long association with modernity in resistance to 'soul' – think George Clinton; think Sun Ra; think hip hop musicians and DJs such as OutKast or DJ Spooky; think the eighties Jamaican dub maestro Scientist. And yet Hebdige's account of relations between two subcultures formed around music is instructive because it suggests how effectively music can form identities that have political and even spiritual dimensions, and how those identities may be articulated in complex interaction with one another. And how music can form a bridge, a basis for sociability, between groups of fans with no 'organic' association with one another – including indeed academic and non-academic fans.

Modern folk music or commercial product?

Hebdige's understanding of music is so richly nuanced because he was clearly so smitten by the styles and music he wrote about. But it has to be said that much cultural studies writing has been more detached and has circled around a small number of tensions and debates which confront the discipline in relation to popular music. The first, which I have already mentioned, is the tension between music as an authentic, self-driven collective expression (as if it were a kind of folk music) against music as commodity or industry product. This tension works in other domains of commer-cialised culture too of course, but it is particularly intense where music is produced under the sign of rebellious authenticity. It's because cultural studies' own claims to being a dissident discipline have, in part, been borrowed from the rock rhetoric which vernacularised transgression that the commercial versus 'real' music issue is so highly charged, and efforts to get beyond it so difficult (see Beebe, Fulbrook and Saunders 2002 for an anthology of essays that attempt to deconstruct this division, and also Grossberg 1994). One reason for this is that many cultural studies academics them-selves identify with forms of popular music and the subcultures that they nurture. But the commercial/authentic distinction also organises so much music-making and marketing because it is expressive of friction between musicians (who form them-selves typically in live bands who move from amateur to professional status) and record company executives who think money. It is also expressive of the differences between listeners who are really into music and those who are less so. No amount of critique or wishing it away will undo this division – it structures what Larry Grossberg has called the 'rock formation'.

Yet one way of moving past these arguments might be to accept, as Will Straw does in a widely read article on heavy metal, that music needs to be understood not from below or from the fan's point of view but institutionally and economically (Straw 1998). Thus he argues that heavy metal fans do not constitute a subculture at all but are the consequence of a precise moment in this history of the music industry – when the tendency towards oligopoly (the control of the industry by a few players) and the emergence of FM radio stations and play lists met a suburban but not upwardly mobile audience. (In fact the question of industry consolidation remains an open one: Peterson and Berger [1990] have shown that it is not necessarily inexorable. Amalgamations occurred in the fifties and mid-seventies that were later undone by shifts in consumer taste.) But, for Straw, on the one side, heavy metal was a uniform style which overrode local differences, partly as a result of centralised radio program-ming – a process which is much more extreme today than in the eighties when Straw wrote his essay. On the other, it provided its fans, most of whom were not going on to tertiary study, with a form of masculinity that stood against educated forms of self at a time when the economic value of a higher education certificate was fast increasing.

Another way of dealing with the relation between commercialism and amateur expressivity is to rethink their relations in terms that do not emphasise their (struc-tural) tension with one another. Perhaps the most convincing work from this point of view has come out of commentary on rap music, which has been extraordinarily commercially successful but which (in certain of its domains at least) has retained its connections with the street movement from which it emerged during the seventies. (Rap has replaced reggae as the music which represents black resistance globally: there are now Polynesian, Melanesian and Aboriginal rap groups just as there used to be reggae groups, and rap is fast hybridising with other styles – as for instance [at the time of writing] in the New York dance craze 'reggaeton', a fusion of Latin, reggae and rap from Puerto Rico, popular with 'perreo' underground Latino/a youth.)

Hip hop – which included fashion styles, graffiti art, break-dancing, scratching or turn-tabling and (later) free-style (the improvisation of rhymes on top of rhythm tracks, sometimes collectively [in 'cyphers'] and sometimes competitively [in 'battles']) – first appeared with a strong intellectual and political charge (Wimsatt 2001). After all, rap is poetic and verbal in ways that most other popular music forms (except toasting and ragga) are not. Certainly in many cases it has been produced differently to rock music. Its beats or rhythms are produced separately from the lyrics and vocals in what is effectively a different section of the industry, although dividing responsibility for the production of different elements of a track has become increasingly common in mainstream commercial music too, where producers of a track's total sound have become industry kings. Nonetheless at rap's core are loosely affiliated groups of performers and producers pulled together for particular projects. The most organic of such groups is the 'crew', mutually supportive performers often with long-term roots in the same neighbourhood, often in the same schools – the schoolyard being a nursery for free-styling, and free-styling being a nursery for recorded hip hop.

The Wu Tang Clan, many of whom come from Staten Island, have been probably the most successful, artistically if not commercially, of these crews. And to stay with the Wu for a moment, it is also the case that their record label, Loud Records, half-owned by the multinational BMG, was a pioneer in so-called street marketing. This was a form of retailing that replaced or supplemented radio and video promotion by swamping select sites in the young, urban, black public sphere – basketball games, local stores, schoolyards, clubs – with sales material. Marketing and community merge here and street credibility becomes both a marketing tool and a commitment to a social sector and to 'being real'. These sophisticated marketing techniques have been key to the gangsta rap which emerged in Los Angeles in the late eighties, also operating in a complicated zone where the commercial image and the lived meet. But it was the Wu who were pioneers in what has become a big industry in US black markets: fashion franchises branded and 'designed' by music stars. In sum, hip hop reminds us that anti-commercialisation is in itself more characteristically a white bourgeois attitude than an African American one, despite a vibrant African American counter-culture based on spirituality and poetry.

With rap the question of audience is especially debated. It is more usually produced by independent labels than by majors, although majors often distribute and market music produced independently. Some argue that this is because the independents are closer to the street, others that a great deal of independent rap is produced for middle-class and educated audiences (black and white) by producers and artists who have the capacity to maintain their autonomy. There is evidence that the majors have under-supported the genre because of (racist?) fears that it has less 'catalogue value' (potential for future sales) and international appeal than rock, and thus they have allowed production to remain in independent hands (Negus 1999, 498–500). As Tricia Rose has pointed out, breakdowns of sales figures may not be especially helpful in sorting out this debate, since so much music is now disseminated outside of quantifiable and official channels, especially among black youth (Rose 1994). And of course, since the late nineties the downloading and swapping of MP3 tracks over the Internet also means CD sales are decreasingly a good indication of listenerships.

Over the last decade rap has itself split into numerous genres and audiences, from mass market figures such as Jay-Z or Eminem whose relation to their labels is conventional, to entrepreneurial collectives such as Wu Tang, to regionally situated independent crossovers into the big time such as the duo OutKast, to an increasing number of avant-garde and out-there artists whose appeal is indeed largely middle class, to those producing versions of canonical genres such as Prince Paul of the rap-opera, *King of Thieves,* and, lastly, to fusions with ragga and other genres. (As I write the number one single in the USA is by Sean Paul, a Jamaican ragga artist who has crossed over into both soul and rap.) Yet despite this segmentation, critics can still regard hip hop as primarily oppositional in its force, a case made most cogently by George Lipsitz (1994) and Tricia Rose (1994). Rose argues that hip hop is at the very least ambivalent about commodity culture and is to be understood as 'urban renewal' – a regrouping of devastated communities. For Lipsitz, on the other hand, in a reprise of Hebdige on punk, hip hop's fascination with commodities (gold chains, fast cars, etc.) is a playful and hyperbolic mimicry of dominant culture, an expression of adolescent fantasy which contains within it a subversive sense of its own extravagance.

Such analyses do need to be qualified, especially in relation to the macho slanging of bitches and hos which constitutes one dominant commercial rap convention. Of course that convention works precisely because it scandalises women, liberals, family values and so on: it performs rebelliousness. But it possesses other functions too: it provides the constraints within which it is possible for a rapper to assert his mastery of a specific rhetoric. And, more problematically, it may express a certain crisis of masculinity among urban African Americans too: a kind of sadism from a social position that combines systemic subordination with widely recognised glamour and street cred as well as the capacity to create fear among middle-class whites. Where in all this does the commerce/real distinction come into play? Or the subversive/dominant opposition?

Another genre that brings the tension between commerce and underground expressivity into the open is dance music. Dance music, like punk and rap, begins with a marginal youth cultural formation, this time the 'rave scene'. The rave scene emerged, more or less simultaneously in Ibiza, the Spanish holiday resort, and in Manchester around 1987 when house music first met the drug ecstasy. House, which had been developed out of disco in Detroit and Chicago, was a music style which synthesised and sampled all kinds of sounds including Eurodisco, Kraftwerk and Anglo synthpop, linking them through dub effects and percussive breaks. It quickly spread to London and Germany, and by the early 1990s was established in California and New York. And, at least at first, it had a specific market: it was played on 12-inchers distributed to DJs, becoming a favourite in clubs such as Chicago's Warehouse and New York's Paradise Garage whose clientele included blacks, whites and Hispanics, straights and gays.

Raves, on the other hand, were large parties, news of which were spread by word of mouth or on pirate radio stations, generally organised without official sanction, dedicated, not to put too fine a point on it, to dancing to techno music while stoned on ecstasy or sometimes (mainly in the States) on acid. The drugs were as much a key to the scene as the music, if not more so: they helped confer its subterranean and illegal status. And the dancing was key to the culture too: a new style without partners, trance-like and radically expressive. But the music soon evolved into different genres in the UK and Europe, breaking with its early dependence on US beats partly as computers and music software became cheaper and cheaper. House and acid house jostled with Detroit techno, hardcore techno, breakbeat, jungle, drum and bass, trance.... And in the early days this combination of mega-parties, techno music and drugs was connected to a discourse of paganism, nomadism and spirituality which clearly remembered the sixties hippie movement and which, for many, was (like punk before it) a conscious repudiation of Thatcher/Reaganite neo-liberal individualism.

In the summer of 1992, at the movement's height, a rave party in Castlemorton Common in England's West Country drew about 40,000 people across six days of illegal partying. But the rave movement as such was not very commercialisable: its tracks were too meandering and samey and it was too drug-orientated for that. Nonetheless popularised versions of music styles formed within it entered the hit parade and club music of the nineties, and in particular the corporatised club world of the late nineties with its star DJs producing endless CDs and special nights (let Ministry of Sound stand as the exemplar) were a mutation of the rave scene. The movement's decline was more due to the logic of exhaustion familiar from the sixties hippie culture: repetition, continual and escalating drug usage, increased invigilation by authorities and the widening of the movement from an avant-garde into a wider, more pragmatic and commodified leisure culture, all degraded it. This is to return to the question of authenticity since dance music's history was one of what Simon Frith and Andrew Goodwin have called 'progress by attrition' – where (as the story goes, sometimes more persuasively than at other times) what starts out real ends sold out (Frith and Goodwin 1990, ix).

More specifically: what was important about the rave scene and its music was that, unlike reggae, punk and hip hop, it had absolutely no organic base, no community defined in terms outside of itself which it could claim to articulate and express. It was drawn together by the music and the drugs – and only by the music and drugs. This meant that its politics (to the degree it had a politics) were not the politics of identity but of pleasure and (to some degree) of mood/spirituality. Yet its music was not expressive of individual talent as communicated through traditional musical instruments; at this level it had lost all folkish resonances. It came to represent a connection between anti-neo-liberal celebration of empathetic collectivity and the highly technologised world of the sample, the turntable, the digital track (even its drugs were the result of sophisticated industrialised pharmacology). Perhaps what was most remarkable about it in hindsight was its lack of political point and ambition. Perhaps today it is best read as a failed but bold experiment in empathy and pleasure as resistance (see Reynolds 1998; Malbon 1999).

Art or pop?

The second tension which besets popular music, and which has helped organise a great deal of academic writing about it, is that between the aesthetic and the popular. Older analyses of rock, whether for or against, tended to stress its rebelliousness, ephemerality, standardisation and domination by fashion. But they have been proved less than adequate since rock too has been produced, consumed and appreciated in an enormous variety of ways. For example, a sector within the rock world has always reached out to more 'serious' music: let's not remember Rick Wakeman but offer Radiohead's *Kid A* and *Amnesiac* as instances instead. And the academisation of rock music since the eighties, both as a topic of analysis and a set of skills in which to be schooled, twists the music away from simple popism. (The professional journal *Popular Music* was founded in 1981; in the USA, a professional association for the study of pop music was established that same year; now seminars on music, which bring together academic and industry types, have become routine and, conversely, rock musicians write cultural studies essays – see R. J. Warren Zanes of the Del Fuegos' piece in the anthology *Rock over the Edge* [Beebe, Fulbrook and Saunders 2002] – or they produce culturally sophisticated art fiction – see the stories by Dean Wareham of Luna and Rhett Miller of the alt-country group Old 97s in *MacSweeney's*, issue 12 [2004].)

Another example: boxed sets were first produced to outflank bootlegs and then, with the advent of the CD, flooded the market in the early eighties. As a result a whole set of quasi-aesthetic and canonising practices which previously had been restricted to domains such as literature (the 'collected works') entered rock 'n' roll not so much against rock's saturation by market forces but because of it. Connoisseurship, collecting and completism are energised by the short shelf life of much product in music retailing outlets and the spottiness of distribution outside the major labels as well as by a thriving black market. From one point of view, these sets are celebratory mausoleums to artists and closures on their reputation and reception. From another they merely show the logic of cultural distinction at work once more. And from yet another side they are simply a great idea, allowing fans to fulfil their desire to enjoy, know, commemorate and collect (Fenster 1993).

Indeed a certain aestheticism is integral to the popular music markets insofar as they are dependent on reviews and criticism. Reviewers make value judgements to guide consumer choices, and they do so by virtue of what are, finally, aesthetic criteria. Let's take a (shortened but still long) instance of a review, written by an employee of the independent San Francisco record store Aquarius Records and pulled off the Web. Here rock's aestheticism is made quite clear, as is the unease between it and popism (as well as the speed with which genres are formed).

LOVELIESCRUSHING 'Glissceule' (Sonic Syrup) cd 9.98

Shoegazing – originally the derogatory term applied to bands such as Ride, Slowdive, and My Bloody Valentine for their lackluster stage presence – had developed into an impressive aesthetic during the early '90s whereby the jangle of '60s psych-pop had been married with Brian Eno's notions of ambient music as an oceanic/prelingual return to the womb. After its gilded crescendo from a couple of records (most notably MBV's 'Loveless'), shoegazing as an artform faded away, with many of the original proponents shedding the layers of distortion to concentrate upon their songwriting. Loveliescrushing – the post-shoegazing US duo of Scott Cortez and Melissa Arpin-Henry – disagreed with this trajectory away from etherealism and towards songsmithery, thus centering their music around only the faintest residues of melody and ghostly reminders of what might be a song somewhere within all of their bleary-eyed guitar washes. Their first two exceptional albums ('Bloweyelashwish' and 'Xuvetyn') found their way onto Projekt, the stalwart proprietors of America's darkwave/goth scene, although they didn't readily fit with Projekt's aesthetic for black lace and blood red roses. The only connection with Projekt may have been in the mutual affinity for the Cocteau Twins, whose glossalaic siren songs certainly resonate within the incomprehensible siren-like vocalisations of Arpin-Henry. Yet Loveliescrushing has little use for a rhythm section, presenting that soft female voice floating way off in the distance amidst oceans of radioluminescent layers of guitar reverberation. In all probability, this will stand as one of my favorite 'pop' albums of the year, even though there's nothing 'pop' about it.

(http://aquariusrecords.org)

'Glossalaic', 'radioluminescent', 'ghostly reminders of what might be a song' – all this is aestheticism of considerable refinement, and yet, almost ironically, pop too. And traces of a liberal arts education are surely apparent here. But the discourse of appreciation, which is also a marketing pitch, gels with the music itself. This is aestheticised experimental music that carefully negotiates a balance between pop pleasures, avant-garde hermeticism and disturbance of dull normativity. This may be the most aestheticised sector of the rock spectrum but, as Bernard Gendron points out in his insightful book *Between Montmartre and the Mudd Club: Popular Music and the Avant-Garde*, the founding move of rock culture – the rejection of bland singers such as Pat Boone in favour of ebullient weirdos like Little Richard – itself implies aesthetic distinctions, an aesthetic, of course, of energy, authenticity and dissent (Gendron 2002, 214).

The difficulties of accepting the art-values buried in popular music are apparent in a great deal of cultural studies work on the field. For instance, an excellent essay by Angela McRobbie on British drum'n bass regards the genre as a black British aestheticisation of popular music styles (McRobbie 1999, 14–16). Much drum'n bass, she notes, is anonymous and not aimed at a market, but rather is performed and created for its own sake. It's a genre that is also marked by the inability of outsiders to assess or otherwise come to terms with it, precisely because of its inward turn:

> The music functions as a record of the lives of its producers. It is extraordinarily self-reflexive, continually redressing itself, telling and re-telling its own story. It combines elements of improvisation, uplift and utopia inscribed within its practice and performance (and described by Gilroy as a part of a black Atlantic musical aesthetic) and also something newer, darker and different. A shot of fear, even terror, runs through the core of drum'n bass music, Virtually without voice or lyrics, except for the commands and commentary from the MC, there is also the underside of racial memory where there is no community, not protection and security – only paranoia.
>
> (McRobbie 1999, 19)

McRobbie believes that drum'n bass is a neglected form, which does not get the attention it deserves because it has few links with mainstream public culture or the academy, in comparison to Brit Art for instance, which she regards as a superficial and cynical drift outward from the art world into popular culture (McRobbie 1999, 18). The assumption here is that sub-cultures such as drum'n bass need official imprimatur, media attention: it is unjust if they don't have any. Which is certainly not the view of many practitioners. Indeed the excitement, experimentalism and 'integrity' of drum'n bass in the late eighties was predicated precisely on the absence of attention which McRobbie understandably deplores.

Conclusion

Popular music is crucial to cultural studies because it provides a strong example of how art forms nurture particular cultural formations through processes of division and attraction, and because music fandom crosses the border between academic and non-academic so easily. But popular music's aesthetics challenge reductive forms of populism (including the rock world's own) while the way that its commercialism is so closely bound to its creativity and rebelliousness also challenges analytic structures that place the market in opposition to authentic dissidence.

In a recent essay on cultural studies and popular music, Lawrence Grossberg suggests that it is important their relations remain political (Grossberg 2002). His argument is that, under neo-liberalism, youth (i.e. American youth) are being squeezed between policies which jeopardise their economic and social future and policies that demand they take more and more responsibility earlier. In this situation, he contends, a theoretically informed understanding of youth culture, and especially of music, will help scholars in the field act as advocates for youth. It's an intriguing notion which chimes with some of my own arguments for the role of cultural studies in this book. But still I wonder what OutKast and their fans, or Michael Jackson and his fans, or Avril Lavigne and her fans, would make of it. Finally, for all cultural studies' long intimacy with pop music, they do belong to different worlds and that difference is more essential to what energises them than any alliances. If that is the case, a cultural studies understanding of popular music, although it may express fanship or even a desire for advocacy, leans finally towards being academic knowledge like any other. The discipline's engagement (as in cultural studies is an *engaged* discipline) with music does not have the political force that it does with topics such as gender, ethnicity, race and sexuality, because these are much more nearly political through and through. When it comes to music, cultural studies can celebrate, critique and try to understand and explain, but it does so at some distance from its topic, and necessarily with a limited political agenda.

Further reading

Beebe, Fulbrook and Saunders 2002; Frith 1996; Frith and Horne 1987; Frith, Straw and Street 2001; Goodwin 1992; Hebdige 1979 and 1987; Ross and Rose 1994.

The Internet and technoculture

In 1999 Indra Sinha (known online as 'the Bear') published *The Cybergypsies: A Frank Account of Love, Life and Travels on the Electronic Frontier*. It is a semi-fictional memoir of nights spent playing and messaging on the Net between about 1987 and 1991. This was before Windows and the World Wide Web turned cyberspace into a mass media. In the late eighties, the Net feels gothic – hyper-gothic. Its characters – Jesus Slutfucker, Lilith, Hagstor and Metibal – prowl virtual space like it's a dangerous, mysterious netherworld. Some are virus writers who meet in places such as nuKE, plotting to burn and destroy; some are role-playing S&M-ers clustering at sites such as Madame Pompadora's on the Vortex; some become addicted to Shades, a MUD site, sometimes spending days at a time sleepless at the keyboard. Obsessive hackers go after nerd nets such as Fidonet (which started in the USA in 1984 and marks the beginning of this community) as well as the university system, the JANET. More riskily, they try to track the daddies of the Internet, both managed by the US Department of Defence, MILNET (the military network) and ARPNET (the research network which was the first Internet system of them all).

Yet access is through modems that take minutes, sometimes hours, to make any connection at all. Phone bills bankrupt some players. Bear owns a computer called an Apricot (Britain's answer to Apple) with 128k of memory and a 16-bit microcomputer, cutting-edge at the time but mind-numbingly slow and perpetually suffering cardiac arrests. All this to enter a world made up primarily of bulletin boards that don't have any capacity for images or sounds at all (Sinha 1999).

At one level what is remarkable about Sinha's vivid evocation of the old Internet is how dated it all seems. For instance: no hard-core porn, and it's porn that will kick start the Internet boom once images are available. Nothing becomes obsolescent quicker than cyberculture. But at another level it is strangely familiar. Who, among those who lived through it, can forget the apocalyptic rhetorics of doom, estrangement and revolution that accompanied the emergence of technoculture? And the opposing rhetorics of renewal, magic and technological bliss which combined sci-fi futurist motifs with the Californian new-age libertarianism most notoriously promoted by the magazines *Mondo 2000* and *Wired* in the eighties. All this reached a climax with the hollow utopias of the dotcom boom and pundits for a new stage of capitalism, which in turn was mirrored negatively in crazy predictions of the millennial crash on 1 January 2000.

The difficulty with technoculture is that no one knows exactly where it is heading or indeed exactly what it is. Just after Sinha's time, or, more specifically from 1990 onwards, the Web as such meant something very specific within the larger Internet. It meant the World Wide Web, which at first was just one service on the Net, the user-friendly one with pictures and (later) sounds that many old-time Net people then despised. (Technically the WWW was a global hypertext system based on HTML; see www.w3.org/history.html for a good Web-history timeline.) Today the Web can signify the whole thing: it's interchangeable with, and is taking over from, terms such as 'Internet' or 'Net'. And the Web does not just belong to culture: it is as much a business, an administrative and a military tool as a personal, leisure one. It is not just a service either. It absorbs and transforms most of the old communication technologies – telephony, broadcasting, mail, publishing – and adds some new ones – audio downloading, linking (which used to be called hypertext, the topic of a plethora of optimistic futuristic writings in the early nineties), info-tracking (to give a name to its capacity to record and publish usage immediately). To use the old Hegelian lingo: it sublates the old media, preserving them and lifting them up to a higher power. But in doing so it also hybridises and mutates them. E-mail, for instance, is a form of post but in its speed, its de-individuating capacity to reach many addresses at once, it can become something like a broadcast, albeit an 'interactive' broadcast.

Because the Web is still developing and because no one knows exactly what it will turn out to do or what its social effects will be, its critique and theory routinely lapse into speculation and prophecy. All the more so because the digitisation of information and communication, although separate from the Internet, is itself closely connected to the Net's extension, since everything that can be digitised can, in principle, be put on the Web. At the moment however digitisation has its own effects independently of the Web, including important implications for copyright, as in the case of MP3 sharing. To cite a case that Steven Feld has discussed: a song 'Rorogwela' sung by Afunakwa, a Solomon Islands singer, had originally been recorded by an ethnomusicologist employed by UNESCO and then sampled in a CD by Deep Sound (Feld 2001). It then took on a life of its own: a highly produced version became a world music hit, a video for which was made. The music was licensed for use in television commercials by a number of transnational corporations including Sony and Coca-Cola. The jazz saxophonist, Jan Garbarek, sampled it in a record of his own, under the impression that he was appropriating 'pygmy music'. At this point a controversy about royalties flared up. Afunakwa had no economic rights to the song, since it (like a great deal of third-world indigenous music) was regarded as 'oral tradition'. And Garbarek had obviously paid no royalty to her or to the Solomon Islands, although it turns out he had paid 50 per cent of the total royalty to a fund to promote 'folk music' as the Norwegian collection agency required. But the real questions were: what recognition was given to the original singer in this drift of digital sound from CD to CD and from web site to web site? And what control did they have over the song's submersion into a soft, commercial 'one worldism'? Here is a case in which a work's original context of production is forgotten and ignored as it is digitised and more or less immaterially disseminated. Nonetheless, although the situation is new, the issues of responsibility and control that it raises are not unique to the digitalised era and the ethical categories that we have can cope with them, although, admittedly, this is less certain for legal structures (see McLeod 2001 for an excellent discussion of the challenges that new technologies pose for issues of intellectual property).

Here digitisation and the transmission of sounds across cultural and national borders test cultural rights and the law. The Web accelerates such tests and uncertainties. Yet, at the moment, attempts to chart the impact of the Web also are constrained by the Web's being a technology-in-process. How it is used now and how it impacts on lives now is not necessarily a good indicator of what is to come: the Sinha example is evidence of that. Or, to give another example, in 1997 Louise Woodward, a British nanny living in the USA, was accused of murdering a baby in her care. The case attracted a great deal of Internet activity on her behalf. She became an early web celebrity and, as such, the object of considerable cultural studies analysis (see Senft 2000). In particular the case has been seen as a harbinger of web activism's nascent power to work for justice. Leaving aside questions of the relations between the Woodward campaign and more conventional media (especially 'Court TV'), it seems as if her case will never be repeated. Today, six years later, the Internet is simply too big for that; there are too many such cases. It has no more relation to social justice (if that was what was in question at all) than it does to the Christian right, political advertising and fund-raising, gambling or to libertarianism, say.

Then too, Internet sites that were once outrageous have now become orthodox. Take another instance from 1997 – the case of Harry Knowles and his web site, http://www.aint-it-cool-news.com, which became famous after an early review of the Hollywood dud *Batman and Robin*. A kid from Texas, Knowles became an important player in Hollywood via the Internet, the first to make that move. At that time his relative imperviousness to the big studios' spin; his fervent love of movies, past and present; his use of leaked insider e-mails about scripts, productions and test screenings; his intimate knowledge of Hollywood marketing techniques, all made the site important as a space outside Hollywood's own presentation of itself, and therefore a threat to the big studios. All the more so because informed and unbiased information about movies before the all-important 'first weekend' is especially damaging. That weekend is crucial to the US film industry because it is a measure not of reviews and word of mouth (over which the studios have little control) but of marketing strategies and star power (which they can control) and can become the basis for further marketing campaigns. But today Knowles' site is commercialised, containing some of the most sophisticated studio advertising of the moment. If it marks itself off from Hollywood in any way, you'd have to be closer to Hollywood than your average movie-goer to notice. The web independent has been brought into line with established media interests.

So, accounts of the Web have moved on from early utopian or future-shock discourses. Academic surveys have followed them. A recent summary of social-scientific research on the Web's social and cultural impacts presents its findings in the field under five headings: (1) the uptake and use of the new technologies depend crucially on local context and don't 'undermine socially normative behaviour'; (2) the fears and risks associated with new technologies are unevenly distributed in social terms; (3) virtual technologies supplement rather than substitute for real activities; (4) the more virtual the more real, which means that the new technologies actually encourage more traditional activities (as in the publishing industry, where the digitalisation of book production has made the process cheaper, quicker and more flexible, increasing the number of books published per year); and (5) the more global the more local, which means that technologies which seem able to transcend location can actually produce its re-inscription. A good example would be the community web sites that provide an effective means of communicating images and attractions of, and activities in, particular localities. There is evidence that connecting neighbourhoods to the Web can increase local pride through the very sense of being globally wired (Woolgar 2002, 14–20). Indeed Net usage can seem to confirm long-seated cultural practices. Daniel Miller and Don Slater's study of Net use in Trinidad, for instance, shows that there the Web was experienced not as a break with tradition but as 'naturally Trinidadian', conforming both to local cosmopolitanism and to local chatty sociabilities (Miller and Slater 2000).

Nonetheless, it won't be the case that the Web marks no break with the past, any more than electricity or cars or telephones (which are equally important, now more or less settled, technologies) did not result in a shift in the patterns of society and culture. And yet to the degree that these technologies become part of the armature of life, they evade study. There is simply no point of view that can analytically transcend them or, pretty much, which is interested in doing so. (Television is an exception because, as we have seen, it remains poised between being a structuring force and being one media among many.) Social scientists examining the impact of new technologies on the community at large are likely to miss important features of that impact, since it is a small number of relatively privileged 'early adopters' who first live out the transformations involved in usage of technologies. But early adopters' experiences will not necessarily be those of later generations.

I do not claim to be an expert and avant-garde web user, but I am more wired than most in the community at a moment when the Web represents approximately 11 per cent of total media consumer time in the USA and obviously much less than that globally. (The United Nations Development Program's [UNDP] 1999 *Human Development Report* noted that by the late nineties, OECD countries constituted 19 per cent of the world's population but 91 per cent of Internet users: this is the figure that measures the global digital divide, i.e. the massive inequality of Net access across regions.) My personal figure for the percentage of media consumer time spent online is closer to 50 per cent, which may be where we are heading – and this means that my personal web usage may have some merit as a predictive case. So let me offer a little auto-ethnography of my web usage on a particular and specific day (yesterday, 28 May 2003). I checked my e-mail first thing after breakfast and then once every couple of hours or so. I ordered some books and while doing that fiddled with my want lists on Amazon and ABE. I opened up the bbc.com news site a couple of times during the day to make sure no big disaster had hit the world while I was doing something else, and read through the headlines at Slate.com. As I'm writing this book I find myself googling sometimes to check out information about topics and importing bibliographical details, usually from the Library of Congress via Endnote. I logged on to Limewire and tried, mainly unsuccessfully, to download some Son Volt tracks because I came across a reference to them which seemed intriguing. I thought about an old colleague and wondered what he was up to, scouring the Web to find out, encountering frustrating dead-ends, out-of-date sites and then some more recent ones. I randomly browsed through some blogs, bookmarking those I might want to look at again. I published some stuff on my own blog and then spent time on Apple Music listening to thirty-second samples of tracks, following the trail of 'people who bought this also bought this' into albums I didn't know.

Not every day is like this of course. And I know I am not typical in that for instance my access to the Internet is at home rather than through work or e-gateways (cyber cafes, universities, etc.) which remain important for accessing the Net among those who can't afford computer access from home. Nor am I an online gamer, involved in so-called 'massively multi-player' online games that deliver role-playing scenarios which take the Bear's old-style virtual fictions onto a whole other plane. More technically, I have a broadband service with a wireless router at home feeding an up-to-date and fast computer, which is still uncommon. But the spread of wireless links to the Internet is increasing and is likely further to popularise web access.

If I were to extrapolate from this account of web usage, my prediction for the technology's social impact would begin with more time available for consumption and a decrease in the contingency of real-space retail commodity selection (it doesn't really matter what books are in particular bookshops since almost everything is easily available online, and that now holds for many commodities). So it would also seem to mean the privatisation of certain public activities, notably shopping. At the same time the Web means increased access to the mass of commodities and information, including access through serendipity. And the increased fragmentation of leisure activities: television, reading, movie-going have a real competitor in the Web – indeed there is now significant evidence that TV viewership is being hurt by web browsing. It also means that barriers to entry into publishing- and broadcasting-like activities (such as blogging) fall so low that the rarity value that marked media/published content collapses, requiring either new techniques of selectivity to guide and form audiences, or a wholly new relation between the public and the private. The technology is beginning to make it easy enough to become a producer for the division between production and consumption, so vital for traditional views of culture, to lose its edge.

My usage hints at an increased porousness between work and leisure too. Yesterday, work and 'private' time overlapped and intersected for me from home, but it would not have been all that different had I been at work. This leads to certain tensions both in that domestic time is more open to work demands, and work time is more exposed to leisure interests. And given that every act on the Web can be monitored and leaves its traces, it means that privacy (understood as the absence of potential observation) is under jeopardy: work and consumption are both more able to be monitored than previously.

It also suggests the emergence of a new domain between the public and the private – the domain of the web log (or blog): web-posted diaries on individuated web sites (with the most popular of many blog providers, Blogger, having over a million registered users at the time of writing). The blog radically democratises web publishing since it makes it both easy and free. There are blogs of all kinds: celebrity blogs, commercial blogs, journalistic blogs, weird obsessive diary blogs, boring blogs, pseudonymous blogs, signed blogs, politicians' blogs. Almost all of them fall into a strange space where they are lost in the vastness of the Web's chatter, and enabled by that. They are neither secret nor public; they are part of everyday life like a diary but at the same time are also statements to and for the world.

Finally, time (for the moment at least) works differently on the Web than it has for traditional media and cultural forms. As Michael Warner has noted, digitisation allows culture to exist in an eternal present in which it is less (but not *not*) organised around 'punctuality', the temporality of print and broadcast media where texts (news programmes most of all) are presented in regular intervals and at specified times (Warner 2002, 97–98). It twists us away from the temporality of broadcasting back to

141

something like the null temporality of the library (as in my search for traces of an ex-colleague). Websites rarely mark their time of origin clearly, and they are there as long as their server remains connected.

Certainly the ongoing triumph of the Web does not seem to mean a victory of dematerialisation or virtuality, those catchphrases of early technoculture theory. The fact that the Web has the particular relation to space that it does, while essential to its operation, seems not to be of primary importance to its users. It does not de-spatialise them, it merely changes the kind of spaces they typically inhabit. The whole 'virtual' thing was something of a red herring (although it retains more point as a category of digital gaming). Likewise affirmations of a wired community and wired democracy, and claims that the Web would increase our power to communicate with one another in such a way as to strengthen the public sphere, seem to have been massively overplayed.

Indeed, against such arguments, Jodi Dean has recently argued that the increased capacity to communicate that comes with the Web actually functions to degrade democracy because it submerges the individual voice in a mass of information and communication without order. Digital network boosterism, according to Dean, helps disable the kind of deliberations that might actually make a democracy out of technoculture (Dean 2002). This argument acknowledges that the Web does not constitute a public sphere of the kind that much enlightened political and social theory assumed: a finite number of individuals capable of sharing communications, and who either constitute the population of that community or who represent it according to an agreed form of representation. Yet as we have seen, the Web is probably not the most important force in degrading a formal politics based on that myth: the older broadcast media, especially TV, played key roles in that.

In sum then, the discourses that have surrounded the Web have tended to exaggeration touching on hysteria, whether for or against. As the Web increasingly structures social and cultural relations, its effects will need to be carefully monitored, its risks guarded against, its pleasures and possibilities disseminated and critically expressed. At the moment the main dangers that the Web poses seem to be the digital divide; its power to shrink the public geography of culture; and its capacity to turn online behaviour into action which is at once a commodity (available to marketing agencies) and an object for surveillance. On the other hand, the Web's promises include the formation of new collectivities and identities, new forms of online sociability and new ease of access for all kinds of information. But conclusions like these necessarily sound lame since, as I say, no one knows yet where digitisation and the Web are leading us. Here's a topic where students – now and to come – will lead the way.

Further reading

Bell and Kennedy 2000; Herman and Swiss 2000; Lovink 2002; Miller and Slater 2000; Plant 1996; Winston 1998.

Part 5

IDENTITY

Debating identity

Identities are conceptually more complex than they may at first appear. From one point of view, they define *who somebody is* in terms of a trait, which might be anything from, for instance, a physical feature of the body, a belief, a genealogy or a cultural preference. In effect they identify by placing individuals into groups who share that trait. And this has a consequence: it means that identity is won at the price of reducing individuality. My identity as a man, for instance, both defines me and lumps me with 50 per cent (roughly) of the population, radically reducing my particularity. Furthermore the traits chosen to ascribe identity to an individual are always contingent, since whatever trait is chosen to fix identity, another one could have been chosen, even if it seems 'natural' to identify people by, for instance, their gender (and it seems as if all known societies do in fact identify people by gender). Identities, then, are not given in terms of what individuals are as a whole, but in terms of more or less arbitrarily selected features that they possess. For the most part, individuals have little power to choose what features will be used to identify them – these are determined socially, from the outside.

From the point of view of individuals, it may seem as if, because identities are external, partial and collectivising, they dislocate one from oneself. They anchor who you are to only a part of yourself. Yet, from the other side, of course, because individuals exist socially in and through their identities, without an identity there is no such thing as a socially situated individual. Societies, identities and individuals do not exist independently of one another, and at a theoretical level, it is meaningless to criticise identities in general for depriving individuals of individuality, just as it is wrong to contend that individuals comprise nothing but their identities. Identities are not so much the mediation between individuals and society as constitutive of that relation.

However this is still a little too simple. Individuals don't have a single identity, they have *identities*, and they do so just because identities are based on partial traits (skin colour, socio-economic status, gender, nationality, region, profession, generation and so on). I am a man and a New Zealander and an ectomorph and bourgeois and an academic and Aquarian, etc. But not all identities carry equal weight in particular circumstances or have the same social consequences. Gender, race or ethnicity, and class are the identities, most of all, by which we are placed socially. And the relative weight of identities changes across time and space. For instance, in many nations the county in which one was born used to matter a great deal in terms of identity. Now (generally speaking) it matters much less. On the other hand, once nationality carried little weight as an identity trait; now it marks the identity with which states are most centrally engaged. Or take being a 'man', which, in the West, has been transformed over the last thirty years or so from an implicit universal (everyone was regarded as male unless otherwise marked) to being merely one identity among others.

Then, too, the terms by which identities are ascribed do not usually describe traits and groups neutrally. They are culturally inflected, and in the last instance are determined by power relations within a community, especially how these shape social relations between those using the identity-descriptor and those to whom the descriptor applies. Thus, for instance, it matters a great deal whether an American black person is called a nigger, an African American, a black, a Negro, etc. Each of these terms marks an identity which is both the same as (in that it marks out the same group) and different from (in that it has different connotations) each of the other terms. And each of these terms may change its meaning depending on who is using it, and in what context. Some identity words are used affirmatively by the groups they describe (and thus they mark 'self-identities'), others are not. Quite often, words used by others to define a group insultingly or prejudicially are appropriated by the group themselves and turned into a term marking self-identity, usually after passing through a brief phase where they are used ironically: hippie, punk, nigger itself, for instance.

The fit between an identity and an individual self is, therefore, structurally loose, and is often thought of as requiring processes of 'identification' in order to be sealed (Fuss 1995). Certainly individuals differ as to the degree of intensity with which they connect to particular identities. Indeed, significant numbers of people struggle to 'dis-identify' from – detach themselves from – given identities, with transsexuals the most famous of such groups. (In this case we have an identity based on dis-identification since, according to the cultural logic of gender-identities, an individual born a man can never wholly become a woman.) And where identities have a low cultural value, individuals ascribed such identities can internalise negative images of themselves. In such cases, the process of identification can cause psychic damage.

Identification remains something of a theoretical enigma: we saw earlier how, for post-Marxists, identification with any subject position can never be complete, since, from their perspective, the subject as subject is constituted by lack. But leaving aside this theoretical analysis, in many situations, identification can be accounted for more simply. People identify with their identities to a greater or lesser degree because identities constitute the framework of their lives, and also, on occasions, because pleasures and rewards follow from so doing. It is important to distinguish between given or inherited identities, many of which are based on corporeality (a Maori, a woman), and chosen identities, many of which are based on cultural, material or ideological choices or preferences (a conservative, a waiter, an opera fan). This distinction (while by no means watertight: what about religious identities for instance, which seem often to be indeterminately inherited *and* chosen?) is useful insofar as it reminds us that there are many kinds and intensities of identification which no theory of identification is able to cover. And as Franz Fanon has pointed out, negative identities can be internalised as powerfully as positive ones (Fanon 1966).

Furthermore, because identities are partial, they leave spaces outside of themselves. Not all of me is covered by my being a 'man' – or by any other of my identities, or by all of them together. There is something in me, a self or 'interiority', that has no identity: it belongs to me as an individual with a proper name but slips away from any interpersonal recognition at all. This is the world of private moods, desires and thoughts, which may not even be consciously articulated at all, where I may seem to be most myself. Sometimes this space is associated with freedom or resistance, but there is no particular reason why that should be so. At best, if social identities are conceived of as limiting rather than enabling (and it makes more sense to regard them as simultaneously limiting and enabling), then the self outside identity escapes the limits of identity. But at a cost – precisely because what lacks identity cannot form a social persona.

There has been an increasing interest in identity since the seventies as a result of what has come to be called 'identity politics', a politics with which cultural studies has been aligned, as we know. Identity politics means, of course, a politics engaged on behalf of those with particular identities (usually historically disempowered ones) rather than a politics organised on the basis of particular social policies or philosophies. In fact these distinctions are somewhat nebulous since even traditional left/right politics was loosely organised around class identities.

The origins of identity politics are murky: it is often said that they begin with the civil rights movement in the USA during the early sixties, after which groups with specific cultural and social identities increasingly made political claims on the basis of those identities – in particular, African Americans on behalf of their racially defined community and feminists on behalf of women (Omi and Winant 1986, 75). These claims were connected to an analysis at once political and historical. In terms of history, it became apparent that for centuries in the West the values and attributes of a particular group – white, heterosexual men, and especially white, heterosexual, bourgeois men – had been taken as the norm. They exemplified what it was to be a human being as such – universal humanness. The Enlightenment, as the historical moment that deprived religion and tradition of their social and political authority, had ironically (so it was argued) consolidated the normativity of the white male by default – with God and history out of the picture, he stood at the world's centre as the privileged bearer of reason. Certainly – and this is the more important political point – the white heterosexual man was the locus of authority and power, with an access to the public sphere and to political and economic goods granted to no other group. Armed with this strong interpretation of history and politics, identity groups, including feminists, gays and lesbians, and various ethnic groups, have increasingly since the sixties been able to find spaces within the public sphere and even the formal political apparatuses to assert and struggle for wants and needs that they have by virtue of their marginalised identity or to resist constraints imposed upon them by virtue of their identity.

It is also sometimes said that identity politics are fuelled by the desire for 'recognition' (Taylor 1994) (the street word for which is 'respect'), but in most cases they have also been motivated by more than that – by the desire for access, liberty and fair, unprejudiced treatment. Nonetheless to the degree that identity politics does involve the claim that a certain cultural invisibility of the identity-group be rectified, it will contain a component of recognition that is lacking in other forms of politics, and it is important not to undervalue respect's value. Furthermore, where particular identities have been marginalised or demonised by the most powerful groups in a society, identity politics can involve 'consciousness raising', that is the critique of negative stereotypes and undoing the psychic damage involved in identifying with them.

It is worth pausing a moment to consider in more detail why identity politics became so familiar a part of the social and political landscape in the last decades of the twentieth century. In general there are two kinds of explanations for the emergence of political formations of this kind: one stresses the agency of the community and individuals involved; the other analyses the larger social conditions that made the new politics and its forms of association possible. Thus, to take a famous instance from history, was the British abolitionist movement empowered by slaves and their supporters or is it to be understood as a consequence of the relative economic inefficiency of slavery (see James 1963; Blackburn 1988)? In terms of modern identity politics: did African Americans, women, gays and lesbians, and the disabled form political associations on the basis of their autonomous will for liberation, or did they organise themselves politically because they were enabled to do so by circumstances? In fact we don't have to make a hard decision between these alternatives. The will and energy of marginalised groups has been crucial to identity politics but, nonetheless, such politics occurred when it did because of larger forces and openings, with the balance between 'push' and 'pull' factors differing in different circumstances.

The emergence of Occidental identity politics in the seventies can be regarded as a moment in a long history during which the authority of various national and colonial hegemonic 'ruling blocs' (in Anglophone countries WASPS [White Anglo-Saxon Protestants]) was gradually diminished. We are already quite familiar with this history, which shares many aspects with the history of postmodernism and globalisation: World War II was a key moment in the decline of elite hegemony for various reasons. The early Japanese victories in Asia showed that the West was not invincible. The US military's dependency on African American troops and the subsequent GI Bill (which helped racial equality in the North but not in the South) helped re-energise the civil rights movement. And the revelation of the Holocaust significantly diminished the appeal of racist politics, basically casting it beyond the pale of the respectable at least in its most overt forms. The decolonisation of the fifties also dented European hegemony, and the South Asian sub-continent's long struggle for independence was especially important to that, as was, later, the victory of Vietnamese communists over, first, the French and then the USA. More concretely, the women's movement was enabled by a series of economic and technological developments: relative affluence, new devices for washing, cleaning, cooking, the oral contraceptive and so on, all of which gradually shifted the balance of power between the genders in everyday life – or at least did so in advanced industrial nations. Similarly suburbanisation played a key role in the emergence of the gay liberation movement since it allowed strong gay communities to flourish in certain inner-city neighbourhoods. And as we have seen, the culture and media industries themselves accelerate segmentation and identity formation by quickly targeting particular identities as specific, de-limited consumer markets.

Cultural studies has often been regarded (and especially in the USA) as the academicisation of identity politics (and therefore an inheritor of this history), but in fact it has been split between two sides: one that has allied itself with marginal or subordinated identities; another that has understood identities as forms of constraint and rigidity or even as part of the social structuration of hegemony. Hence there have been repeated attempts to articulate a 'post-identity' cultural politics by turning to concepts such as hybridity, attempts that became more and more influential through the eighties and nineties, fuelled by an increasingly concrete sense of identity politics' conceptual and political difficulties.

We can summarise these difficulties as follows:

1   Identity politics tends to erase internal differences. Thus feminism failed to mark the difference between women of different classes or of different ethnicities, or indeed different attitudes towards femininity itself, a failure that almost crippled the movement.

2   A very similar point: identity politics often assumes that an identity is an essence – that there exists an essential (or authentic) way of being a woman, a Maori, an Asian, etc. Hybridity theory helps disabuse us of this notion, as we shall see below.

149

3   Identity politics tends to work by the principle of exclusion. Identities tend to be structured by reducing or demonising particular others, either in cases where socially dominant identities are being formed (the concept of the white was largely based on vilifying groups with other skin colours) or in cases where identity–groups are engaged in a politics of emancipation (feminism was under pressure to represent all men as sexists).

4   Identity politics tends to overlook identities around which lives are actually lived. In everyday life, one of the more important identities that individuals have is determined by the paid work that they do. (This has been of more interest to sociology than to cultural studies, in part because cultural studies has often been driven by the will to politicise identities and has been relatively uninterested in questions concerning paid work.)

5   When a political or social movement is grounded on identity, the content of the 'identity' tends to be emphasised and the importance of organisation and process in achieving political ends is neglected. This is because identity politics are often simultaneously concerned to increase the intensity of group solidarity and to fulfil claims to rights. Furthermore, because identities in identity politics are neither negotiable nor (within limits) able to be expanded to include those who don't share the identity, identity politics can lapse into rigidity and cause fragmentation of the shared ground that politics in certain conjunctures needs to operate within. This tendency is most marked when an identity is ascribed in terms of a culture, as we will see in the section on multiculturalism.

6   Identity politics tends to invent legitimating histories or traditions which can be politically (then commercially) exploited. Perhaps national identities are the most obvious instance of this, since 'invented traditions' have been especially strong in their case. The most famous example is the 'invention' of the Scottish tartan and kilt as an important signifier of national identity, first by English clothing manufacturers during the eighteenth century and then by Sir Walter Scott's work on behalf of cultural nationalism during the early nineteenth century (see Hobsbawm and Ranger 1983).

Perhaps cultural studies' strongest attempt to address these problems was to try and rethink identity in such a way that the concept lost its rigidity. This attempt took various forms, the most widely disseminated of which is the category of 'hybridity', but another is what Stuart Hall called 'unities in difference' (Hall 1987, 45). In both cases, identity is conceived not as a fixed marker but in terms of the processes or performances by which identities are formed. According to this theory, these processes are continual: the meaning and force of all identities are in constant mutation (although they sometimes change more slowly than at other times). Identities are not just given or chosen, they have to be enacted, but this means that they have to enter into negotiation with the situation in which they are performed or otherwise acted upon. More than that: in a post-Marxist turn, it is supposed that individuals and groups can assert their identity all the more intensely because identity as such is always a little out of reach – no identity orders a whole subjectivity or forms a secure ground for all life-practices. To put this in other terms: hybridity theory thinks of identity not as a marker, a stable trait shared across groups, but as a practice whose meaning and effect is constantly mutating as its context changes.

But why 'hybridity'? For various reasons. Let's first take up the concept's theorisation by the influential postcolonial critic Homi Bhabha, who came to the question of identity through his interest in colonialism. Bhabha argued that 'subaltern' identities are regularly articulated in terms that are not their own but are those of the dominant faction. ('Subaltern' is a term used originally by Gramsci but which now usually refers to those social groups with the least power of all, especially colonised peoples.) Under colonialism, subaltern identity is not a pure expression of its own distinct character. Rather, the identity of subaltern groups is articulated in signifying practices that imitate and displace concepts (or discourses) that have been articulated by the coloniser. In imitating and deflecting dominant identities and discourses, so Bhabha's argument goes, the hybrid subaltern subverts the oppressor outside any formal political struggle. Hybridised identities acquired by the dominated cause ambivalence. And they call into question the naturalness and legitimacy of hegemonic identities (see Bhabha 1994).

Second, in a rather different account, hybridity is a useful concept because groups and individuals do not have a single identity but several. In particular, as Stuart Hall argued in his work on ethnicity, the term 'black' in Britain pulled together various very different groups coming from various places around the world. And its heterogeneity lent it power. It meant for instance that the 'black' identity could not call upon myths of a past to consolidate itself, and that it could not easily settle back into assumptions of shared culture. This 'difference in unity' demanded a politics of process in which what was different between members of one identity was as important as what was shared, and which prevented any kind of monolithic culture becoming its objective (Stuart Hall 1992). It required alliances and exchanges between different groups in situations where a political group was formed on its basis.

These concepts have been criticised because, for all their openness, they remain based upon a logic and politics of opposition in which identities remain, at base, distinct from one another and determining of social action. Thus, in the words of Robert Young, hybridity 'always reiterates and reinforces the dynamics of the same conflictual economy whose tensions and divisions it re-enacts in its own antithetical structure' (Young 1995, 27). The concept of hybridity does not move sufficiently past identity politics. But this critique is rather removed from everyday life where so much is ordered by identities. It seems to be making a theoretical and utopian rather than a practical point.

151

Furthermore, to critique hybridity as insufficiently disengaged from the category of identity itself is to forget that subject-formation requires identity. It is impossible to exist in society without a proper name, without being located within the set of identity-granting institutions into which one is born: family or kin-group, nation, ethnic community, gender. And this is not just an inescapable social structure. Many individuals are seriously attached to at least some of the identities given to them as members of a particular family, ethnicity, nation and/or gender, and want these not to be fluid but stable. It is in and through their identities that they belong to communities. And they may find the traditions clustered around such identities to be empowering and an aid in the construction of strong and vibrant communities and futures. Can such cases be excluded from emancipatory politics?

Maybe what is most striking about both many celebrations of identity and its critique by hybridity theorists is that neither offers a central role for what is surely one of the core categories for politics as such and for the articulation of subordinated identities in partic-ular: struggle. But struggle's logic is peculiar. During a struggle, enemies invariably appear from within the struggling side: between different inflections of the identity. (An obvious example is the feminist movement, which quickly fragmented, as we shall see in Part 6.) This leads to splits and purifying exercises and, often, banishment of renegade members of the identity-group. And when the struggle is over, especially if it results in a victory, identi-ties lose their charge and coherence; assimilation and indifference begin their work. (Think of Irish migrants to the USA or Australia for instance.) In the debate over hybridity this particular dynamic of identity politics is lost, partly because, for hybridity theorists, concepts such as subversion and resistance are *cultural* and able to use cultural modes such as mimicry, ambivalence, irony and so on as weapons. Thought about in the hard light of active liberation movements, hybridity can seem a wishful rather than a material concept.

In sum, although arguments over identity politics have lost the intensity of the seven-ties and eighties, they remain important to cultural studies (which is removed from active liberation struggles) as one of the debates around which the discipline continues to develop. There is no getting away from identities – even being a cultural studies student or teacher forms one. One way to present what is at stake in this issue might be to ask: do we in the discipline prefer to proliferate new identities, or do we try to combine and mutate established identities? Or do we work towards a post-identity politics open to forms of rationality that (seemingly?) don't presuppose any identity whatsoever? That's the kind of question which cultural studies is especially well positioned to address since it sets a cultural problem in a political frame. And arguably identity, most of all, is where culture is joined to society and politics.

Further reading

Fuss 1995; Gilroy, Grossberg and McRobbie 2000; Hall and Du Gay 1996; Papastergiadis 1998.

Multiculturalism

In 1991 Irving Kristol, one of the founding fathers of American neo-conservatism, published an editorial think-piece in the *Wall Street Journal* headlined 'The Tragedy of Multiculturalism'. Its main claim was that, although multiculturalism is mainly criticised because it is 'illiberal', in fact it is primarily an invention of educationalists and, as such, is a 'desperate — and surely self-defeating — strategy for coping with the educational deficiencies, and associated social pathologies, of young blacks' (Kristol 1995, 50). By shifting the curriculum towards African American history and culture, Kristol argued, multiculturalists were debasing the civilisational value of the heritage. In words that seem to prophesy the heightened rhetoric of the war on terrorism, he declaimed: 'What these radicals blandly call multiculturalism is as much a "war against the West" as Nazism and Stalinism ever were' (Kristol 1995, 52).

Kristol's essay was written in the heat of the culture wars of the early nineties, and it may seem hard to imagine such statements, with their racist overtones, achieving this level of prominence anywhere else in the West today, except of course in the USA. But that would be to forget the French and German far right (Le Pen and the Republikaner party) or one-time Professor of Greek, Enoch Powell's famous 1968 'rivers of blood' speech in the UK which predicted that the continuation of Caribbean and South Asian immigration would lead to anarchy or worse. Yet it is also true that multiculturalism in the US political arena tends to mean something rather different than it does in, say, Europe or Australia: it is somewhat less connected to issues of immigration and more focussed (as in Kristol's case) on accepting blacks and Hispanics into the mainstream. (Thus it was that Spike Lee became a hero of US multiculturalism during the late 1990s.)

Yet it is salutary to recall Kristol's piece not just because it demonstrates conservative thinking on this issue but because it succinctly points to two of the major critiques

153

of multiculturalism. According to its conservative critics, multiculturalism threatens: (1) a return to cultural barbarism through a lowering of standards or a debasement of values; and (2) illiberal coercion, since under particular policies designed to enable the survival of minority cultures, limits to individual freedom may be imposed (for instance, the law in Quebec, Canada, requiring all firms of over fifty employees to conduct business in French). And they often add a third argument, neglected here by Kristol, namely that multiculturalism will lead to a fragmentation of languages, religions and cultures within the nation so as to unravel the binding threads required for national unity.

The first of these arguments will largely be dealt with in the section on cultural value below since it turns around the proposition that value is not relative to particular cultures. But it is worth noting that the idea that multiculturalism equals barbarism is odd even in terms of the progressive vision of history that the distinction implies, given that multiculturalist policies are features precisely of the most developed, indeed of hyper-modernised, states. Multiculturalism is much weaker in the peripheries of the developed world: even an advanced industrial state such as Japan barely accommodates it, retaining an official monoethnicism which downgrades the lives of migrant Koreans and Chinese, as well as indigenous Okinawan, Ainu and Burakumin peoples. Similarly, ethnic cleansing, to take the most extreme form of anti-multiculturalism, is today more common in states where modernisation is lagging than it is in hyper-modern nations.

The second of these conservative arguments has only a tangential relation to cultural studies as such. But the third is relevant since it returns us directly to the question of the relations between nation-states and culture. Of course, what we might call hard monoculturalism – the idea that for every nation there ought to be just one culture – has obvious problems from a historical point of view. Almost all nations are, and always have been, multicultural in the sense that they contain a multitude of cultures and usually of languages and dialects. In fact, if we accept Reinhart Koselleck's theory of the emergence of the modern state then the modern state exists *because* of a particular form of multiculturalism. Koselleck argues that the state separated itself out of society and culture at the point (after the Thirty Years War in the mid-seventeenth century) when it became clear that national territories would have to include two religious confessions (Protestantism and Catholicism, or, in Britain's case, varieties of Protestantism), religious difference being no less a crucial indicator of difference then than ethnic difference today (Koselleck 1988). The modern state was brought into being in order that individuals of different religious creeds could live peaceably together as citizens.

Indeed as the Swedish sociologist Ulf Hannerz has carefully argued: all modern societies do not just tolerate, but are built around, meanings and values that are not shared by all members (Hannerz 1992, 44). A commitment to a nation can encompass differences and indeed may be strengthened by them. Perhaps nowhere is this truer than in the USA, where 'American culture' stands for a relatively restricted set of attachments that can co-exist with a number of very different religious, taste, moral, etc. preferences. This implies that the term 'culture' in 'multiculturalism' may be used fairly lightly. At any rate nationalism plays a role in unifying communities with different cultures. So we can think of nationalism either positively or negatively: as an ideological formation that prevents recognition and expression of unshared values or as an ideological formation that allows for a sense of collectivity across unshared values.

The situation changes somewhat when multiculturalism becomes official policy since such a move accepts a model of society in which various communities embrace their cultural differences. The primary point of multiculturalism is to grant full (and not just formal) citizenship to those of different cultures, in a way similar to how religious belief (within strict limits) began to cease being a criterion for citizenship in Protestant states around the end of the seventeenth century. And culture becomes important in this context because citizenship is not just a matter of holding a passport, possessing the right to vote and so on. It also consists of the capacity to contribute one's heritage, looks and beliefs to the national identity: the British 'national character' or 'national body', for instance, needs to cover its citizens of colour as well as whites. At a governmental level, multiculturalism thought such as this requires accepting notions of citizenship that actively affirm difference, and needs to be articulated in terms of citizens' participatory rights alongside governmental responsibility to uphold those rights (Bennett 2001, 61). This would allow us to include within *European* culture the contributions of the Muslims, people of African descent and Asians who live and work in Europe: a mosque in Marseilles is as French – and by the same stroke as European – as the Prix Goncourt.

Official multiculturalism emerges out of the intense difficulties faced by European politicians when they divided Central Europe into new states after World War I. The League of Nations ratified 'minority rights' for communities who did not form majorities in the new states, although as late as the thirties in Europe, communities that we would think of as ethnic minorities were called 'religious minorities' by administrators (Arendt 1973, 267–290). But minority rights were soon exposed as unenforceable. A situation developed in which many nations – from Germany to the USA – denaturalised ethnic groups or migrants, often condemning them to statelessness. After WW2, policies of denaturalisation were illegitimate (since they had paved the way for the Holocaust) while international protection of minority rights was moribund. States had to manage their own multiculturalism, although they were often slow to recognise that culture or even ethnicity was what was in question. Official multiculturalism was spurred on by large-scale immigration in and after the fifties when improved and cheaper global communications allowed migrant communities to stay in touch with their home states and maintain their old cultural interests and dispositions. (For an excellent account of the effects of modern media flows on diasporic identity see Naficy 1999). Diasporic communities often have a more rigid sense of their traditional home culture than those who stay behind because nostalgia plays so important a role in their relation to it, and because they do not experience ongoing changes at home. At any rate, to some degree multiculturalism is a consequence of globalisation.

On one level multiculturalism is a governmental tool for managing difference, as when states contain large minorities with irredentist (i.e. separatist) ambitions (for example Canada). Or, as I say, when a state contains non-hegemonic and minority communities of different races – here multiculturalism can be a means of managing not just monoculturalism but also racism (as in the USA). Conversely, in all these cases it is the state's acceptance of cultural difference under multiculturalism that triggers the conservative backlash, since such acceptance seems to loosen the grip of hegemonic groups on the apparatus of government.

It is not as if the conservatives are multiculturalism's only critics. From the left, multiculturalism has come under attack for rather different reasons. First, so the claim goes and in an argument that should by now be familiar, in appealing to the concept of 'culture' and imagining a nation-state composed of a variety of equally empowered cultures, multiculturalism closes down on differences within particular cultural groups. That is, it does not provide sufficient room for hybridity and 'identity-in-difference' in the terms spelt out in the last section (see Bharucha 1999). Second, multiculturalism tends to propose cultural solutions for political problems, by emphasising recognition and freedom of expression rather than power and economic equality (Critical Cultural Studies Group 1994). This argument is a version of the old new left complaint against cultural studies outlined in the introduction to this book.

Another version of this argument is that states promote multiculturalism to exhibit their tolerance rather than to promote difference, as is instanced when relatively trivial cultural modes – ethnic restaurants or festivals – are lauded under the banner of multiculturalism (see Hage 1998). And third, multiculturalism which comes under attack from the right when it is authorised and organised by the state comes under attack from the left when it is authorised and organised by the market, as instanced by the so-called 'Benetton effect' or by internal corporate diversity policies applied for commercial ends (Gilroy 2000, 242; Critical Cultural Studies Group 1994, 115). We are familiar with this logic: in aiming to market to different communities, corporations will incorporate personnel and values connected to those communities. And a few global companies, such as Benetton, have gone further: they have incorporated a multicultural 'we are the world' feeling into their branding so that their advertisements function as advertisements for multiculturalism itself. More recently too, in a merger of market and public multiculturalism, some urban governments have promoted cultural diversity in order to make their cities attractive to globally mobile companies and highly skilled labour. Finally, there is a left argument that multiculturalism encourages essentialism: it freezes different cultural communities into their differences, and conceives of cultures not as dynamic, ceaselessly transforming themselves, but as fixed traditions. This kind of cultural essentialism can encourage ethnic and racial prejudices (a notion which is also peddled by conservative critics).

It seems as if both left and right critiques have created an image of multiculturalism which implies a nation wherein a finite number of cultural groups remain inside hard and fast borders, living in terms of cultures that were more or less fixed either in their home countries or in times past. But it is important not to let that imaginary multiculturalism bewitch us. For, in the real world, each multiculture contains a variety of perspectives and values, some in conflict with others, and some mappable onto other multicultures. (A conservative Islamic father and a conservative Anglican one in Britain may share something that their more open and questioning daughters do not.) And we need not to forget that individuals can belong simultaneously to different multicultures and engage in activities which are not covered by any 'culture' at all. Such possibilities need not be ruled out by multiculturalism.

Because it is so beset by enemies, multiculturalism remains a vulnerable concept and, in recent years, has often (especially in Europe) been replaced by the somewhat less contentious term 'cultural diversity'. It is sometimes claimed that 'cultural diversity' is a more appropriate term because 'multiculturalism' implies a bounded border within which different cultures co-exist, and (as we have seen) increasingly nation-state borders do not provide the framework within which cultural relations have to be considered. But it is hard to resist the sense that multiculturalism is being let go simply because it has become too controversial and beleaguered a term.

One of the problems that multiculturalism faces is that it does not fit the liberal paradigm. That is to say, if multiculturalism were simply a matter of allowing different cultures to be acknowledged, and to participate, in the nation, there might still be perceived problems of fragmentation, but policy could always be legitimated by a classically liberal paradigm of tolerating differences within unity. This would be a non-individualistic liberalism, of course, which acknowledges different collective or cultural identities and interests rather than different personal identities and interests. But, as we have begun to see, this is not all that contemporary multiculturalism requires. Multiculturalism is articulated against prejudice, invisibility and exclusion, but not *only* against these things. It addresses the question of the *survival* of particular cultures within advanced commercial media cultures and under hyper-powerful governments, and not simply the question of the right of different cultures to free expression and acknowledgment unconstrained by official indifference or efforts at repression by monoculturalists and racists. For if the state does not support, say, the French language in Quebec or help maintain the Hmong language in the US Midwest or, in general, examine different curricula for different ethnic groups, then diasporic cultures may disappear. In this situation active state intervention may be required.

157

Leaving aside the empirical question as to whether in fact globalised capitalism works in the interests of multiculturalism (and as we know there is a case for arguing that it does), the theoretical question that this 'will to survival' poses is a complex one. Is cultural diversity in and of itself a good, and worth preserving if, under ordinary social conditions certain traditions and identities might disappear without coercion? This is certainly the view of the main international organisation concerned with culture, UNESCO, which recently declared that cultural diversity is 'as necessary for humankind as biodiversity is for nature' and its defence is an 'ethical imperative' (UNESCO 2001b, Art. 1). Here we are in the realm of cultural rights once again. Whatever line on this one takes, the argument is overshadowed by a more practical one, since cultures are unlikely to survive in anything but a museumified and gestural form if they are simply propped up by governmental policy. Cultural survival of particular communities cannot be guaranteed simply by state agency and intervention.

Furthermore, multiculturalism challenges one of the core notions of European Enlightenment in that it may require different groups of citizens to be treated differently. Should Islamic women be allowed to wear the *hijab* (scarf) at school? Should workplaces and schools respect the Chinese New Year? To what degree should the state expect of its citizens that they speak the national language? Should, to take a still more extreme case, Islamic citizens be allowed to live under the *sharia* (Islamic law) if they so wish? These issues become more difficult when customs such as female circumcision come into question. Female circumcision (now usually called female genital mutilation [FMG]) is common in many North and Central African cultures (although not unknown elsewhere): it's a dangerous, extremely painful operation in which the clitoris of pre-pubescent girls is removed, usually to prevent them later feeling sexual pleasure. FMG is not limited to any particular religion: it is primarily a regional and cultural practice that immigrant Africans have brought to the West. Because it affronts so many Western (and not just Western) values, it demands that we ask: what happens when cultural traditions don't respect 'human rights' as these have come to be understood in the West and by the major international organisations? From this point view, these women's rights to their body (at the very least) are being abused. Should universal rights override cultural rights?

In this raft of difficult issues at least one thing seems clear and needs to be returned to over and over again: nations do not require common cultures anymore than they required common religion. Indeed, they do not even require common laws: there is nothing in principle preventing different groups of citizens operating under different legal systems, as indeed happens already routinely and on a large scale (if controversially) in countries such as India, and on a more minor scale in postcolonial countries such as Australia where Aboriginal law is now applied to indigenous offenders in some places under certain circumstances. Nor do nations require a common language; in fact, very few states have ever been monolingual, and bilingualism or multilingualism is an established reality in most Asian nations as well as in New Zealand for instance, where Maori and English are now both national languages. In Europe, Switzerland is the key example of the multicultural, multilingual state, historically validated as such. Belgium is another such example.

So the ideal of the monoconfessional, monocultural, monolegal, monolinguistic state cannot be defended on pragmatic grounds since other kinds of states work also. Which means that in this context nation-states are best regarded as political and economic units rather than as cultural ones. And as to the question of when the state ought to intervene in cultural practices in the name of human rights, I would suggest that a case-by-case approach is what is required given that the question of what exactly constitutes a 'right' is so uncertain (see Arendt 1973, 290–302). It is possible, for instance, to question whether one has a 'right' to speak just the language one is born into – even while accepting that multilingual states are more than viable. Yet with an extreme instance such as FMG, there would seem few grounds to defend culture over rights. What is important is to recognise that intervention in the name of rights in specific cases need not undercut multiculturalist policies, particularly when these are not based on static or monolithic concepts of 'culture'.

One particular problem remains when we think of multiculturalism in countries with relatively recent histories of settlement and colonisation and where colonised communities remain intact. If we take multiculturalism simply as a movement that endorses, promotes and nurtures cultural differences, then the difference between indigenous, settler and more recent migrant cultures can be lost. One of the effects of the term 'cultural diversity' is that it makes this forgetting easier: it is notable that in Tony Bennett's 2001 policy document, presented to the Council of Europe as *Differing Diversities: Transversal Study on the Theme of Cultural Policy and Cultural Diversity*, indigenous peoples become just another culture to be managed under the umbrella of diversity.

But the fact is that colonised people have a different relation to the settler-state and to the land than do post-settlement migrant communities and this needs to be recognised at all levels including government ones. In Australia the multicultural policies that were embraced in the 1970s did little for indigenous peoples; if anything such policies held Aborigines back. Against this, in New Zealand the official policy is 'biculturalism', which divides citizens into either Maori or Pakeha (whites). Proponents of biculturalism (and especially the Maori) have rejected multiculturalism and cultural diversity as policy options precisely because they would diminish the Maori special relation to the state and land. But indigenous exceptionalism can lead to problems of its own: Auckland, New Zealand is now a multicultural city with thousands of South Asians and Taiwanese and Hong Kong Chinese residents whom the policy of biculturalism, split as it is between Maori and Pakeha, leaves peculiarly adrift. Even more problematic, Auckland is a major Pacific Islander centre with major populations of

Samoans, Tongans, Fijians, Tuvaluans and Tokelauans living there, some driven out by rising ocean waters as a result of global warming. More Niueans, for instance, live in Auckland than in Niue itself. But these peoples, ethnically close to the Maori if often quite antagonistic towards them, have little or no official recognition in part because of official biculturalism. In this situation, at the very least, cultural diversity needs to punctuate biculturalism.

To conclude then, the common US identification of multiculturalism with cultural studies as such, while over-simplistic, seems to me not wholly misplaced. Multiculturalism *is* a core value of the discipline. But this is so because multiculturalism need not in itself be a static concept – or a static set of policies. Future work in this area is necessary to align the critiques of identity politics outlined in section 5.1 to the politics of multiculturalism, that is to address the question: is it possible to be *for* multiculturalism against the monoculturalists but also *against* essentialising identity politics? And it will be important to understand multiculturalism as a site where two very different – if interconnected – force fields meet. First the increased mobility of populations around the world and the pressure on migrant rights that this involves, and second, the corporate welcoming of difference and otherness on commercial grounds. In this nexus, by far the most urgent political problem is that concerning undocumented migrants or migrants who are not full citizens and whose population share in the richer countries is on the increase. What kind of policies, recognition or representational structure might draw these almost invisible and unjustly treated people into the official problematic of multiculturalism? That's another core question to which cultural studies can make a contribution.

Further reading

Bennett 2001; Goldberg 1994; Gordon and Newfield 1996; Hollinger 1995; Naficy 1999; Papastergiadis 2000; Zizek 1997.

5.3

Race

Race differs from concepts such as gender, class and even ethnicity in that there is a question as to whether it is real at all. Nobody doubts that the difference between men and women has a biological basis (even if there is huge debate about what that difference means, or ought to mean, socially). Few people doubt that the category of class is necessary to an accurate account of modern societies (even if there is a great deal of debate as to what actually marks one class off from another and how deep class divisions actually go), and ethnicity too is generally assumed to be more simply a piece of ideology. But race, it seems, is nothing but a dangerous product of prejudice or, at least, of false thinking. Racism is, at its heart, the belief that the human species is constituted by a number of separate and distinct biologically discrete sub-species: i.e. races. But, as almost all scientists agree, there is no such thing as race in this sense. Tellingly, even at the height of scientific racism, racists found it difficult to decide how many races actually existed.

Yet race as a category refuses to disappear. There are several main reasons for this. First, it can return to its pre-scientific roots, to the conceptual machinery of xenophobia, to old notions about 'savages' and to long-term popular imaginary of racial characters (see Jahoda 1999; Hannaford 1996; Todorov 1993). In this context, races consist less of people joined by deep-seated biological traits than by the sharing of particular kinds of personalities, values and dispositions, bound to particular body types, often marked by skin colour. That kind of racism can create hierarchies and build apparatuses of oppression and discrimination almost as effectively as racism based on deep biology. Hence the South Asian caste system is effectively racism since different castes are deemed to have different body types and capacities.

Second, race remains a powerful but barely visible referent in concepts such as ethnicity and multiculturalism and thence even in the concept of culture itself. Cultural differences, when they are deemed to be based on the rooted or 'ethnic' differences between peoples, are often displaced forms of race differences. In practice, it is often difficult to disjoin what is called culturalism (that idea that different peoples have different inherited cultures) from a racist node, since different cultures so often implies different kinds of people with different kinds of bodies.

Third, racism is difficult to uproot since it is based on look – the visual differences between different groups of peoples. These differences often (but not always) have a relation to differences in history, culture, language and geography, which are basically accidental or contingent, and yet at another level are not contingent at all, since a great deal of human history across the globe has been based on discriminations based largely on bodily visibility. Race may not be a true way of dividing the species but nonetheless it has helped to organise human history.

Last, and most importantly, race is experienced as such by many on a daily basis, although not by same-race majorities in most communities (which is why travelling to China, for example, can be such a powerful experience for Europeans: there they can understand what it is like to be a member of a group with a different body type who doesn't necessarily get understanding or respect). The everyday experience of race is extraordinarily complex but it often involves being the object of continual slights, petty exclusions, changes of tone, avoidance of the gaze and over-hearty responses as well as a sense of oneself based around feelings, bodily self-awareness, values, expressive forms and manners that are not shared by most of the people you encounter. In this experience, race and culture are wholly fused.

At one level the only way to avoid racism is simply to stop using racist concepts. This would require removing the markers of race, and in particular that of skin colour, from discourses about social groups and individuals so that these markers become as meaningless a criterion for distinguishing between people as, say, shoe size. It just would not matter whether people were black or white or whatever. Another way would be to follow Toni Morrison in her argument that, for instance, Bill Clinton was, as she puts it, 'our first black president'. Morrison reads 'blackness' not as skin colour but as a socio-cultural position. Clinton came from a single-parent household; he was a 'born poor, working-class, saxophone-playing, McDonald's and junk-food loving boy from Arkansas' (Morrison 1998, 32). Not to mention a big, hyper-sexually-active boy. In Southern racist mythology, all this added up to blackness, which, Morrison persuasively contends, helps account for the fury and vindictiveness that he stimulated among his enemies and the loyalty he found among the black community. Blackness, for Morrison, becomes detached from race: it is a cultural attribute which can be disseminated widely enough to help undo racism.

But is it possible, at the moment, to imagine a world in which racial markers either float freely or are diminished to the level of shoe size? Probably not: just because culture and society are still too organised around them; experience too is filtered through them.

The history of Western racism is not yet well understood by cultural historians. It is clear, however, that something remarkable occurred during the second half of the nineteenth century: a previously fairly unimportant idea (if a not unimportant prejudice) began to control a great deal of the human sciences, and thence government policy. Around 1850 the British Prime Minister, Benjamin Disraeli, could declare, 'Race is everything, there is no other truth', words that are cited repeatedly by the apostles of racial sciences (cited in Hannaford 1996, 352). By 1900, eugenics, for instance, which aimed to protect race purity (and hence social improvement) by controlling 'breeding', was a respectable science, attracting serious research funding and being implemented, albeit fitfully, across the West. How was this possible? Conceptually race was, in Disraeli's terms, 'everything' because it conjoined nature and society: in its terms the human species was, by nature, divided into different races, and those races each had their own 'natures' which determined history, culture – everything.

As I say, this was historically unprecedented: previously race had been but a minor category in thinking about how society worked, even if not a minor category in organising actual social relations. What changed? The most important of the various historical forces propelling race into this central position was Darwinism. Charles Darwin's theory of evolution as published in *On the Origin of Species* (1859) was not itself inherently racist since it did not rely upon the subdivision of species into races for its explanatory power (although Darwin himself did think of some races as more evolutionarily advanced than others). Rather, Darwinism allowed society and politics to be understood not as the outcome of human choices (under the sway of particular interests) but as subject to invariable, determining biological laws, and, in particular, the laws that ordered the transmission of inherited traits across populations. This was the basis of what has come to be known as 'scientific racism'.

But scientific racism itself implied an older concept that we can think of as Romantic. At its basis, it rested on the philological notion of the *Volk* community (as first theorised by Herder during the late eighteenth century), a community distinguished by its authenticity and bound together by a cultural tradition – by values, myths, language and a spectrum of character types and capabilities unique to it. As it turned out, after Darwinism, races were figured as biological versions of Herder's *volkish* cultures.

Scientific racism needs to be thought of in functional terms also: it cannot be regarded simply as the outcome of Darwin's theory of species-formation. It became such a powerful idea because it fulfilled particular ideological needs in the age of imperialism, and most of all because it helped legitimate the domination of the globe by whites (although, at the same time it created new hierarchies among Europeans – as between the Anglo-Saxon and the Celts for instance [Fèuredi 1998]). It also allowed whites to continue to dominate African Americans in the Americas where, even after the ending of slavery, a whole set of Jim Crow 'race laws' were established to prevent blacks participating fully in society, politics and the economy. Racism also helped to unite groups of Europeans dispersed across the globe under the impulsions of capitalism and colonialism. Certain Europeans, of whatever nationality or religion or class or gender or even culture, were joined together globally as members of the 'white' race (even if, once again, whiteness was not a marker of race at all and various whites, according to scientific racism, belonged to various races). Rather paradoxically, racism was also propelled by egalitarianism. It is as if once all human beings were deemed equal, systemic inequality could only be maintained by declaring some kinds of people less than fully human – and racism could do that.

One key effect of racism was radically to downgrade the lives and identities of mixed races. Demonised as 'half-castes', *metis* (people of mixed blood) were a particular affront to racism, not just because, in cases where whites had sex with people of colour, the assumption of white superiority and autonomy was threatened, but because they provided living testimony of cross-racial sociability and mixing, and indeed of the artificiality of hard biological definitions of race-purity.

Today, as we know, racism works purely ideologically. Inside a shared culture, in most cases it works by distinguishing other peoples by virtue of their race, so that people 'like us' are unmarked by race. However in cases where whites are under threat and/or in hard competition with people of different skin colours and ethnicities (poor whites in the industrial USA or white workers today whose jobs are threatened by coloured immigrants or by job-flight to Asia), racism can help whites ascribe imaginary freedoms and superiority to themselves, and white racism can flare up (see Frankenberg 1997; Allen 1994; Roediger 1991). And racism, in the era of post-racism, works differently in different nations. As I have said previously, it is widely dispersed globally but (in China) Han racism works very differently than does say German racism in relation to Turkish immigrants, which is different again to the milder quasi-racism of fair-skinned people of colour in relation to those of darker skins in the Caribbean and South America. Here something like a race difference involves no cultural difference.

Most powerfully and typically, racism organises certain stereotypes: races are regarded as groups of similar individuals who possess a narrow set of traits, usually, but not necessarily, negative traits. Notions such as 'all Africans have got rhythm' or 'Asians are brainy' are racist, although not as dangerous as notions such as 'Jews are dishonest and mean' or 'Indians are lazy'. Some people will even claim that they're not racist *because* they so admire Asian diligence for instance. Racist imagery of this kind regards individuals not so much as individuals as such or even as belonging to other collectivities (to localities or classes say) but primarily as members and representatives of a race imagined as a bundle of stereotypes and dispositions. Groups or individuals within racialised communities whom these stereotypes cannot cover become more or less invisible: thus, for instance, one of the more under-mediatised groups in the USA is the African American upper-middle class.

Racial characteristics infuse gender stereotypes in particular: African American masculinity (hyper-virile and threatening), Asian femininity (hyper-feminine and submissive) being two key instances. This melding of race and gender intensifies differences on both registers. Furthermore, it is not just the case that racialised individuals are read through and measured against stereotypes but that their behaviour is likely to be regarded as 'typical', as confirming such stereotypes. This kind of cultural racism survives the downfall of institutional racism – that is, racism that formally disbars some races from access to jobs, neighbourhoods, clubs, etc. And cultural racism is especially damaging in that it can so easily be interiorised by members of oppressed races themselves.

The primary difficulty with the concept of race today is that it is so tightly connected to that of ethnicity. As we know, formally the concepts seem easy enough to distinguish: race is a biological notion while ethnicity is a cultural one. And yet ethnicity is in fact very connected to filiation and blood: people of the same ethnicity share not just cultures but a network of family relations, roots, a more or less primordial – if often mythical – connection to a particular home territory. If race mediates between society and nature, ethnicity mediates between race and culture. Leaving aside particular cases where epidermical hierarchies exist outside of ethnic differences, the key distinction between race and ethnicity is that ethnicity seems not to be tarnished by the history of racism, so that while today race is almost never a source of individual or group pride (and, when it is, it is treated with intense suspicion), ethnicity *can* be just such a source of pride. Indeed, the distinction still works divisively: people of African descent are much more often represented as sharing a race (especially in the USA where racial difference between blacks and whites is routinely conceded) than, say, whites or Jews who are represented in terms of *ethnicity*. Out in the streets in Anglophone countries, an 'ethnic' is a member of a migrant community. Australians with a British genealogy, for instance, are not ethnics at all so far as most Australians are concerned.

The difference between ethnic cultures and other kinds of subcultures (such as those formed around taste or generation) is that, being so deeply embedded in history and geography, they are particularly powerful markers of identity ('I'm Serbian' implies more than 'I'm a punk' ever did). And they can be figured as forms of resistance to the processes of modernity. Indigenous ethnic cultures exist as survivors of the destructive power of colonialism, while more mobile and metropolitan ethnic cultures exist as 'differences' that need to be preserved against homogenising global flows. Multiculturalism, as we have seen, is the state's recognition of the power of ethnicity to establish identity. Yet ethnicities are not simply positively affirmed; they are also often responses to the past discriminations that defined them. To put this slightly differently, many ethnic identities are not so strong simply because they are self-generated, but because historically they have been used by dominant groups to pick out and subject particular groups of people. Communities such as the Romany and the Jews who have survived millennia of severe, often murderous, even genocidal, exilic prejudice, are perhaps the most notable instances of this complex dialectic of ethnic self-affirmation and external discrimination, and, ironically, have often been blamed for failing to assimilate.

Racism and ethnicism are both, then, forms of identity politics, and like all identity politics (as noted above) they neglect the history of interactions with others out of which particular ethnicities and cultures emerge and within which they are maintained. Since the eighties there has been a fascination with moments of 'first contact' – the first time indigenous peoples from wherever encountered whites for instance. Such encounters represent moments of purity: a glimpse of true mutual otherness. These moments form the mythic foundations for a politics of difference. But such moments are very rare. In fact, what history over and over again reminds us is that peoples are interconnected: the sweep of cultural exchanges has been much wider, covering greater distances, than localist and ethnically orientated thinking has typically acknowledged. This means that interrelatedness (imitations, distinctions, transformations, mixings) is the norm of cultural formation. It follows from this that 'hybridity' is not some valuable and counter-hegemonic exception. Rather, it is a norm. Almost all races, ethnicities and cultures are hybridised – which makes it a weaker, more banal concept than cultural theorists such as those discussed in the previous section have supposed, while at the same time it undermines the case for monoculturalism and ethno-racist purism.

Racism poses a challenge to cultural studies because it represents an impossible form of identity politics. It is because of this that it has been especially important to the development of the discipline. In Britain the realisation that racism was used routinely by government (and in particular the police) to produce law-and-order panics that confirmed bourgeois hegemony (Gilroy 1987) quickly led to critique of the intimate relation between race and nation (could a black be a Brit, from the position of cultural orthodoxy?) which further led to the theorisation of hybridity. But the idealism of those forms of critical theory which argued that a progressive practical politics could be mounted via concepts such as 'identity in difference' and the emphasis on how individuals uneasily combine various subject-positions has long been apparent. Hence anti-racist analysis has had to follow another path. No one has been more important to the articulation of anti-racist analysis within cultural studies than Paul Gilroy, whose *Against Race* presents the case against promoting and accepting identity based on race (by which he also means ethnicity) with most rigour, although it must be noted that the work focuses almost completely on black identity.

Such a case might seem to be uncontroversial, but, as Gilroy implies, those who identify themselves as blacks, Jews, Irish, Chinese and so on (which, of course, means pretty much everyone across the globe), by appealing to racial categories, belong to the history of what he calls 'raciology' – the legitimation of what Franz Fanon called the 'epidermidalization of difference' (i.e. basing human differences on skin colour). Vernacular forms of identity, therefore, share something with fascism and Nazism, and Gilroy's book explores what that something is. Part of Gilroy's argument is the familiar one: that all racial/ethnic thinking relies on the values of groundedness, rootedness and traditional community – values which ignore, first, the dependence of modern racial identities on advanced technology and commercial culture and, second, internal differences within racial groups. He emphasises the way that, since the Nazis, race-thought has emphasised the visual rather than the discursive (despite many of his examples of contemporary black culture coming from the world of music).

The most interesting part of Gilroy's thesis is his account of what is happening to black culture now. For Gilroy, strong contemporary black culture has moved far away from Afro-centrism. It has accepted its diasporic status. Indeed it has lost the political and utopian longings for freedom that suffused slave societies (the crucial moment here being the ending of South African apartheid in 1989). Longings for freedom have been displaced onto what he calls 'a radicalised biopolitics', a fervent concentration on and celebration of the (heterosexual) body and sexuality, in which identity becomes attached to the body (Gilroy 2000, 185). Radicalised body politics does not belong to the 'street' (which, he argues, has stopped being a locus of community and has come to be regarded as a site of conflict and danger and the object of policing) but in settings on the boundary between the public and private, for example the basketball court. And aspects of black body culture have entered global consciousness in alliance with US cultural power – most notably, through sports superstars such as Michael Jordan and commercial rap music. Here blackness has come to represent a 'strange, hyperhuman hybrid of ultramodern and ultraprimitive' (2000, 347).

Gilroy's argument urges the end of raciology, and yet his book, like others on African American culture in particular, leaves the reader with the sense that globalised societies and cultures are finding more and more ways to *use* race: as a niche for marketing; as a source of commodifiable, imaginary representations which can ener-gise popular cultures; as a way of dividing and weakening the transnational labour force; and as a source of identity pride especially, but not only, for the marginalised and unprivileged. What is perhaps most useful about Gilroy's work is its insistence that racism changes constantly; reading this as a sign of its continued strength, only the most vigilant politics and critique will ever be able to unravel it.

Further reading

Back and Solomos 2000; Baker, Diawara and Lindeborg 1996; Banton 1998; Dyer 1997; Gilroy 2000; Rattansi and Westwood 1994.

Part 6

SEXUALITY AND GENDER

Feminism's aftermath: gender today

One of the most remarkable phenomena of recent (Western) history has been feminism's rise and fall. Certainly a fall has been much publicised. In 1998 *Time* magazine ran a cover story: 'Is Feminism Dead?' which concentrated more on Ally McBeal and the Spice Girls than on Gloria Steinem or Betty Friedan (founders of American feminism), and which obviously thought (hoped?) the answer was 'Yes'. For *Time* the anti-feminist backlash was sweeping all before it. Yet 'fall' is harsh, since the feminism that emerged so startlingly in the late sixties and early seventies and which, for so many women seemed to change everything, did indeed change if not everything, then at least a great deal. And it is not as though its work is done, as women such as Susan Faludi and Naomi Wolf, lashing against the backlash, tirelessly remind us (see Faludi 1992 and 1999; Wolf 1991 and 1997).

In the West women are not subordinated and discriminated against to the degree that they once were. The once widely accepted notion that a 'woman's place is in the home' has been relegated to the political fringes. Most nations have legalised abortion and provide maternity leave. Child care provision is commonplace. Young women often claim to feel more or less as empowered as young men (remember 'girl power'?). Women are, formally at least, equal participants in the education system, in most workplaces and in, say, the dance/ecstasy scene (as they were not in the hippie or even punk movements). The media no longer treats women's sexuality as if it were simply passive and private. Dating practices give more agency to women. Sanctions against sexual harassment have become routine. Women's contribution to the cultural heritage has been retrieved from profound neglect, and in particular a whole canon of women's writing has been returned to literary memory. Gender is now a core category for social and cultural analysis in a way it never was previously.

On the other hand, positions of real authority are still dominated by men who monopolise the most senior positions in most institutions. In the home the gender division of labour continues so that, for instance, women still cook more meals for men than vice versa even in households where both work. Women continue to bear the brunt of child rearing. In the world of sport, women have taken giant strides but men still crowd them out as a commercial attraction. In show business, women's careers are shorter and if they are young they are under continual pressure to present themselves in hyper-sexualised styles. In fact commercial culture and marketing is more plastered with images of hot babes than it was before the feminist movement began. (Ironically feminism seems to have helped further to [hetero-] sexualise the culture in this way.) Divorced women struggle economically in ways their male ex-partners do not. And of course beyond a tiny strata of Westernised women (and strenuous policy initiatives, especially from transnational non-governmental organisations), in the non-European world feminism has made little headway. Even in affluent countries with a long-standing women's movement, such as Japan, gender relations remain remarkably stable and unequal. In many of the poorest countries as well as under Islam, harsh forms of patriarchy continue (see Buckley 1997; Narayan 1997).

Given all this, it is surprising that feminism as a movement has all but withered. Feminism is no longer cool. Most young women routinely declare themselves not to be feminists, irritating many of their mother's generation who fought so hard to secure the rights and possibilities that helped make this rejection possible, and who know their work is not complete. The tension between feminism's accomplishments and its current public neglect is often covertly expressed in popular culture. Take the career of an actress such as Julia Roberts, currently Hollywood's biggest woman box-office draw. In the movie *Pretty Woman* she plays a woman character who is empowered and tinged by feminism but who is also contained by pre-feminist images and values. And in *Erin Brockovich* her role hangs on a working-class woman's struggle to obtain some job satisfaction and a strategic sexualising of her body to get what she wants. But these themes are treated as if no gender-based political movement – to whom they are key – exists (Brunsdon 1997).

The reasons for feminism's withering are various: as we shall see, the movement tore itself apart through internal debates. Its own relative success de-energised it – indeed, logically speaking, one outcome of the movement's utter success would be its redundancy. It was outflanked by less mainstream identity politics, including multiculturalism and the queer movement. It was a victim of popular culture which routinely regarded it as an enemy, reducing it to a bunch of stereotypes. Perhaps, too, feminism brought new stresses to bear, particularly on middle-class women among whom its impact has been greatest; namely, the demand that they have careers in an environment where careers are more and more demanding and insecure. Women are having babies later, and increasingly not at all, not simply because that is their choice but because to do otherwise would be to invite real, everyday life pressure. And this is a situation exacerbated by feminism's loss of ideological clout, since these stresses are caused in part by continuing gender inequities in the distribution of domestic labour.

Finally the politics of feminism led to strange places, especially when it came to sexuality. In this context, the importance of the Monica Lewinsky case (which had global repercussions) can barely be exaggerated. A majority of women inclined to feminism found themselves taking the side of a president who was relatively liberal on issues such as reproductive and women's rights but who was revealed to be a sexual predator, if not a harasser. In Australia, the 'Ormond College Affair' became a big news story when a prominent one-time feminist, novelist Helen Garner, defended a university administrator who had harassed students in his care on the grounds that his punishment (dismissal from his prestigious post and permanent disgrace) did not fit the crime (getting drunk at a student ball and attempting to grope a group of young women). And it seemed that many women of Garner's generation, who had been through the liberation movement, agreed. In such cases, it seemed to many as if sexual realities and the feminist ethic clashed in ways that could lead to miscarriages of justice.

In this situation one way we might begin to restore a sense of feminism's importance is through an overview of its longer history, that is, of its causes and motivations.

Feminism's past

Although traditional, pre-industrial societies are routinely thought of as 'patriarchal', that is as dominated by men, it seems that modernising capitalism, if anything, has intensified women's subordination, especially among the middle classes. Outside capitalism, aristocratic women could acquire considerable independence and power, and even under industrialisation working-class women often worked outside the family. Not so middle-class women – they were exposed to new forms of submission. So it is not surprising that it was a middle-class woman who presented the first modern feminist arguments. During the early years of the Industrial Revolution and inspired by the French Revolution, Mary Wollstonecraft applied an Enlightenment account of human nature and Enlightenment principles of justice and equity to gender divisions. Her primary targets were the kinds of femininity that reduced women's rationality: the emphasis on sexual attractiveness, on 'sensibility' (something like modern sentimentalism), and on meaningless or frivolous accomplishments.

Her book, *A Vindication of the Rights of Women* (1792), quickly became notorious but had little immediate impact. It was addressed to a society in which patriarchy – thought of simply as men's domination over women – was almost invincible, albeit uneven. Invincible and uneven? In the country, working men and women had different roles but they also shared tasks, including heavy outdoor labour. Workplace and home were not usually separated, which drew men and women together into familial productive units. But with urbanisation and the spread of wage labour, things changed. By and large, it was men who sold their labour into offices and factories, and women who were required to carry out the tasks back home that sustained the household. Where women did work for wages, they were excluded from the more skilled jobs. There were, however, regional and industry variations in this process: jobs such as coal mining were entirely male whereas weaving in the factories was largely carried out by women, with men often dependent on their wages. This helped to politicise some women workers. Thus – to take a British case – in nineteenth-century Lancashire, where the weaving industry was concentrated, women were well organised industrially, and at the turn of the nineteenth century became active in the suffragist movement which politicised women's demands for the first time (Massey 1994).

By and large working-class women who worked for wages, and who acquired the status and power of breadwinners, were under sustained attack from social managers and theorists. The main reason for this was not mere prejudice, although sexism played its part: men and women were seen to be in competition for wages, and middle-class and ruling-class men took the side of working men against women. Middle-class women's worldly goods normally belonged to their husbands. There can be no doubt either that the Victorian home – the woman's sphere – was often maintained as such by male violence. No women were permitted to vote. They were prevented from joining the professions (save governessing) or from going to university. Bourgeois women were educated in 'accomplishments' (singing, piano-playing, drawing, sewing, flower-arranging, maybe a little French and Italian…) designed to increase their appeal as spouses. Few had any classical or scientific education. (This was one of Wollstonecraft's most heartfelt complaints.)

In more general terms, the will to harden gender divisions between work and domesticity belonged to the movement of social 'reformation' which dated back to the late seventeenth century, and which attempted first to restrict public drunkenness, prostitution and gambling, and second, to improve hygiene and individuals' sense of civil participation and responsibility. This movement had its basis in Protestant churches, where women were often relatively empowered. And of course many public spaces had long been barred for women, who courted insult and violence on the streets unless accompanied by men. The argument was that ordered domestic environments, each under the subordinated control of a wife and mother, were the most effective seedbeds for a reformed society. In sum, for almost a century the new industrial and professional workplaces, male solidarity and violence, along with the ideology of civil reform, marginalised the kind of feminism that Wollstonecraft represented (Caine 1997).

Sixty years after Wollstonecraft, in the late nineteenth century, the 'woman question' re-emerged, with renewed efforts to award women the vote and to allow them access to divorce and to the higher-education system, and thence to the professional workforce. But perhaps the most significant contribution to what is sometimes called 'second-wave' feminism, was Virginia Woolf's *A Room of One's Own* (1927), an innovative polemic very different from Woolf's earlier Bloomsbury elitism. Here culture and society are seen to be divided between men and women, in such a way that men restrict women's possibilities. Woolf contends that men have continually written and talked about women but that their occasional idealisation of them merely masks women's actual subordination. In the end, hers is a materialist argument: women do not have freedom of expression because they do not have access to property, which has been monopolised by men. For women to participate productively in culture they need access and money – a 'room of one's own'. If this were to happen cultural values and imagery would be revolutionised. Furthermore, for Woolf, male-dominated culture is saturated in values and styles with which women feel uncomfortable. It represses the basic bisexuality of human nature, an androgyny which functions in her later writings as both a utopian ideal and, more conservatively, as a lost totality (Mulhern 2000).

The depression of the thirties, World War II and the immediate post-war 'reconstruction' period put the feminist agenda on hold, but in the late sixties it re-emerged as the women's liberation movement. Influenced by the social theory of the time, it attached three new elements to the old demands for more participation by women in the economy, the workforce, the education system and the formal political system.

The first was a critique of representation: women, so the claim went, were demeaned by being represented, especially in the commercialised public sphere, as primarily sexual objects for the male gaze. More than that, 'femininity' and the feminine ideal were ideological constructs, circulated within patriarchy, which now came to mean not a particular social structure associated with pre-modernity but the cultural formation within which men remained dominant and which prevented women from being who they wanted to be. It was in this context that 'gender' was first separated from 'sex'. Women, so the argument went, were biologically different from men, that is to say they were of a different sex, but that didn't commit them to a particular way of being feminine, to a particular gender. To put this slightly differently: sex is a biological structure, gender a social and ideological one, and there is no natural relation between the fact that women bear children, for instance, by virtue of their sex, and the insistence that they are, say, supposed to be relatively demure in public and have a particular role in the private / domestic sphere by virtue of their gender.

Nonetheless many women had internalised their femininity under capitalist patriarchy, so that 'consciousness raising' (which in this context meant learning about the history of female subordination, acquiring basic skills of ideology critique and understanding how history and women's image today affected you personally) became a key tool of early 'third-wave' feminism in undoing the power of conventional gender roles (as they now began to be called). Consciousness raising, which quickly became a media joke, was in fact an important moment in the early history of a cultural studies approach to the contemporary world: an engaged analysis of current cultural forms, designed to change both you and the world.

The third innovation of third-wave feminism was a rethinking of the public/private division. One problem with Woolf's 'room of one's own' approach and its ethic of retreat and autonomy was that it did not sufficiently contextualise what by the sixties was seen to be a central strut in women's subordination: the gendering of the division between the public and the private, through which women were restricted to the private realm. As Carol Pateman put it: 'the dichotomy between the private and the public … is, ultimately what the feminist movement is all about' (Pateman 1989, 135). That kind of thinking, in which the domestication of women was open to contestation, led (especially when tied to consciousness raising) to the famous apophthegm, 'the personal is the political'. That phrase was to become a central strut of identity politics as a whole.

As we have already noted, feminism fell apart at least in part because it split into various schools. This is not surprising since its programme pointed in a number of different directions. Most importantly it was split between, on the one hand, the objectives of Wollenstonecraft's older feminism – the attainment of equality between men and women, which concentrated primarily on questions of social and political access and participation – and, on the other, the impulsions of new identity politics by which women asserted their difference from men, and which focussed on culture expression and private self-fashionings.

The second split within feminism concerned sexuality itself. The issue can be put this way: to what degree was heterosexuality itself part of the problem? To what degree was feminism a politics of sexual desire? And more concretely, was moving beyond heterosexual norms the answer to the universalising of the male gaze, the sexualising objectification of women's bodies and women's entrapment in passive, privatised, hetero-versions of femininity? Anti-heterosexual politics, in its weak form, would attempt to downgrade sexuality's role in women's lives (in a move which seemed to repeat old Puritanism) and, in its radical form, would insist upon the political efficacy of same-sex sexuality between women. But of course many women could not accept either of these programmes. Nowhere was the debate over sexuality more fierce than in relation to pornography: an issue where pro-sex feminism looks most fragile, yet over which it has basically won out, if at some cost to the movement's coherence.

The third split, closely linked to both the above, was in relation to femininity. Did feminists need to reject conventional femininity or could they inhabit and enjoy it in new, perhaps more ironical and certainly more empowered, ways? Here too the less radical position won: femininity was first recuperated, in the academic world, by the argument that it could be not so much interiorised as impersonated, and then by insisting on its specific pleasures (Brunsdon 2000). Young women from the eighties embraced femininity in fairly (if often slightly ironised) traditional terms, declaring the difference now was that *they chose it*. One doesn't have to be too well versed in the theory of hegemony (which argues that victims generally may consent to their oppression) to wonder about that.

Finally, too, the core notion that the personal is the political led in two directions. As Lauren Berlant has argued, relations between the political and the personal changed under the sway of the conservatives in the nineties. The old division between public and private selves was downgraded to a form of what Berlant (1977, 1) calls 'public intimacy', in which the intimate private life is made publicly accessible for political purposes. This means not only that the private life of politicians is exposed and at stake in their public careers, but that political issues are increasingly centred on intimate familial relations. In particular, social policy is increasingly based on the effects of policy on children and mother–child relations, all the more so since marriage is an increasingly impermanent and unstable institution (Shumway 2003). But this is to take power away from feminism's emphasis on the personal and to produce tensions between feminists who wish to redraw firm lines between the politics and the private (a return to the liberal distinction of the personal nature of private life and its lack of relevance to public life) and those for whom the conservative appropriation of the 'personal and the political' does not mean the promise of that phrase for women should be jettisoned. It might even be that emphasis in the public sphere on the intimate expresses the possibility (or hope) that intimacy is where the closest and most fulfilling human relations can develop (partly because women have power in this realm), in ways that provide a template for political desire and judgement.

The question now is: what does feminism want? Feminism's early forms had clear visions: equality of rights and opportunities; an end to the dominance of the male gaze; the unfolding of a woman's culture on its own terms. The rights and opportunities agenda is (albeit slowly) being met, and the culture of gender and sexuality has been transformed since the advent of feminism, although not in ways that the early feminists would have foreseen or for the most part approved. But what now?

One of the problems in answering this question is that, as post-structuralists have long suggested, 'women' is too large a grouping to be analytically useful, and this becomes more obvious as globalisation proceeds. Women of different races, places and classes live under different conditions; and it is impossible to generalise across these. While it is obviously true that women share a body that menstruates, is capable of bearing children, goes through menopause and (in the case of heterosexuals) draws them sexually towards men, it is no less obviously the case that upper-middle-class, white, American/European women, for instance, are closer culturally and economically to their male equivalents than they are to poor, South Asian, peasant women. Across cultures, ethnicities and classes, solidarity between women, which is the foundation of a feminist politics, has something of a strained and abstract character unless it has a firm footing in a set of shared restrictions, unless it has an actually existing patri-archy firmly in its sights. Partly for this reason, and partly because popular culture has proved quite immune to feminist reform, cultural studies has by and large lost its focus on women's liberation.

Instead feminism has developed in an adjacent academic field – gender studies – to which I now briefly turn.

From women's studies to gender studies

Feminism was not primarily an academic movement, even if it popularised certain forms of self-education and even if, across the developed world and even in many poorer nations, it led to the entry of hundreds of thousands of women into the univer-sity sector from the seventies onwards. As a result of this transformation of the academy, a new discipline, that of women's studies, was slowly established, often against obdurate resistance. But since the nineties, perhaps partly because of femi-nism's loss of steam and the backlash against it, women's studies has been mainly transformed into gender studies.

Gender studies has moved through a number of positions very rapidly, positions which recapitulate the debates and flows of the women's movement in the outside world. Drawing on Angela McRobbie (1999), we can enumerate the most important of these, even though in most cases they repeat formations mentioned above (and can be read as a micro-history of third-wave feminism's intellectual shifts).

1 The analysis of women's docility and its contemporary conceptual underpinnings. Betty Friedan's *The Feminine Mystique* (1963) remains the classic of this moment.

2 The attack on widely distributed images of conventional femininity which were produced for men from men's point of view, and the simultaneous de-stigmatisation of unattractive or otherwise negative images of women as seen from that point of view. Robin Morgan's anthology *Sisterhood is Powerful* (1970) helped popularise both this and the following movement.

3 The critical analysis of patriarchal ideology as an overarching symbolic structure through which identities are granted to both men and women and in which social norms are organised in the interest of maintaining male domination. Key to this move was the insistence on the sex/gender distinction.

4 The development of Marxist feminism which regarded the modern subordination of woman as a function of capitalist social relations, and concentrated on women's material inequities and struggles, especially in the workplace, rather than on issues such as femininity. Juliet Mitchell's *Women's Estate* (1971) was an important contribution to this form of feminism.

5   The psychoanalytic analysis of female pleasure and psychic structurations: here woman is conceived to be 'other' to masculinity, and, hence, not under control of patriarchal ideology. Juliet Mitchell's *Psychoanalysis and Feminism* (1975) pioneered this mode of feminism.

6   The reclamation of women's genres – melodrama, soap operas, weepies, romance – as indirectly acknowledging women's oppression, or at any rate as expressing women's fantasies and emotions as oppressed subjects. This was probably the moment at which women's studies and cultural studies intersected most specifically.

7   Feminist post-structuralist anti-essentialism (aka 'French Feminism'): the argument that the category of 'woman' is not a natural or essential one and that it is important to resist using it as if it were, even in resistance to patriarchy, since to do that only fixes the identity more firmly. This argument, which was put forward in various forms by thinkers such as Julia Kristeva, Luce Irigaray and Hélène Cixous, cannot, by its very nature, ground a movement based on identity. So it leads to the queer movement that theorised a politics of sexuality outside of essentialism. Retrospectively at least it can be seen as a moment in the dissolution of women's studies proper (Oliver 2000).

8   The broadening out from women's studies as such to gender studies. The women's liberation movement had successfully decoupled sex from gender and one of the least anticipated consequences of this was that it became possible to devote considerable analytic and critical attention to masculinity as a gender as well as to think more carefully about the processes of identification through which individuals became gendered. Judith Butler's *Gender Trouble* (1990) was particularly important to this. Butler theorised gender not so much as a subject position externally imposed by ideology or as able simply to be chosen, but as found and improvised in embodied social action by individuals and mediated through sexual desires which were not themselves simply biological.

Masculinity

As I state above, masculinity appeared as a topic of academic analysis from within the logic that transformed women studies into gender studies. But the next step was for it to form a field of its own – masculinity studies. Within masculinity studies, the white body has been particularly important, not just because the academic movement has been predominantly Western (more so even than feminism), but because white masculinity has been so hegemonic as to constitute a transnational norm. Although women's liberation has been primarily a first-world movement, feminism does have a global reach and women's issues are firmly on the agenda of many international NGOs, human rights agencies and so on. This is much less the case for masculinity. As a very rough indication of this, googling 'third world feminism' results in almost 2,000

179

hits, whereas 'third world masculinity' results in only one. Let's hope this situation changes; certainly there is lots of work to do. But it does mean that to mark it out the history and specificity of the white male body has an immediate political energy.

Historically that body has been relatively invisible, as if the power attached to whiteness and maleness would be at risk were the actual flesh to be presented in public. Characteristically, up until the sixties (and despite the popular 'physical culture' movement which stressed fitness and musculature from the early 1800s), white men normally appeared in public fully clothed. It was young women and men of colour who could be presented closer to nakedness. Even male clothing has been relatively unspectacularised (that is, not presented to attract visual attention).

The greying of male attire happens in a process known by historians of fashion as the 'great renunciation', which began in England in the 1820s when modern trousers emerged and the dark suit began its career as a uniform for middle-class men. This marked the effective end of the aristocratic display of power and prestige through male clothing, and the emergence of a de-individuated style of dress which signalled and performed an extended franchise of power: the power not of families and individuals but of a gendered collective, that is, of men. It also represented the ascetic ethics of saving, restraint and carefulness associated first with the Puritan tradition and then with professionalism, both being tied to a gender regime in which men increasingly were required to control their emotions, especially their spontaneous feelings of suffering and empathy. The late eighteenth-century 'man of feeling' who cried when he saw animals and children in pain, in the next century became the efficient and composed professional. Or he became the competitive participant in the public world, calling upon his masculine toughness to jockey for success in the cruel marketplace, and trained into that role at school and on the sports field (Miller 2001). Women were assigned the work of sympathy and feeling as a kind of gender specialisation. And this form of masculinity marked the white man out from the man of colour, who was under less – or no – injunction to compete, to remain stoical, to button up his emotions or to adhere to ascetic norms and practices of self.

This structure began to change during the sixties, partly as a result of feminism but also because of the increased engagement of the gay movement in public culture. At this point, at one level men became, as they say, increasingly 'feminised', sparking off what was widely represented as a crisis of masculinity. This too was a stimulus for the emergence of masculinity studies, which appeared not just at a time when gender was disconnected from sex, but at the same time as white man's privilege was being brought into question.

Probably the key contribution to the emergence of masculinity studies was the work of the Australian sociologist Bob Connell, who used a version of Gramsci's theory of hegemony to argue that white masculinity had played a crucial role in the West's global dominance and in securing consent to its imperialism (Connell 1987 and

180

1995). At the same time, Connell drew attention to the relations between masculinity and homosexuality. This is a topic which will be dealt with in more detail in section 6.2 – it is enough to say here that he showed that homophobia played a key function in Western straight masculinity. A man was really a man to the degree that he wasn't gay (even more than he wasn't feminine), gayness being as it were the zero degree of masculinity, further down the scale than being an asshole, a prick, a cunt, a wimp, a pussy, a wuss, etc. So modern masculinity was established by othering homosexuality in a process that was all the more intense because, as the literary critic Eve Sedgwick most lucidly demonstrated, masculinity required forms of homosociability (bonding between men in segregated places such as the sports field, club, workplace, school, etc.) in which affections could easily take a sexual turn (Sedgwick 1985 and 1990). The argument is: because homosociability and same-sex desire are so closely bound, the latter has to be repressed all the more violently.

As I say, the tectonic shifts in society and culture that somewhat weakened the hetero-sexual white man's privileged position also transformed his masculinity itself. There had always been many ways of being a man, but from the fifties onwards, in the West, styles of masculinity proliferated. Examples include: the house-husband, happy to keep home fires burning while his spouse worked; in Britain, working-class dandyism emerged in subcultures from the fifties onwards, first with the Teds and then with the Mods (although both were associated with violence); hippie masculinity went down a particular path of mellowing. Meanwhile in Australia a style derisively (if sometimes also affectionately) called the 'straight poofter' emerged: heterosexual men who had all the mannerisms of stereotyped gayness. And remember the sensitive new-age guy, the right partner, or so it was supposed, for an assertive but also sensitive new-age woman?

Perhaps the most important aspect of masculinity's transformation has happened in relation to emotion. Post-war Western masculinity began the process of re-attaching itself to affect, as figures in popular culture such as James Dean, Kurt Cobain and even Elvis demonstrate in their particular ways. What seems to have happened is that adoles-cent styles were becoming mainstreamed on the back of new media genres, notably rock music and the teen movie. At the same time, however, and in reaction to this, forms of hyper-masculinity began to develop – whether in the post-Schwarzenegger pumped-up body (which was by no means a simply heterosexual body) or in those movements in which heterosexual men were encouraged to reconnect to their masculinity in reaction to a modern, feminised society that was supposed to prevent the reproduction of male strengths and essences. Robert Bly's book *Iron John: A Book About Men,* which appeared, tellingly enough, in 1990, the same year as Judith Butler's *Gender Trouble,* helped inspire that movement, giving birth to thousands of men's groups. Men could now consciousness raise too.

Masculinity studies has been especially engaged, then, in analysing the trajectory of maleness and its various modes in the post-feminist epoch. Hence to give one example of work in the field: in a subtle essay, Sean Nixon has argued that maleness is especially important to old-style working men, men involved in strenuous physical labour (Nixon 2001). The economic and cultural value of this labour has decreased: those kinds of jobs have largely been taken over by machines and migrants. But this has intensified the investment in masculinity: masculinity here becomes less a crypto-norm and more a marked signifier of identity. According to Nixon the softer new masculinity is a response to this: it highlights masculinity, it is self-conscious about it, but it creates an alternative masculinity, a stylised one which is both different from the tough, old-style masculinity of the labouring body and draws something from it. This is a masculinity for the young service classes, which has severed its hard alliance with heterosexuality.

As I asked above, what does feminism want? Can the same question can be put to men? What does masculinity want? In one sense it cannot, since the study of masculinity is disconnected from efforts to secure further rights and opportunities. On the contrary, it wants to marginalise men somewhat, to see them as limited and historically formed, as a gender-marked social identity amongst other social identities. But since there are still many men who do not regard their masculinity as specifically gendered but as a norm, the study of masculinity continues to have real political meaning.

Yet the politics of masculinity also revolves around the same question that split feminism – Do we want more or less gender difference? On this my own view is: the ultimate, rather utopian objective of gender studies is to help produce a future where less subjectivity is organised around gender. This is not to support 'androgyny' like Virginia Woolf, or 'bisexuality', or even those 'queer' identities where forms of masculinity or femininity are unravelled or made ironic or hybridised (more on this in section 6.2). Rather it is to work for modes of selfhood that don't attach to gender at all: to increase the parts of oneself that aren't either masculine or feminine or any mix of the two or any relation to either. Of course there are limits to this project since most of us are committed to sex, and sex is linked to gender in fact if not in theory. So thinking about sexuality in order to reduce the role of gender, if taken to its endpoint, would lead us to demand forms of sex that aren't gendered. To what degree is that possible?

Further reading

Adam, Beck and van Loon 2000; Brunsdon 1997; Felski 1995; Gardiner 2002; Massey 1994; McRobbie 2000; Morris 1988; Nixon 2001.

Queer culture

The term 'queer' has often puzzled outsiders. Why call yourself *that*? This too has its story. For a long time 'queer' was, of course, a derogatory term for male homosexuals. That began to change when it began to be widely used in a new, affirmative sense among activist organisations that confronted politicians and the media in relation to the AIDS epidemic. In particular, it emerged in the USA out of ACT UP, which was established in 1987 to respond to the safe-sex movement. The safe-sex movement had attempted to close down on sodomy as an unsafe practice, in a strategy that risked echoing old-fashioned homophobia. ACT UP argued that the HIV virus should not be confused with the sex that spread it ('Fight AIDS, not sex') and that the solution to the epidemic was a medical one, which need not in any way encourage gay-bashing. Driven by this programme, it came to distinguish itself from the discourses and objectives of the gay and lesbian liberation movement that had appeared in the seventies dedicated to strengthening and winning acceptance for gay and lesbian identities (see Berlant and Freeman 1993). ACT UP quickly internationalised itself, and formed the institutional nucleus for what became queer politics and a collectivity sometimes then known as 'queer nation'. While it would be wrong to think of queer politics as globalised (it has made little or no headway in Africa or in nations with Islamic traditions, which have remained severely homophobic), queer movements have appeared in parts of Asia, Latin America and the old Soviet bloc (see Patton and Sánchez-Eppler 2000).

It is important to distinguish queer culture from the various sexual liberation movements that preceded it, and which have now developed into the GLBT (Gay Lesbian Bi and Transgender community) – of which the gay liberation movement was the first, and has had the widest cultural impact. Along with the feminist movement described in the last chapter, one of the most stunning transformations in late twentieth-century culture has been the emergence of gay and lesbian public cultures – or, to put this another way, the prising open of the closet. Homophobic prejudice and persecution did not cease but for the first time in modern Western history, the lifestyles that clustered around same-sex desires could be lived publicly. News-stands sold newspapers for gays and lesbians. Celebrities came out. Gay clubs, dance parties, holiday resorts, bars, whole neighbourhoods became part of the 'normalised' social fabric. Gay voting blocks emerged in certain cities (first of all San Francisco, where reputedly about a quarter of all voters are gay); and along with them openly gay politicians. Marketing and advertising agencies recognised the 'pink dollar' as a distinct market segment. Festivals such as Sydney's Gay Mardi Gras, which celebrated gay and lesbian culture, attracted wide public, even governmental, support. By the late nineties, gay characters were appearing neutrally, even affirmatively, in mainstream films and TV sitcoms.

History and theory

This movement is often (if rather mythically) traced back to a particular moment. On 27 June 1969 the New York City Police raided the Stonewall Inn, a Greenwich Village gay hang-out. Such a raid was by no means unusual, but this time, to everyone's surprise, the clientele, which included gays, lesbians and transsexuals, fought back, starting what came to be known as the 'Stonewall Riots'. These were followed by the first 'Gay Power' rally the following month and by the establishment of a more militant group, consciously based on feminist radical activism, which dubbed itself the Gay Liberation Front. A number of similar organisations were formed across the developed world with various time lags. Thus, for instance, almost twenty years later, in 1990, another group, Outrage!, was established in London as a response to the queer-bashing of the actor Michael Boothe and the lack of police response to this. Outrage! upped the ante on the more sedate British gay liberation movement by embarking on a programme of outing famous gays, organising public 'kiss-ins' and 'queer weddings' to highlight discriminatory legislation.

The gay movement's political programme turned around two main demands, the repeal of laws criminalising same-sex acts and the admission of full civil rights to self-identified gays. These demands (and especially the first) were not new, although the openness and confidence with which they were pursued was. What was new, however, was the formation of a new public culture around gayness, underpinned by a new theoretical understanding of homosexuality. (Even here the term 'new' needs to be qualified since groups such as the Los Angeles-based ONE Institute had theorised 'homosexual culture' in sociological terms during the fifties.)

The new culture embraced gayness as an identity that became not a more or less shameful and mutated internalisation of negative images of homosexual identity beamed in from the straight world, but self-generated and proud markers of who you

184

were. Until now, in mainstream society but not only in mainstream society, male homosexuality had been associated with feminised masculinity: stereotypes of limp wrists, aestheticism, a predilection for the colour pink, and so on. After Stonewall, in the seventies a new style of gayness came to public attention: an assertively macho style, with cowboy hats, pencil moustaches and blue Levis. It was a style that simultaneously sent up and joyfully embraced conventional Marlboro man masculinity as well as defiantly overturning old stereotypes. Post-seventies gayness has opened itself up to a plethora of styles.

Homosexuality itself was not an old concept: it was invented during the last decades of the nineteenth century from an amalgam of academic medicine and social science which has come to be known as sexology. For its first theorists, homosexuality was a form of social pathology, which was also conceived as being a form of 'deviance'. It was in this context that Michel Foucault's revisionary history of sexuality made such an impact in the seventies. Famously Foucault argued that what he called the 'repressive hypothesis' needs to be turned inside out (Foucault 1978). He contended that sexuality should not be regarded as a force of nature that our ancestors censored and distorted, and which needs to be liberated within us. Instead sexuality (like all concepts) is produced in discourse, in 'talk about sex' – and, he boldly argued, the increasing public attention given to sexuality across the nineteenth and twentieth centuries, especially the emergence of a science of sexuality in the late nineteenth century, in fact produces modern sexuality. In these terms there was more rather than less sexuality under the repressive Victorian regime because, for instance, masturbation, adolescent sex and commercial sex were more strenuously invigilated. And, for Foucault, there is no sexual life-force in human beings awaiting liberation from social bonds: once again there are just various 'discursive practices' in which the 'truth' about sex is formed and connected to social practices, interests and power structures. And (in a conceptual move we can recognise as post-Marxist), because the various components of sexuality – pleasures, desires, drives, objects – are so elusive, 'truth about sex' proliferates in search of a disappearing object.

These lines of thought led to Foucault's second main argument: from the late eighteenth-century onwards the status of sexual desire and practices between men changed. They became not bodily or psychological acts (albeit ones with relations to sin and crime) but central signifiers of identity. By around 1900, if a man preferred sex with other men to sex with women that now made him a 'homosexual' (and not just, for instance, someone who had sex with other men more or less often). It did so to such a degree that anything else he might be – a member of this or that nation, class, locality, profession and so on – was secondary compared to his sexual orientation in marking his identity. Foucault argued against the sexualising of identity at all: for him what was important was not public recognition, official sanction for desires and personhood, but rather the capacity to nurture and experiment with sexual styles and pleasures outside of the constraints of normalising or inspectorial pressures. And the invention of homosexuality intensified homophobia. Hatred of men who committed sodomy had long formed part of popular culture (men convicted of the crime had often been hounded by women prostitutes in particular, who saw them as competitors), but now homophobia acquired new social functions. Indeed its intensification during the last decades of the nineteenth century is linked to similar shifts in sexism and racism. All these modes of thought represent some human beings (women, people of colour, homosexuals) as less than fully human, and all emerge in their modern form alongside democracy as a way of maintaining those social hierarchies under threat by means of formally egalitarian policies and doctrines.

Foucault's intervention (itself heavily dependent on the gay liberation movement) helped the gay movement repudiate 'homosexuality' as a paradigm. It helped develop the notion of 'compulsory heterosexuality' through which it became clear that the total heterosexual domination of the social and cultural order was not a fact of nature or biology but of history and convention. Very similarly, Foucault's intervention lay behind the concept of 'heteronormativity'. This pointed to the way that, in our society, concepts of the normal and the heterosexual are almost impossible to separate. But it also indicated how heterosexuality almost invisibly supports a number of other norms – it is (or at any rate has been) the key to social acceptance, and remains one of the mainstays of family values. That is, heteronormativity as a concept makes it clear that compulsory heterosexuality is socially invisible because it has embedded itself into the culture's sense of the normal across so many registers and formations that alternatives look like pathologies rather than viable alternatives. And it helps show how dependent the regime of compulsory heterosexuality is on its 'other': what normalises heterosexuality is continual differentiation of itself from, and management of, what is not 'normal'. But this works the other way too: homosexuality, or any sexual practice or orientation, cannot be pulled out of the system within which it exists. There is an important sense, so the argument goes, in which to transgress or critique heteronormativity is to do so in terms which, in part, belong to it. This need not be regarded as limiting critique, but it does mean that notions of radical autonomy and difference, and any politics founded on them, have a phantasmal quality.

Leaving these rather recondite arguments behind, we can summarise: after Foucault, sexuality was taken out of the realm of nature and placed at the very heart of modern history, society and politics, allowing new relations between sex, society and politics to become imaginable, and with them, some claimed, new kinds of sex. In particular, after Foucault, in arguments developed by Leo Bersani, sex no longer had to be primarily conceived of as connected to love, joy and expressiveness, or even pleasure (as it is for dominant post-repressive ideology). It is just as connected to loss of control, disorder, aggression and shame (Bersani 1990). And obviously no less seductive (or obsessional) for that.

These lines of thought, however, exacerbated internal divisions within the gay and lesbian liberation movements. In their basic form these divisions repeated those that had already appeared within feminism and, in this context, can be boiled down to the question: did gays and lesbians want to be accepted as 'normal', to be granted the same rights and to embrace the same values and styles as any other citizen? Or did they want to maintain their difference and, specifically, their transgressive relation to heteronormativity?

The movement for difference institutionalised itself, as we have seen, around the response to the AIDS epidemic, since it was then that a conservative, normalising wing of the gay liberation movement was able to enter into negotiations with governmental agencies. On the other side, cultural studies intellectuals such as Paula Treichler, Cindy Patton and John Erni critically examined the discourses and politics of the AIDS response. In one important contribution Erni, using a methodology derived from Foucault, showed how the search for a 'cure for AIDS', although on the face of it a medical project, was in reality a set of discourses and power relations which continued to express traditional homophobia (Erni 1994). Taking a more utopian standpoint, drawing on Eve Sedgwick's work, and moving towards queer theory, Cindy Patton argued that the gay body is 'written by science' (Patton 1990, 129) and that the official response to the HIV virus was a culmination of the scienticised gay body. Now medical science was essentialising the relationship between homosexuality and a disease, as though the first simply caused, and was expressive of, the second. Her answer? To take advantage of gaps and fissures in science's hegemonic discourse and find new forms of identity in the spaces that remained invisible to public surveillance and outside of official sexual identities – 'queer identities' in other words.

In a later intervention in the debate, Michael Warner has suggested that what differentiates the conservative and the radical movements are their relation to the state. The gay and lesbian movement is happy to present itself as an interest group representing a constituency of citizens lobbying for policies meant to improve the welfare of its constituency; the queer movement is suspicious of the politics of representation and of the state welfarism that such a politics presupposes (Warner 1999). Indeed, at least from one side of the spectrum, queer covers a wider range of sexual acts and identities than GLBT, since, in the wake of Foucault and post-structuralism, it rejects identity politics as such. It is even possible to be interested solely in sex with people of the opposite gender and queer, which is not the case for those who identify as gay or lesbian.

The queer movement has met with a great deal of resistance within the gay and lesbian movement. In the USA the anti-queer case was put most popularly by Andrew Sullivan in his book *Virtually Normal* (1995, but based on a 1993 *New Republic* essay). As we might expect, Sullivan argued that most gay people want to be normal like everyone else and that the linkage between sexuality and 'cultural subversion' has alienated not only the wider society but most gay people too. Indeed, from within the more consumerist and conformist side of the gay community there is a sense that we have already entered the 'post-gay' moment, which is to say the gay community has effectively been de-politicised (Warner 1999, 62–64).

At any rate, for Sullivan the gay movement should be overwhelmingly concerned with two issues in particular: gay marriages and the right to join the military. Leaving aside the fact that these are issues which raise negative passions (to the degree that they do raise passions outside of the world of formal politics and the mass media) mainly in the USA, this kind of thinking has led to a quite widespread feeling that the gay liberation movement has only a small number of goals to meet and therefore can soon be disbanded. Against that expectation, many take a queer position to argue that, were gay and lesbian marriages to be legally recognised, this would cast an invidious distinction between married and non-married couples within the same-sex community itself. Marriage legitimises sexual relations, and by the same stroke de-legitimises other – extra-marital – relations. And same-sex marriage would make increasingly precarious queer intimacies that don't involve the kind of love which sanctifies marriage. Do queers need this? That question faces the strong liberal riposte: Even so, if we want to get married who are you to stand in our way? Or the more radical riposte: wouldn't same-sex marriage change and widen the institution of marriage by de-coupling it from traditional gender roles? The difficult politics of this issue, which have had the effect of further radicalising the queer movement, have not, as a matter of fact, helped energise the queer cause in the USA (see Warner 1999).

Against this background, the radical queer movement has moved into increasingly utopian politics. In one of its moves, drawing on Leo Bersani's work mentioned above (itself dependent on Lacanian psychoanalysis), it has embraced sex as abjection. It is in these terms that Michael Warner can write: 'In those circles where queerness has been most cultivated, the ground rule is that one doesn't pretend to be *above* the indignity of sex' (Warner 1999, 35, original emphasis). And then in response to the movement against public sex (the cleaning up of porn shops, clubs where sex takes place, cruising haunts, etc.) which has been supported by some in the normalising gay movement, it has argued for a rethinking of the public/private division. In doing so it rebukes that long Western history in which sexual acts are the most private of all. Indeed, it can be argued, in which they form the nub of privacy as such. Here is Michael Warner:

> As it happens, an understanding of queerness has been developing in recent decades that is suited to just this necessity: a culture is developing in which intimate relations and the sexual body can in fact be understood as projects for transformation among strangers. (At the same time, a lesbian and gay public has been reshaped so as to ignore or refuse the counter-public character that has marked its history.) So too in youth culture, coolness both mediates a difference from dominant publics and constitutes that difference as the subjective form of stranger sociability.
>
> (Warner 2002, 122)

This is an attempt to affirm, on political grounds, casual sex between strangers (more common among same-sex partners than of heterosexual ones) by aligning it to edgy styles – here 'cool' – where strangers recognise themselves as alike and thereby connect. Warner hopes for a connection between the kinds of sociabilities formed around such styles and the queer movement as such. But to what degree do forms of 'stranger sociability' have to be *organised* effectively to differ from 'dominant publics'? And anyway (if one wants to engage in this kind of utopian political calculation), isn't it as rebellious to be uncool as to be cool, even if the uncool don't form any kind of social association?

In a nutshell: what queer theory teaches us is that nothing is certain about sex and sexuality and that the social categories we have to organise, use and police it are contingent (they might be different and indeed are always in the process of becoming different). And the same is true, at the level of individuals and their bodies, for the pleasures and other intensities we take from sex, which although they may be offered to us as mediated through sex's social categories, are also open to modification by new ways of incorporating and acting out (or performing) gender as well as sexual drives.

This mode of analysis – which emphasises the contingency and performativity of gender roles and which was pioneered by Judith Butler – owes a great deal to poststructuralism and often seems more appealing as a theoretical model than useful for the analysis or enactment of actual, existing, sexual cultures and politics (Butler 1989). This means that queer theory has not been absorbed easily into cultural studies proper as we have been thinking of it here. In literary studies, queer theory has generally involved a re-reading of the heritage so as to uncover previously secreted moments of same-sex desire, sometimes, it has to be said, on a pretty flimsy basis. It has, as it were, outed the canon. Some cultural studies work has taken the same tack: thus Richard Dyer in one essay in his *The Culture of Queers* focuses on our uncertainty about whether certain film noir movies, which like so many American fictions involve close relations between 'buddies', are to be read as representing erotic flows between these buddies or not. He argues that this uncertainty is itself a generic feature of noir, one of the ways in which it unsettles and destabilises the status quo (Dyer 2002).

But the step beyond textual interpretation and theory-production has yet to be fully taken in queer cultural studies despite groundbreaking work by figures such as Lauren Berlant, Michael Warner and others. That remains a task for cultural studies' future; but one made all the harder because it is apparent that in the ebb and flow of academic fashion, the tide is going out for queer thought and practice, however much political work remains to be done.

Further reading

Abelove, Barale and Halperin 1993; Butler 1990; D'Emilio 1998; Dyer 2002; Halperin 2002; Jagose 1996; Patton and Sánchez-Eppler 2000; Sedgwick 1990.

Part 7

VALUE

Culture high and low

Why study popular culture? Basically because it is by definition the main cultural expression of our time. Like television, still its primary medium, it is everywhere. We who live in developed nations (well almost everyone) live our lives around and partly through it. It's a bank of pleasure and meaning. It's the mirror in which the culture recognises itself. It peoples the world: for many, celebrities and fictional characters are like distant acquaintances. It draws national – and international – communities together, dotting conversations and private and communal memories. For some (and just about everybody at some time or other) elements of popular culture become an obsession or help form an identity. What would society be without television, sport and pop music? Different hardly catches it. And of course it is also a huge business. In the last instance, popular culture demands teaching and research, just because it's so *there* (Lewis 2001).

Yet relations between academic disciplines and popular culture remain contentious. To begin with, academic writing about popular culture risks pompousness, especially when it claims progressive clout for the popular, as it often does among those called 'cultural populists'. Who hasn't been embarrassed by the pontifications of cultural theorists on hip hop say, or *Dr Who*? The reason for this is not, of course, that academic work is too rigorous and profound, and popular culture too trivial for the two ever to be compatible. Or that popular culture is so accessible that academic commentary of it is redundant. Rather, inside popular culture itself, intellectual self-regard is a systematic target of deflating ridicule. Since, in most of its forms, popular culture is committed to immediate pleasure, it wraps its seriousness in entertainment. However powerful and insightful it might be, its first requirement is – generally speaking – to be consumable now.

193

Popular culture also unsettles the academic bias towards weightiness because its works and styles tend to be current for so short a time. The academy is structurally attuned to what endures, and it is itself a key instrument of cultural preservation. And those forms of academic enquiry that are determined to extract an uplifting, progressive, political cum moral message from their topics have a commitment to the future that popular culture mainly lacks. It does not help that academics are, by virtue of their job, middle class and connected to authority, while a great deal of popular culture emerges from, and is addressed to, those who have no post-compulsory education. Indeed, it is often, at least on the surface and especially in genres such as hip hop or punk, anti-authority. All this means that much of the most insightful work on popular culture is closer to the culture itself than any academic theorists can be. Journalists such as Greil Marcus, Anne Powers or Lester Bangs generally write better about it than academic theorists. Much academic writing strains to join the popular but it doesn't often (ever?) happen. (See the introduction to Jenkins, McPherson and Shattuc 2002 for a recent manifesto of academic popism; for a good discussion of the structural divisions between fans and academics, see Hills 2002, 20.)

Popular culture in history

When it comes to popular culture, just as elsewhere cultural studies can use a historical sense of its object, so let me present a micro-history of relations between high and low culture. Students are often amazed to learn that the division as we know it is quite recent. It did not exist when a culture of the aristocratic elite, based on a classical education and patronage and centred on the classical (i.e. Greek and Latin) canon, was counter-posed by a people's culture which was largely non-literate and centred on non-commercial carnival, communal sports, festivities and rituals (Stallybrass and White 1986). From the mid-eighteenth century, that structure was transformed so that two literate cultures existed, one elite, the other not, both increasingly commercialised and available in the vernacular (i.e. in living rather than dead languages). In this situation, elite culture became organised around distinct moral–aesthetic principles, which included the notion of the timelessness of culture, culture's responsibility for the provision of moral guidance, culture's capacity to harmonise and fulfil the self, the individuality of the work (art or literature) and the genius of its greatest producers (Guillory 1993).

Popular culture, on the other hand, became organised around the market, with little legitimation and few constraints on production, except those imposed by censorship. It provided pleasure and entertainment. Insofar as these were seen to require passivity and moral vacuousness, it was feminised (Huyssen 1986). And yet the cultural hierarchies and divisions characteristic of the first half of the twentieth century were still not fully established: snippets of Shakespeare were still presented in the popular theatre of the mid-nineteenth century for instance (Levine 1988). Modern divisions really became set when, late in the nineteenth century, high culture was defended by professionals in reformist or oppositional terms. Aesthetes such as Walter Pater began defending art without claiming any social usefulness for it all. Among what was called the 'art for art's sake' movement, art, at most, allowed its fans to live intensely, hard in the moment. It provided a mode of radical sensation (Pater and Phillips 1986 [1873]). More conventionally, the so-called 'apostle of culture', Matthew Arnold, thought of culture not simply as 'the best that is known and thought' but as a form of criticism that could be directed against Puritanism, commercialism, aristocratic brutality and arrogance, as well as vulgarities of any kind. It could also enable people to see 'the object in itself' (Arnold and Collini 1993 [1869]). Soon more and more of the education system was devoted to propagating culture in these terms (Arnold was himself a school inspector).

These defences of high culture, if anything, increased strong demand for it from working-class men and women (Rose 2001). Certainly there was little sense that the division between elite and popular cultures was itself a form of social domination. This allowed governments and philanthropists to win widespread approval when they funded high cultural institutions: schools, libraries, concert halls, art galleries and museums, in order to disseminate hegemonic forms of civility, as well as to increase communal cultural capital generally. This intervention, however, had the effect of consolidating cultural divisions and tying high culture to middle-class respectability more tightly. And that in turn paved the way for another twist in our story: an experimental and (sometimes) subversive avant-garde split off from established high culture, often by appropriating elements of the popular. We can take the nineteenth-century French Romantics' celebration of puppets and popular-theatre characters such as Pierrot as an example (Storey 1985).

By 1970 (when cultural studies was emerging) this whole system had begun seriously to break down under the pressure of the extension of audio-visual culture (radio, film, television) as well as of the extension of secondary and post-compulsory education. At this point, defenders of high culture began to look like a beleaguered minority whose powers, although still in place, required shriller and shriller defence. On the other side, what we might call popular-cultural connoisseurship (a recondite familiarity with performers, conventions, texts) became the basis for more popular culture reception and production, allowing for a much more variegated and self-reflexive popular culture. At the same time, texts that combined high and low elements became commonplace once again. Clear binary differences between high culture and popular culture began increasingly to break down. The modern canon was dispersed so that, today, publishers such as the Oxford University Press can label reprinted Zane Grey novels as 'classics' even though they belonged to the mass culture of their time. Likewise museums regularly present exhibitions on past (and sometimes present) mass or commercial culture and non-canonical artists. It is harder to come up with examples from 'below' that incorporate high-cultural motifs or references, but, as we shall see, a large body of culture today exists in a zone between or reaching into both high and low (to use those loaded terms).

At any rate, by the sixties the high culture canon had lost certain of its functions. It was no longer required to maintain social hierarchies (society had stronger means for that) or to guide contemporary cultural production, which began once again to 'appropriate' or adapt, rather than to defer to, the canon. What effectively organised the popular/high division was, on the one hand, the distinction between old, or historical, culture (cultural heritage) and contemporary culture, and on the other, the distinction between old art media (namely literature and fine art) and audio-visual and new media.

These new and mixed cultural preferences began to change the way people grouped around their cultural preferences. Jim Collins uses the term 'taste cartographies' to describe the 'ways critical distinctions are now being made in reference to different configurations of taste, value and class affiliations' (Collins 1995, 188). It's a concept that allows us to see how, in contemporary culture, tastes are more than tastes for objects. They assemble and connote the groups who have them, even if many (but by no means all) taste groups are still linked to class or sexuality or ethnicity or gender. Yet as tastes became less connected to class in particular, the sociabilities they stimulated became increasingly important as identity markers and life practices – most of all for that minority whose sense of themselves was formed around these very tastes.

This is of course a summary of events in the West, but similar (if not identical) logics now work outside the West, especially in Asia. Conservative ideologues in both Japan and China have appealed to traditional arts requiring training and scholarship as a bulwark against Americanised mass culture, and – to take just one example – since the seventies Korea has appealed to its own high cultures against commercialised Japanese popular culture (animation, karaoke, computer games, popular music, melodramas). Meanwhile teen sociability in particular is organised around shared tastes within the various strata of commercial culture, which regularly involves appropriations of imported forms, against the supposed values of their elders.

Mass culture

Traditionally academics have distinguished between *popular* and *mass* culture. Popular culture meant culture of and by the people (if not merely folk culture as such). Mass culture meant culture produced industrially on a mass scale. But that distinction has lost its force. In cultural studies, the term 'mass culture' has fallen out of use because it was generally a term of abuse (see Denning 2004, 97–120). It denoted an exploitative, mechanical, empty culture, one often thought to pedal cheap fantasies and to pander to impossible desires. That kind of theory failed to account for nuances, differences and qualities within the domains that it named, and did not even pretend to share whatever pleasures and benefits mass culture provided for its audiences. One important moment in the lifting of the negativity that surrounded the notion of 'mass culture' (thus allowing it to be refigured as the popular) was Fredric Jameson's recognition (riffing on the German theorists Ernest Bloch and Herbert Marcuse) that much industrialised culture contained a 'utopian' charge. It may have offered food for fantasy and wish-fulfilment but by soliciting its audiences' 'libidinal investments' it also provided glimpses or tastes of what the good life could be. These glimpses or tastes might even motivate political energies. Or so the argument went (see Jameson 1992).

The problem with jettisoning the concept of mass culture once and for all is that not all popular-cultural products are equally popular. Some are much more widely consumed than others. Skateboarding is a form of popular culture, but not as many people enjoy it as enjoy watching or playing football. Heavy metal is popular culture but it isn't anything like as popular as hip hop (of which some genres are much bigger than others anyway). So it remains useful to think of something such as mass culture as culture that accesses audiences across a variety of cultural sectors and is part of almost everyone's cultural literacy within a particular society. It's a sub-section of popular culture, where we think of popular culture, simply, as all culture that is not regarded as, or does not consider itself, elite culture. (And it's worth remembering that elite and popular cultures, as opposites, need each other to be defined in those terms.)

Cultural populism and the canon

Cultural studies' embrace of popular culture does possess a certain political valency, albeit one that full-blown cultural populism exaggerates since, as we have seen, the academicisation of popular culture fits the logics of contemporary capitalism rather than stands against them. The political force of cultural studies' affirmation of the popular is closely tied to a 'critique-of-the-canon' argument that goes like this: the canon is that select group of texts, artworks, etc. conventionally regarded as representing the highest achievements of the culture, and often discussed and disseminated as such in educational and high-status cultural institutions. But a culture organised around highly selective canons is unable to ascribe full value to what lies outside the canon. The canonical does not have more absolute value than the non-canonical – it is simply that the particular criteria, attitudes and training that it implies form the culture of the dominant classes.

Those, for instance, who are profoundly moved by great works of art, who have strong opinions about why some canonical works are greater than others and who want to study them in depth and communicate their findings and opinions are not so much wrong (there is no way of telling right or wrong in this context) as failing to address a bigger and ultimately more important picture. They are ignoring the two-way flow between class and

197

ethnicity on the one side, and culture on the other; the way in which the prestige of the canon is transferred onto the educated and/or rich (and especially the *white* educated and rich), while at the same time the prestige of the educated and/or rich is transferred onto the canon. And, more, the way in which appeals to the canon still feed modes of cultural conservatism that remain important to the right. In fact, entrenched as it is in the business of creating hierarchies, and necessarily restricted in its circulation, appealing as it does only to a few usually highly educated fans, canonical culture has a great deal less vitality and genuine power than popular culture. By embracing popular culture and its particular modes of reception, cultural studies is thus making a political intervention against the structures which hierarchise society around money and culture simultaneously.

This is a rather complex argument that branches out in a number of different directions and has attracted a number of ripostes. The most obvious and important of these ripostes is that anti-canon argument omits the main problem with popular culture – which is that it is not the spontaneously produced culture of the community, but instead is the product of commercial enterprises whose ultimate measure of success is profit not quality. Thus, this argument goes, modern popular culture is structurally inclined to the superficial and the false: indeed it blands out social contradictions, differences and injustices, and hobbles critique and rational understanding of the society to which its audiences belong. So it is possible for critics to suggest that the reason why revolution is unimaginable in the USA is because its anodyne popular culture is so powerful (Brennan 1997, 257). Another and barely less traditional way of putting this is that popular culture is aimed at those who do not have a serious interest in culture: it is the culture of people seeking to relax, forget work and have a good time in their leisure hours. They do not require a probing, enlightening, contemplative culture; they forego aesthetic responses based on a 'disinterested' and informed relation to works, since they look to the cultural domain mainly for recuperation and distraction. (The least forgiving critique of mass culture in these terms remains that of Theodor Adorno and Max Horkheimer, for whom, as we've seen in section 4.1 on television, popular culture commands distraction rather than sustained attention in ways that weaken real individuality, satisfaction and liberty [see Adorno and Horkheimer in During 1999].)

One populist reply to these critiques is to celebrate the terms in which popular culture is consumed for their very lack of seriousness and ambition; to celebrate, for instance, what Iain Chambers has called the 'mobile orders of sense, taste and desire' focussed on 'the tactile, the incidental, the transitory, the expendable, the visceral' which make up the culture of distraction – and we could add to this list, fun, pleasure, goofiness, whatever (Chambers 1986, 13). Another reply is to turn to the argument that we should not seek political solutions and engagements in cultural forms against the anti-populists. Is popular culture the best site for nurturing the critical faculty? If not, why not leave it alone? Another is to contend that popular culture has a social value in that its consumption is in itself a form of participation in a public sphere – our collective identities are formed through our immersion in the popular. But the most common argument is to point once again to the links between subject positions and cultural tastes and to maintain that a taste for the canon is at base the expression of particular identifications, closely linked to class and ethnic stratification.

In fact the debates over academic cultural populism seem to me limited and repetitive, since they do not have a clear enough sense of the forces that are transforming popular culture. These forces have been discussed at various points in this book, but it is appropriate to rephrase them at this point.

Popular culture

Popular culture has become segmented into a myriad of forms, genres, audiences, tones, styles and purposes, so much so that it cannot meaningfully be talked about as a monolith. While, as we have seen, some so-called 'popular culture' is produced *en masse* (and has certain of the characteristics of mid-twentieth-century mass culture that cultural critics of the period complained about), a great deal is produced for relatively small numbers of people who are familiar with, and more or less passionately interested in, the genres involved. And a great deal of popular culture – such as hip hop for instance – does retain links with geographical communities. Yet, at the same time it is increasingly finding new links between sectors and ways to market one set of products in terms of another. Branding across formats has become increasingly important with tie-ins: comics, computer games, books, films, music CDs, music videos, TV shows can all be produced around the same characters and 'brand'. From the industry perspective this is one of the forces driving consolidation as large media conglomerates look for 'synergies' in a quest that has not been as successful in business terms as was once predicted. The point is, however, that both these forces – of segmentation and of consolidation – exist simultaneously and do not have to be thought of in contradiction.

Certainly popular culture is riddled with art niches, in the sense that it produces work which resists immediate pleasures and satisfactions; which is experimental in terms of its media; which is ambitious in that it expresses unusual and thoughtful feelings and messages; which is often conscious of the history of its particular genre; and which requires some familiarity with a wider field than with the piece of work itself. In these terms – to repeat – there exist thousands of movies (David Lynch), songs (Radiohead or the Magnetic Fields), comic books (Chris Ware), even television shows (*The Sopranos*), which hybridise high and low forms. Indeed, art values are not only being democratised but are breaking into new spheres as they colonise fields such as food, car culture, wine and fashion (at the same time as art itself is becoming de-aestheticised). Admittedly these values may be class markers and the products that express them available mainly to the privileged, although not exclusively: take aestheticised or 'custom' car culture as an example of an aesthetic practice that (at least until very recently) has barely been taken up or enjoyed by the bourgeoisie.

From the other side, sectors of old high culture have embraced the instruments of popular culture without losing much credibility. For instance, much art produced by art-school graduates and aimed at the art world has absorbed commercialism and the media. (In fact it is the very strength of the 'art world' as an institution which allows this to happen.) This has largely been Andy Warhol's legacy, and has been taken up, to much controversy, by the Brit artists of the late nineties. Artists such as Damien Hirst and Tracy Emin have become celebrities and cultural entrepreneurs in a way not especially different from any rock star or fashionable restaurateur. Actually, the whole phenomenon of Brit Art is an example of the complex relation between different styles and audiences that cannot be broken down into the high and low division (Betterton 2001).

Modern popular culture has also developed tones and moods unique to itself partly because its consumers know that it is profit-orientated business and that they are being, to some degree, exploited, but generally don't care! The enjoyment and the meaning of the music, the fashion, the movie or the record exist, not despite commercialisation but because of it. To enjoy and consume it is, whatever else it is, to participate in the present. Hence some popular culture is enjoyed in this spirit – 'It's rubbish, but I like it' – and there is often a sense of solidarity between producers and consumers in that they share the joke. A typical example: the laddish British magazine, *Loaded*'s logo, 'For men who should know better'. This is sometimes called irony, but that's not quite right. It's an attitude that does not fit the old categories developed to describe the possibilities of cultural orders still under the grip of the classics and aesthetics.

There is a closely related phenomenon in which conventional images of being a girl or being a boy for instance are pastiched slightly, exaggerated with a trace of mockery, as in the Hollywood teen-movie *Clueless*. This is sometimes read as providing a political space in which new grounds for identity formation can be explored (McRobbie 1999, 127). This is doubtful however. That kind of interpretation falls prey to what we can call the fallacy of progressive self-referentiality or self-ironisation. Being aware that one is being positioned into stereotypes of femininity say, and gently making a joke of it by camping the stereotypes up, implies no liberation from that position. If anything it implies a tolerance of being positioned.

Popular culture often displays its intelligence in the way that it develops new styles to appeal to new audiences. Often these involve the old category of wit. So to riff on an example from Paul Gilroy – that of the early-nineties Californian rapper Snoop Doggy Dog. Snoop was involved in the project of popularising rap, transforming it into a mainstream pop genre. Why did he pass as a dog? Because dogs chase pussy. Because it is a dog eat dog world. Because dogs hunt in packs. Because the dogfather is an inverted godfather. Because a dog is an abject creature and doing it doggy style is thought of by some as gross and as demeaning to women, although (jumping ahead in time) it is also a move in the sexy perreo dance style which caused an uproar in San Juan and looks likely to hit the US mainland (this is written early in 2004). Because, on the other hand, a dog is man's best friend and a favourite of white Hollywood family movies, where no family is a real family without one. Because dogs (like Snoop) are dogged. And because a man impersonating a dog is comic (if a little embarrassing) rather than threatening (Gilroy 2000, 204ff.). Snoop disseminated a trope from the streets in which abjection was turned against itself so as to attract the widest possible audience/market. As Jamaican crossover ragga master, Elephant Man, put it in his recent song 'A Bad Man': 'Here's to all you dogs the world over!'

Popular culture also routinely creates more or less invented notions of tradition and innovation: there are neo-modern, neo-classic and a plethora of retro styles (just thinking of decades, there's a taste for each — thirties, forties, fifties, sixties, seventies, eighties styles, you name it). Of course, there is nothing new in the anchoring of taste formations in the past: neo-classicism, which shifts its meaning and its content across generations in the period between the Renaissance and the mid-twentieth century, is arguably the key taste/style formation of modern Western culture and has always involved elements of 'invented tradition'. Neo-classicism has generally meant order and harmony in turbulent times, and under modern capitalism all times are turbulent, so that one function of taste and style has been to indicate a historically transcendent calm and stability. But in contemporary popular culture, retro is neither a principle of order nor even of nostalgia: it organises fashions which know themselves as such, soliciting complex modes of reception which involve memory, irony, regret and pastiche.

To point to popular culture's rich and innovatory tonal range, however, is not to say that popular culture does not have real limits and problems. But in most cases these are confined to specific occasions or genres and can't be used to demonise the domain as a whole. One of popular culture's more systemic limits is that of obsolescence. In it, individual works or arts do not usually acquire prestige and aura because they are rare and exist at a distance from those who appreciate them, but on the contrary because certain names and texts are everywhere, because they have a culturally saturating fame. It is true that the objects of specific and limited tastes (Lou Reed, *South Park*) can acquire considerable prestige among the hippest taste monitors at a particular moment, but they have, even at their period of greatest acclaim, nothing like the massive popularity (or circulation at any rate) of Madonna or *The Simpsons* at their peak. Yet all prestige and appeal is acquired only in the process which will exhaust it: at a certain point repetition and celebrity turn into boredom and satiety, and the object is trashed into final uncoolness and obsolescence, awaiting its call into history's dustbin — from which it will be retrieved (perhaps) as retro or nostalgia. Only premature death can stop this process it seems: Elvis, Marilyn, Lennon, James Dean.

The transitoriness of much popular culture is linked to its generationalism: massified popular culture is directed in particular to the young, since they have the greatest 'discretionary' spending power, as well as the most need to use it to make social connections. This complicates things considerably since old popular cultures become intertwined with youth memories for ageing generations, and getting into contemporary popular cultures routinely comes to require negotiation with the sense that one is 'too old' for this.

And popular culture can be exploitative – let's call two important forms of this the rip-off and the beat-up. The rip-off appears when marketing efforts are made to entice audiences to consume low-quality work. The sad tale of the *Star Wars* franchise is a good case in point: the most recent films have contained no (good) new ideas and have none of their predecessors' energy. Their main impetus was clearly profit, and my bet would be is that most people seeing them would feel slightly cheated. Almost every franchise (and notably television series) involves a certain rip-off since they are under structural pressure to end a little past the time that they can maintain quality.

The beat-up is the intensifying of prejudices and cultural divisions: in a sense almost all Hollywood production before about 1980 is a beat-up on African Americans. This does not mean that all films that pandered to and intensified negative images of blacks are simply to be rejected on those grounds (as if films that encourage horrible prejudices cannot have other attractive – if not quite 'redeeming' – features), but it does mean that those films were exploitative of white racism. Rabidly conservative talk-show hosts, offering false information, closing down on dissent, bullying and ranting have refined the beat-up into a form all of its own. The effort to end that kind of exploitation is, of course, one of cultural studies' most important and easily defended tasks.

Because, under capitalism, popular culture is fundamentally commercialised, it is a standard bearer for commercial values and the ideology that supports consumer capitalism. This means that it has a somewhat conflictual relationship with publicly funded culture and in particular with public broadcasting. There may, indeed, be good reasons to support the public funding of culture – and, as we know, these reasons usually boil down to maintaining diversity and news services which are not ratings-driven and protecting the poorest in the community from the overpricing of media services. On the other hand public subsidy for middle-class tastes is not so easily defensible. And so in certain contexts, commercial popular culture as an enemy of, or at any rate an alternative to, public culture can work against the best interests of the community.

The big point is, then, that cultural populists need to recognise limits and problems to popular culture as it exists (some of which are open to cultural policy intervention), while cultural elitists need to recognise that those limits and problems do not define popular culture as such.

Cultural value and taste

All this goes to show that it is still difficult to think about popular culture from within the academy without returning to the question of value. But there remains a great deal of confusion about this issue. In making at least a start in clearing it up, it is helpful to distinguish between value, quality and taste, since these are different, if interconnected, categories that have often been jumbled together.

Value is the (supposed) abstract worth of a cultural object or genre or medium in relation to other objects, genres or media. It is fundamentally an economic concept, and classically has been divided in two. Objects have use value (their value as measured by their usefulness) and they have exchange value (their value as measured by what they can be traded or substituted for, usually via money). From this perspective 'cultural value' is really a kind of metaphor since basically culture has neither use nor exchange value as these work in economics. Insofar as value can be ascribed to it, cultural objects possess exchange value rather than use value since the implication is not, for instance, that high culture is more useful than popular culture but that it should be substituted for it. Certainly there are no objective standards for measuring cultural value, nor does culture possess a mechanism like the market to consign quantifiable cultural as against monetary value to objects through the mechanism of supply and demand.

On the other hand, quality is the worth of a cultural object as judged within the institutions from which it is produced or consumed in relation to the autonomous features of its medium. All cultural zones contain works of different quality; indeed all cultural production seems to involve quality judgements, since producers constantly reject their own attempts on the way to finishing a piece. And within cultural zones and genres, there is widespread if by no means total agreement about quality. Every object within a zone or a genre may be different and unique, but it is not completely different and unique, so quality judgements are possible. If someone were to argue that, say, Britney Spears, Vanilla Ice and Boy George were better than, say, Alicia Keys, Public Enemy and David Bowie then they would be regarded generally as being either provocative, perverse, ironic or ignorant.

Each media has different criteria of 'quality'. The term itself is used most in industrialised culture (its usage for culture emerges out of industry itself as in 'quality control') such as the music and most of all television businesses. Geoff Mulgan, for instance, has listed seven distinct senses of the term 'quality' as used within the television industry (Mulgan 1994, 88–115; see also McGuigan 1996, 45–47) which we can reduce to four: (1) quality as an expression of professional production skills, a concept which provides room for producers' creative freedom; (2) quality as measured by consumer response to programming; (3) quality as judged in terms of an aesthetic specific to television; and (4) quality as judged by television's capacity to meet ethical functions, notably truth-telling and cultural diversity. It may be that similar criteria

203

could be produced for less industrialised cultural sectors: the literary novel for instance. Nonetheless, in aesthetic domains where quality cannot be measured by the capacity of an object to perform a specific task there remains structural uncertainty about quality judgements – as there would be in the case of point (3) listed above.

Finally, there is taste. Taste is the expression of an individual's personal cultural preferences. It has an important history since it is so closely related to the development of modern privacy and liberty – let's briefly rehearse this history so as to deepen the story told above about relations between high and low cultures.

In the West, and particularly in France, taste and 'polite' culture become important as society splits more thoroughly into state and civil spheres. As the state takes over the government of life from the church and its care of souls, first by taking control of the police and army, civil society becomes the realm of public institutions: newspapers, books and journals as well as theatres, clubs, taverns, coffee houses, libraries, gambling halls, art galleries, sports grounds, shops, music halls and so on. The old notion of the 'private', which referred to those disallowed access to the public sphere (as in an army 'private'), disappears since these new forms of public life (state and civil) connect to everyone, or at least in theory.

In this process, the private becomes a protected zone for 'opinion' (as theorised by the philosophers John Locke and later Immanuel Kant) and, crucially in terms of our interests, for taste. At the same time, liberal notions of private economic and legal rights to property, personal labour and capital begins to organise modes of production (i.e. capitalism). By 'liberal' I mean: (1) that individuals are defined in terms of their relation to property, even if only their ownership of their own body and its labour power, and (2) that society is conceived as the aggregate of formally equal individuals whose rights to liberty are paramount. Only in the early nineteenth century does the concept of the private become primarily associated with gendered domesticity, as the workplace and the home begin to split from one another and a notion of 'personal life' as distinct from work appears (Warner 2002). But the liberal individualism of nineteenth-century capitalism, although it further damaged social consensus, did not provide markers of hierarchy in the way that the old aristocratic system had.

Taste, rather than opinion, helped meet the need for hierarchy: canons of good taste allowed liberal culture to exist as an ordered, graded structure. As we have seen, it also disseminated civil docility. The individual's right to their own taste (and its free expression), then, is deeply embedded in the liberal theory behind modern capitalism since good taste is key to mediating between the social and economic inequities that capitalism produces and the democratic and egalitarian theses underpinning that theory. The decline of taste as a marker of hierarchy and its loss of social function is partly a consequence of capitalism finding other ways of constructing hierarchies (basically through the extension of an extraordinarily subtly graded consumer market) and partly by egalitarianism colonising the cultural domain after its success in formal politics.

Once the era of good taste disappears it is not just that more objects can appeal to more people but that criteria for taste proliferate. Today sometimes it seems as if just about any signifier whatsoever is available to hang a taste on: How rough and gutsy is it? How smooth? How ironic? How sincere? How hot? How cool? How techno? How natural? How in-your-face? How laid back? How loud? How quiet? How weird? How chic? How queer? How straight? How heavy? How light? How deep? How much glitter? The old signifiers of aestheticised taste – beauty, harmony, order – have lost meaning, but have not of course disappeared. And the more choice one has between taste criteria and objects, and the less that choosing one particular criteria or object disables access to another, the more relaxed it is possible to be about taste's liberalisation. If I can have access to both Henry James and *South Park*, why diss one?

The problem with much thought about cultural value is that it either confuses value with quality or lets taste override both, as if the truism 'everyone has their own taste' is an argument against value or quality as such. Of course, in practice taste, quality and value do intermesh, but value is the most fragile of the three concepts since, at base, in relation to culture it can only be used metaphorically. After all, and to reiterate, commodities have value, cultures do not. In the end taste trumps value, but quality distinction remains unsurpassable.

Bourdieu

Thus it is that the most often cited and sophisticated theorist of cultural value, Pierre Bourdieu, is really a theorist of taste. His basic argument in his major work, *Distinction* (1984), is quite simple and already familiar to us in broad terms: modern society is divided into different and hierarchised taste communities (he reduces these differences to three: 'legitimate', 'middle-brow' and 'popular') whose particular tastes, interests, knowledges and skills are not acquired contingently. Nor do these cultural differences and gradations exist because high culture is 'better' (more civilised, profound, subtle, mature, etc.) than low culture. Rather (in an argument we know) gradated taste differences have a particular social function: they help reproduce those class divisions that they map onto. For Bourdieu, tastes are a key constituent of cultural capital, and everyone has more or less cultural capital. They also exist within and organise what he calls a 'habitus', that is, the set of dispositions, preferences and classifications that people are not necessarily aware of holding and which often seem 'natural', but which are continually acted upon and acted out, even, for instance, in the way we move and care for our bodies. A habitus is the way that cultural capital is regulated and lived, and it bridges the material conditions of existence (class differences in terms of work and money) and the signs and practices through which different groups place themselves within the social hierarchy.

Individuals from the dominant class inherit more cultural capital than those from the dominated class, just as they do more economic capital. They learn to appreciate

205

and contextualise high culture. And they learn the rules and discourses that regulate and legitimate it. In particular, they acquire the skills to recognise the aesthetic domain as aesthetic rather than simply as entertainment or as technical accomplishment. They learn to take a disinterested and mediated attitude to art: appreciating it as an end in itself. Such cultural capital can be transferred to economic capital in various ways (and vice versa), but it is especially important for those Bourdieu calls the 'dominated fraction' of the dominant class, who make up for their relative lack of money and status by acquiring relatively more cultural capital.

There are a number of problems with Bourdieu's argument, and the most telling have often been placed within cultural studies and sociology (see Collins 1995, 194ff.; John Hall 1992; and, best of all, Frow 1995). Most obviously, Bourdieu's theory relies on too tight a fit between class and taste. As we have seen contemporary culture is marked by a proliferation of taste groupings based on a variety of social distinctions (gender, ethnicity, locality, generation, etc.), and in some cases on none at all: groups of like-minded fans may be formed across relatively wide social differences (a taste for fishing, for instance, or for ballroom dancing). This means that the link between high culture and class domination is weaker than is claimed.

Nor does the link between taste and class have the same force in all countries: a large-scale survey in Australia, designed to test Bourdieu's thesis there, demonstrated persuasively that, while certain cultural preferences are very class-specific (providing piano lessons for children for instance), in the main the correlation between class and culture was looser than Bourdieu supposed (see Bennett, Emmison and Frow 1999). One reason for this is that it is likely that culture is a less powerful marker of class difference in Australia than it was in post-war France (much of Bourdieu's research for *Distinction* was carried out during the sixties), or for that matter almost anywhere in Europe and North America. And it is questionable whether Bourdieu's theory works outside the West: in China – perhaps; in Oman, say – much less so.

Bourdieu's theory also assumes that most people in society recognise the same overarching cultural standards; that they have a shared sense of how much or little cultural capital each possesses. This is doubtful: it is clear that, while just about everyone believes that there is more status in owning a Mercedes-Benz than a Toyota, or that a nest egg of a million dollars is better than one of ten thousand, not everyone believes that appreciating classical music or the English literary canon is a mark of status. For many (and not just those in 'dominated' classes) that is simply a sign of being a nerd or a wanker. Cultural capital circulates in restricted channels.

On the other hand, Bourdieu underestimates the degree to which tastes can move across different groups. Some tastes begin in small and elite groups and become relatively massified (classical music crosses over onto the pop charts that happen every few years, and over the long term the taste for impressionist and post-impressionist art increases). Others move in the opposite direction (the cultural power of Elvis-style rockabilly was at first arbitrated by the tastes of black and white teenagers from the USA's south-west for instance). Indeed age lends almost everything, including mass cultural objects, charm to a discrete set of collectors and/or the aesthetically minded. Different groups (and individuals) may value the same activities and objects but in different spirits: Abba fans for instance love the group for all kinds of reasons, and with widely different degrees of jokiness, from zero to lots. And that too isn't accounted for in Bourdieu's theory.

In sum, while Bourdieu's theory represents the most rigorous attempt to connect patterns of social domination to cultural tastes, its ambitions are not quite met. Perhaps most disappointingly of all – what does Bourdieu have to say to individuals who love, say, *DrWho*, Kate Bush, Franz Kafka and Dr Dre? Can their passion be interpreted simply as a (unselfconscious) strategy to acquire cultural capital or to reconcile themselves to a lack of it? (Clearly having a wide range of tastes *is* a sign of cultural capital.) What about pleasure? Understanding the world? Political engagement? Can't tastes carry these too? What about all the uses, buzzes and social connections that come with cultural participation and consumption, and which can't be thought of just as efforts to acquire prestige in a zero-sum competition where winners balance losers? Cultural studies, one might say, begins where Bourdieu leaves off.

Further reading

Bourdieu 1984; Brantlinger 1983; Fiske 1989; Frow 1995; Hartley 1996; Jenkins *et al.* 2002; McGuigan 1992.

The nature of culture

As Raymond Williams noted in his seminal essay 'Ideas of Nature', the concept of 'nature' is one of the most multifaceted in Western discourse, 'culture' being a weak competitor in this respect (Williams 1980a). Indeed, the two words have a twinned history: before it came to mean the institutions, processes and meanings through which we make sense of existence, 'culture' meant something like cultivation, that is, productive human intervention in nature. At any rate, nature exists in what the anthropologist Marilyn Strathern has called a 'matrix of contrasts' — that is, it's defined in opposition to, or in correspondence with, a number of very different categories.

Nature is defined, first, against artifice and technology. In these terms it becomes the domain of what is not under the control of human agency, or even what is produced or marked by human agency. The immediate difficulty with this definition is that today what exists as 'nature' is almost wholly a direct or indirect product of long human manipulation so that, on this planet, there is almost no pure nature in this sense.

Nature too can function as a synonym for life, since it can also be limited to what belongs to biology rather than to physics or chemistry. It exists as the array of *living* things rather than *all* things or, what has almost but not quite the same sense, as what is 'organic' as against what is 'inorganic'. (The rise of organic foods has altered the meaning of 'organic', which previously was used to denote simply what was living, but which now means something like 'what has not been produced by recent agricultural technologies'.) This means that to describe the world out there as 'nature' is to smuggle in a certain life force into the universe, as if the universe itself were animated. This corruption of an animated universe is common across many cultures.

Very differently, nature is also defined against supernature. Here it becomes basically everything that belongs to this world as against the world of gods and spirits. As such it includes rather than excludes what is artificial or technologised. Of course, from the point of view of hard modern rationality, supernature only exists as a human belief and is, therefore, part of nature anyway. From that point of view, then, there is ultimately nothing but nature.

Nature, as distinct from supernature, was once conceived as a world of anarchy, chaos, death. This was the case, for instance, within orthodox Christianity, for which the fallen world of nature and labour awaited redemption upon the Day of Judgement. It was also the case for all political theorists (such as Thomas Hobbes) who believed that the closer human beings were to their natural state the more brutality and disorder there would be. In a different formulation, Horkheimer and Adorno, in their classic *Dialectic of Enlightenment*, argued that modern social domination (the oppression of the poor by the rich in particular) needs to be understood as the consequence and endpoint of that human fear of, and desire to dominate, nature which has always driven the production of technology and rationality (Horkheimer and Adorno 1988 [1947]). But more and more, since the seventeenth century, at least for secularists, nature has been regarded as an order of rational laws and processes, as well as (under the sway of Romanticism) a site of innocence and recuperation. Nature as Eden.

Rational and natural laws may be more or less harmonious. But the most recent versions of living nature – Darwinism and neo-Darwinism – regard the principles that drive organic nature as ordered but not benign. Their nature is conceived in terms of a slow, cruel history in which the struggle to survive under fierce competition determines outcomes. Darwinism turns biology into a form of history, and has the capacity to turn history into a form of biology (as it is for those who believe that social relations are produced by evolutionary forces). Recently, too, under the influence of Norbert Weiner's cybernetics, nature has been conceived not as ordered by rational laws or as a retreat, but as an 'autopoietic' or self-regulating system (see Hayles 1999).

Nature has also become a universal normative concept. We speak of 'natural rights'; we demonise acts as 'unnatural' (famously, until the gay liberation movement, same-sex acts). In ordinary language, phrases such as 'naturally' and 'it's only natural' are used, almost without thinking, as explanations, defences or as praise. The distinction between what is 'natural' and what is 'artificial' almost always denigrates the latter. Nature as a norm is not the same as nature as life itself, but this difference is routinely overlooked. Modern environmentalism in particular merges them, as if protecting a nature conceived as artifice and technology's opposite is in the interests of nature and life as universal norms.

More specifically, ecological thought appeals to a number of versions of nature. Of these the 'quasi-aesthetic' and the 'ethical' (as we can call them) are probably the most widely accepted, partly because the sense of pending global disaster that permeates much eco-politics is too terrifying and too inhuman to enter the mainstream (Latour 2004). Quasi-aesthetic environmentalism aims to preserve species, wildernesses, etc.

209

basically for aesthetic reasons, on behalf of their beauty, or of biodiversity, or of sheer pristineness and so on. Ethical environmentalism puts the case for anti-anthropocentrism. It attempts to limit humankind's lordship over nature or, to put it less forcefully, to restrain the human species' assumption that it exists at nature's centre and that nature exists to meet its needs. Quasi-aesthetic eco-politics is indeed aesthetic insofar as it claims protection of the environment as a final good: for it, preserving a species of bird, for instance, is not an option to be measured against other options through a cost–benefit analysis. It is an end in itself, just as a work of art is an end in itself for traditional Kantian aesthetics (although environmentalism routinely also appeals to the incalculable, as when it makes the argument that we just don't know what will be lost if a particular species becomes extinct).

Aesthetic environmentalism can quickly become commodified and fetishised, as in the marketing copy of the Body Shop, a retailer of 'naturally inspired solutions for skin and hair care', to cite their description of themselves. That's a turn of phrase ('naturally inspired') that carefully negotiates the difficulties both of staying natural and of deciding what the 'natural' actually is. Indeed the Body Shop's marketing appeals not just to nature as such, although that lies at its heart, but to nature's wider connotations. Its advertising can go as far as to masquerade as a political programme. On its web site, the company lists its 'values' as 'against animal testing', 'support community trade', 'activate self esteem' 'defend human rights' and 'protect our planet'. Presumably its main objective is to make a profit, but leaving hypocrisy aside, here nature as a norm is used to back up one of the strongest struts of contemporary ideology: that self-esteem (and faith in one's unique worth) is a necessary – make that a natural – good.

As we have begun to see, nature can also be thought of as the other to morality and civilisation. Nature here is the domain of instincts, impulses and drives which rationality and moral order need to control. Perhaps the most graphic case of this is the relation between the psychoanalytic 'id' (which, for Freud, is where our basic sexual drives and natural drive for pleasure and annihilation reside) and the 'superego' or conscience which becomes strong through a complex process of repression and self-mastery. Freud seems to have sometimes thought that women tended to be less fully socialised than men, as if they were closer to a state of nature, and certainly feminists have argued that under patriarchal ideology women were to men as nature was to culture (and passive was to active) – this phrasing coming from the title of a famous article by Sherry Ortner (see Griffin 1978; Rosaldo et al. 1974).

Another way of thinking about nature, which follows the German idealist philosopher Hegel, makes a distinction between 'first' and 'second' nature. First nature is nature as it exists outside human society and technology; second nature is nature as it exists for and within human societies. Which means that second nature itself takes two forms: on the one hand it is nature as it has been transformed and built after 120 millennia (roughly) of human interaction with it, but it is also 'nature' as a concept and norm for human beings. This Hegelian distinction asks us to think about history as the steady submergence of first by second nature, and for Hegel this was clearly to be regarded as progress. Second nature can have another sense too: it can describe the naturalisation of society and politics, the passing off of social or political constructs as natural. Perhaps the most common form of this is to think of the family as a fact of nature rather than of society, and then to model society as a whole in familial terms. The word 'culture' itself, with its historical sense of 'cultivation', has a residually naturalising force: it is as if the formation of collectivities and individuals were like the cultivation of a crop.

Nature, then, is what the structuralists used to call a 'floating signifier': it performs different kinds of semantic work in different contexts. Or to put this another way, it promises to be something exterior to the social and cultural which might therefore frame and limit them. But nothing can be unproblematically exterior to the social and cultural, at least insofar as what has meaning for us belongs to the meaning-giving process, that is to culture. So nature is the outside of culture and society as that outside appears from inside, and in terms of, culture and society.

Cultural studies' relations to the meanings and cultural work of nature concepts are various enough but the discipline is structurally inclined to resist claims that nature really does exist as an external source of value whether these claims take the form of aestheticised, ecological thought or of modes of analysis which naturalise society and culture. In terms of this, it is one of cultural studies' most basic and valuable critical moves to argue that conservative thought systematically tends to suppose that what is social, and hence potentially political (the nuclear family, mothers as primary child-care givers and so on), is also simply natural.

This scepticism towards the natural does not mean that cultural studies analysis cannot be aligned to environmentalism. What kind of ecological programme survives the critique of the concept of nature? Perhaps the most sophisticated answer to this question is that of Alexander Wilson in his *The Culture of Nature: North American Landscape from Disney to Exxon Valdez*. There Wilson proposes a 'restoration ecology', which he conceives not as a process of maintaining nature in its pristineness but as a human mimicking of natural systems linked to a strong sense of the history of human–nature interactions (Wilson 1992). This line of argument has itself come under question as remaining too connected to romantic anti-capitalism (Why model ourselves on any concept of nature at all?) (Neil Smith 1996), but since Wilson's nature is more an imagined ideal to be imitated than a ground for action or preservation, it is hard to accuse him of naturalism at all. Nature for him has become thoroughly part of culture and history, but remains capable of organising a certain collective idealism.

In fact cultural studies is in a strong position to examine the cultural and social effects of environmentalism. Thus in a number of works Andrew Ross has criticised the uses to which notions of ecological scarcity and interconnectedness have been put

(Ross 1994, 16–17). He wishes to critique the argument that natural resources are becoming exhausted and that a slight event in one place (a cow's fart) can trigger a larger event (a drought) half a world away – arguments which lie at the heart of some strands of eco-politics. As far as Ross is concerned, such claims often lead to exhortations for personal ethics of asceticism and environmental responsibility, and a vague sense of global citizenship, rather than to a clear-headed analysis of who is actually responsible for global over-consumption. He believes that the culprits are primarily big corporations in the overdeveloped world – a judgement that underplays the contribution of consumers to the problem. Ross also argues against environmentalism's alliances with big business and indeed the military on the grounds of managing risk and damage. 'Sustainable development' is often the rubric under which such alliances proceed. For him it simply enables business and the military to mobilise resources and dominate social discourse (Ross 1996b). Ross fears that, ultimately, environmentalism may allow the authority of science and expertise, especially as funded by multinational corporations, to govern more and more social and cultural activity.

But the most influential of cultural studies' contributions to the analysis of nature has been the category of the post-human. Post-human theory affirms a human being no longer placed in nature conceived of as the opposite of technology and artifice. In her famous essay, 'A Cyborg Manifesto', Donna Haraway posed a trenchant critique of all forms of thought that fetishise nature and the organic (see Haraway 2003). She proposes a way of thinking that does not invoke nature as a value, or as any kind of transcendental – outside the system – signifier at all. In particular she resists thinking of social bonds in biological terms – as 'filiative'. And she refuses to frame sexual relations as primarily reproductive, regarding the reproduction technology which is breaking the nexus between sex and reproduction as liberating (Haraway in During 1999). Had contemporary technologies of genetic implants and genetic code shifting existed when the essay was written, no doubt these would have been affirmed too, as opening up possibilities for human and social agency and experience outside naturalised concepts of identity.

But Haraway is no simple technophile. She believes that the increasingly complex interrelations between human beings and machines need careful inspection and open and collective structures of control in order to prevent them intensifying rather than alleviating inequities of class and gender. In particular, as technology increasingly orders both work and leisure and the relation between them, the border between work and leisure is becoming less clear cut for many – which can be, to put it bluntly, either a good thing or a bad thing, depending on whether work becomes more like leisure (as it may for the privileged) or leisure more like work (as it may for the poor).

Indeed for both Haraway and Ross, who write as socialists, the key term seems to be labour. Haraway argues for the importance of restructuring labour processes in a post-human and post-nature world, so as to prevent a concentration of old forms of oppression. Traditionally, and particularly in Marxism, labour has been figured as the bridge between nature and society, as if nature becomes something else — society — only through work. And the amount of labour that a product required for production was the surest measure of its value. Of course that kind of labour is being downgraded as technology and information order production, and as services and cultural goods play larger and larger roles in national economies.

At any rate it is no accident that labour appears as a crucial category in thought about cultural and social relations to nature, since labour has always mediated the orders of the social and the natural. Indeed what Haraway and Ross remind us is that when cultural studies examines its prime object, culture — whether in the sense of leisure culture or the culture of everyday life, or culture as the struggle over life's meaning — labour tends to disappear as an analytic category. This returns us to one of cultural studies' (and this book's) central concerns: can the discipline claim to be *engaged* if it lacks a firm analytic grasp of labour — the 'natural' basis of social existence — as it works in culture? Or does our deconstruction of nature actually mean that we have to rethink the category of labour too? If nature disappears into its 'matrix of contrasts' (as I am suggesting here), maybe it takes with it any concept that links work to a primordial, *natural*, condition.

Further reading

Franklin *et al.* 2000; Haraway 2003; Hayles 1999; Ross 1991, 1994 and 1996b; Wilson 1992.

Conclusion

I began this book by claiming that cultural studies is an engaged discipline in three different senses. It takes into account the perspective of the marginalised and oppressed; it nurtures cultural celebration and affirmation, and encourages fandom; and it aims to frame its analyses and critiques in relation to everyday life, or at any rate to life outside academia. All this without making knee-jerk negative judgements of any everyday life zone – condescending neither to global export culture industries, say, nor to the local community arts hall. At the same time cultural studies is an academic formation, somewhat reluctantly connected to the enterprise economy and neo-liberalism, which belongs primarily to the classroom and study. Furthermore it is a globalising academic field with a strong commitment to maintaining differences between communities and cultures on the grounds that the transnational imposition of common interests, values, styles, etc. is a mode of hegemony.

All this doesn't quite add up. What's the relation between critique and affirmation? Between a commitment to the sociabilities and experiences of everyday life and academic work? Between the field's transnational extension and its respect for difference? Between its embrace of enterprise and of marginality? In developing my understanding of cultural studies through a series of specific topics and chapters, my sense of the field's loose ends, irresolutions, contradictions and frictions has, if anything, increased. But – and here's the point – this is not to be thought of as a crippling problem or failure but rather as what energises the discipline, what keeps it fresh, exciting, open to the future. It's what ensures that the new generations of students becoming involved in the field will be able to keep its projects going on their own terms.

What kind of work will they be doing? Where is cultural studies heading? It would be easy for me to list here a bunch of topics that seem to need more attention – religion, sport, ageing, travel and so on. Or to point to methodological gaps hidden in all those loose ends and contradictions: the need for more careful accounts of the relation between a passion for particular cultural forms and the articulation of critique; the need for more developed accounts of the 'everyday' itself for instance; a stronger sense of where cultural studies is headed within the Chinese or Islamic traditions. But I suspect that it is less meaningful to gesture at under-examined topics as they appear to me today than to wait for those entering the discipline to tell me what I am going to need to know in the years to come, and, indeed, what I ought to have known all along.

Bibliography

Abelove, Henry, Micháele Aina Barale and David M. Halperin. *The Lesbian and Gay Studies Reader*. New York: Routledge, 1993.

Abercrombie, N. *Television and Society*. Cambridge, England: Polity Press, 1996.

Ackah, William. *Pan-Africanism: Exploring the Contradictions: Politics, Identity and Development in Africa and the African Diaspora*. Interdisciplinary Research Series in Ethnic, Gender and Class Relations. Aldershot; Brookfield, Vt: Ashgate, 1999.

Adam, Barbara, Ulrich Beck and Joost van Loon. *The Risk Society and Beyond: Critical Issues for Social Theory*. London; Thousand Oaks, Calif.: Sage, 2000.

Adams, Rachel and David Savran. *The Masculinity Studies Reader*. Keyworks in Cultural Studies; 5. Malden, Mass.: Blackwell, 2002.

Adorno, Theodor W. *The Culture Industry: Selected Essays on Mass Culture*. London; New York: Routledge, 1991.

Agamben, Giorgio. *Homo Sacer: Sovereign Power and Bare Life*. Stanford, Calif.: Stanford University Press, 1998.

Allen, Theodore. *The Invention of the White Race*. London; New York: Verso, 1994.

Althusser, Louis. *Lenin and Philosophy and Other Essays*. Trans. Ben Brewster. New York: Monthly Review Press, 1971.

Anderson, Benedict R. O'G. *Imagined Communities: Reflections on the Origin and Spread of Nationalism*. 2nd rev. and extended edn. London; New York: Verso, 1991.

Ang, Ien. *Watching Dallas: Soap Opera and the Melodramatic Imagination*. London; New York: Methuen, 1985.

—— *Desperately Seeking the Audience*. London; New York: Routledge, 1991.

—— *On Not Speaking Chinese: Living between Asia and the West*. London; New York: Routledge, 2001.

Appadurai, Arjun. *Modernity at Large: Cultural Dimensions of Globalization*. Public Worlds; Vol. 1. Minneapolis, Minn.: University of Minnesota Press, 1996.

216

—'Grassroots Globalization and the Research Imagination'. *Globalization*. Ed. Arjun Appadurai. Alternative Modernities. Durham, NC; London: Duke University Press, 2001: 1–21.

Arendt, Hannah. *The Origins of Totalitarianism*. New edn. New York: Harcourt Brace Jovanovich, 1973.

Arnold, Matthew and Stefan Collini. *Culture and Anarchy and Other Writings*. Cambridge Texts in the History of Political Thought. Cambridge, England; New York: Cambridge University Press, 1993 [1869].

Arrighi, Giovanni, Beverly J. Silver, Iftikhar Ahmad *et al. Chaos and Governance in the Modern World System*. Contradictions of Modernity; 10. Minneapolis, Minn.: University of Minnesota Press, 1999.

Back, Les and John Solomos. *Theories of Race and Racism: A Reader*. Routledge Student Readers. London; New York: Routledge, 2000.

Baker, Houston, M. Diawara and R. Lindeborg, eds. *Black British Cultural Studies: A Reader*. Chicago: Chicago University Press, 1996.

Balibar, Étienne. *Masses, Classes, Ideas: Studies on Politics and Philosophy before and after Marx*. Trans. James Swenson. London: Routledge, 1994.

Banton, Michael. *Racial Theories*. 2nd edn. Cambridge, England; New York: Cambridge University Press, 1998.

Barr, Marleen S. *Envisioning the Future: Science Fiction and the Next Millennium*. Middletown, Conn.: Wesleyan University Press, 2003.

Barrell, John. *The Birth of Pandora and the Division of Knowledge*. Basingstoke: Macmillan, 1992.

Bauman, Z. *Legislators and Interpreters*. Cambridge, England: Polity Press, 1987.

—'Is There a Postmodern Sociology?' *Theory, Culture and Society* 5 (1988): 217–237.

Bayley, C.A. '"Archaic" and "Modern" Globalization in the Eurasian and African Arena, c. 1750–1850'. *Globalization in World History*. Ed. A.G. Hopkins. London: Pimlico, 2002: 47–74.

Beebe, Roger, Denise Fulbrook and Ben Saunders. *Rock over the Edge: Transformations in Popular Music Culture*. Durham, NC: Duke University Press, 2002.

Bell, David and Barbara Kennedy. *The Cybercultures Reader*. London: Routledge, 2000.

Bennett, Tony. *Culture: A Reformer's Science*. St Leonards, NSW: Allen & Unwin, 1998a.

—'Cultural Studies: A Reluctant Discipline'. *Cultural Studies* 12.4 (1998b): 528–545.

— *Differing Diversities: Transversal Study on the Theme of Cultural Policy and Cultural Diversity*. Strasbourg Cedex: Council of Europe Publishing, 2001.

Bennett, Tony, Michael Emmison and John Frow. *Accounting for Tastes: Australian Everyday Cultures*. Cambridge, England; New York: Cambridge University Press, 1999.

Berlant, Lauren Gail. *The Queen of America Goes to Washington City: Essays on Sex and Citizenship*. Series Q. Durham, NC: Duke University Press, 1997.

—'Affirmative Culture'. *Critical Inquiry* 30.2 (2004): 278.

Berlant, Lauren Gail and Lisa Duggan. *Our Monica, Ourselves: The Clinton Affair and the National Interest*. Sexual Cultures. New York: New York University Press, 2001.

Berlant, Lauren Gail and Elizabeth Freeman. 'Queer Nationality'. *Fear of a Queer Planet*. Ed. Michael Warner. Minneapolis, Minn.: University of Minnesota Press, 1993: 193–229.

217

Bersani, Leo. *The Culture of Redemption*. Cambridge, Mass.: Harvard University Press, 1990.

Berwanger, Dietrich. *Television in the Third World*. Bonn: FES, 1987.

Betterton, Rosemary. ' "Young British Art" in the 1990s'. *British Cultural Studies*. Oxford: Oxford University Press, 2001: 287–304.

Bhabha, Homi K. *Nation and Narration*. London; New York: Routledge, 1990.

—— *The Location of Culture*. London; New York: Routledge, 1994.

Bharucha, Rustom. 'Interculturalism and Its Discriminations: Shifting the Agendas of the National, the Multicultural and the Global'. *Third Text* 46 (1999): 3–23.

Bindé, Jérôme. 'Towards an Ethics of the Future'. *Globalization*. Ed. Arjun Appadurai. Alternative Modernities. Durham, NC; London: Duke University Press, 2001: 90–113.

Blackburn, Robin. *The Overthrow of Colonial Slavery, 1776–1848*. London; New York: Verso, 1988.

Bly, Robert. *Iron John: A Book About Men*. Reading, Mass.: Addison-Wesley, 1990.

Boddy, William. *Fifties Television: The Industry and Its Critics*. Illinois Studies in Communications. Urbana, Ill.: University of Illinois Press, 1990.

Bourdieu, Pierre. *Distinction: A Social Critique of the Judgement of Taste*. Cambridge, Mass.: Harvard University Press, 1984.

Brantlinger, Patrick. *Bread & Circuses: Theories of Mass Culture as Social Decay*. Ithaca, NY: Cornell University Press, 1983.

Brennan, Timothy. *At Home in the World: Cosmopolitanism Now*. Cambridge, Mass.: Harvard University Press, 1997.

Briggs, Susan. 'Television in the Home and the Family'. *Television: An International History*. Eds Anthony Smith and Richard Paterson. Oxford: Oxford University Press, 1998: 109–121.

Brunsdon, Charlotte. 'Pedagogies of the Feminine: Feminist Teaching and Women's Genre'. *Screen* 32 (1991): 364–382.

—— *Screen Tastes: Soap Opera to Satellite Dishes*. London; New York: Routledge, 1997.

—— *The Feminist, the Housewife and the Soap Opera*. Oxford Television Studies. Oxford; New York: Clarendon Press; Oxford University Press, 2000.

Buckley, Sandra. *Broken Silence: Voices of Japanese Feminism*. Berkeley, Calif.: University of California Press, 1997.

Butler, Judith P. *Gender Trouble: Feminism and the Subversion of Identity*. Thinking Gender. New York: Routledge, 1990.

—— 'Contingent Foundations: Feminism and the Question of Postmodernism'. *Feminists Theorise the Political*. Eds Judith Butler and Joan W. Scott. New York: Routledge, 1992: 3–21.

Caine, Barbara. *English Feminism, 1780–1980*. Oxford; New York: Oxford University Press, 1997.

Carey, James W. 'The Origins of Radical Discourse on Cultural Studies in the United States'. *Journal of Communication* 33.3 (1983): 311–313.

—— *Communication as Culture: Essays on Media and Society*. Media and Popular Culture; 1. Boston: Unwin Hyman, 1989.

— 'Reflections on the Project of (American) Cultural Studies'. *Cultural Studies in Question*. Eds Marjorie Ferguson and Peter Golding. London; Thousand Oaks, Calif.: Sage, 1997: xxvii, 247.

Certeau, de. *The Practice of Everyday Life*. Berkeley, Calif.: University of California Press, 1984.

Chakrabarty, Dipesh. 'Provincialising Europe: Postcoloniality and the Critique of History'. *Cultural Studies* 6.3 (1992).

Chambers, Iain. *Popular Culture: The Metropolitan Experience*. London: Methuen, 1986.

Chan, Hoi Man. 'Popular Culture and Political Society: Prolegomena on Cultural Studies in Hong Kong'. *Culture and Society in Hong Kong*. Ed. E. Sinn. Hong Kong: The Centre for Asian Studies, 1995: 23–50.

Cheah, Pheng and Bruce Robbins, eds. *Cosmopolitics: Thinking and Feeling Beyond the Nation*. Minneapolis, Minn.: University of Minnesota Press, 1998.

Chen, Kuan-Hsing. *Trajectories: Inter-Asia Cultural Studies*. Culture and Communication in Asia. London; New York: Routledge, 1998.

Chew, Matthew. 'An Alternative Metacritique of Postcolonial Cultural Studies from a Cultural Sociological Perspective'. *Cultural Studies* 15.3/4 (2001): 602–620.

Chow, Rey. *Ethics after Idealism: Theory, Culture, Ethnicity, Reading*. Theories of Contemporary Culture; Vol. 20. Bloomington: Indiana University Press, 1998.

Clarke, John and Janet Newman. *The Managerial State: Power, Politics and Ideology in the Remaking of Social Welfare*. London: Sage, 1997.

Clifford, James. *The Predicament of Culture: Twentieth Century Ethnography, Literature and Art*. Cambridge, Mass.: Harvard University Press, 1988.

— 'Taking Identity Politics Seriously: "the Contradictory, Stony Ground..."'. *Without Guarantees: In Honour of Stuart Hall*. Eds Paul Gilroy, Lawrence Grossberg and Angela McRobbie. London; New York: Verso, 2000: 94–112.

Collins, Jim. *Architectures of Excess: Cultural Life in the Information Age*. New York: Routledge, 1995.

Connell, R.W. *Gender and Power: Society, the Person and Sexual Politics*. Stanford, Calif.: Stanford University Press, 1987.

— *Masculinities*. Cambridge, England: Polity Press, 1995.

Connerton, Paul. *How Societies Remember*. Themes in the Social Sciences. Cambridge, England; New York: Cambridge University Press, 1989.

Corner, John. 'Television and Culture: Duties and Pleasures'. *British Cultural Studies*. Oxford: Oxford University Press, 2001: 261–272.

Couldry, Nick. *Inside Culture: Re-Imagining the Method of Cultural Studies*. London: Sage, 2000.

Crane, Diana, Nobuko Kawashima and Kenichi Kawasaki. *Global Culture: Media, Arts, Policy and Globalization*. New York: Routledge, 2002.

Critical Cultural Studies Group. 'Critical Multiculturalism'. *Multiculturalism: A Critical Reader*. Ed. David Theo Goldberg. Oxford: Blackwell, 1994: 114–139.

Cunningham, Stuart. 'TV Violence: The Challenge of Public Policy in Cultural Studies'. *Cultural Studies* 6.1 (1992a).

— *Framing Culture: Criticism and Policy in Australia*. Australian Cultural Studies. North Sydney, NSW: Allen & Unwin, 1992b.

—— 'From Cultural to Creative Industries: Theory, Industry and Policy Implications'. *Media International Australia* 102 (2002): 54–65.

D'Emilio, John. *Sexual Politics, Sexual Communities: The Making of a Homosexual Minority in the United States, 1940–1970*. 2nd edn. Chicago: University of Chicago Press, 1998.

Dean, Jodi. *Publicity's Secret: How Technoculture Capitalizes on Democracy*. Ithaca, NY: Cornell University Press, 2002.

Deelman, Christian. *The Great Stratford Jubilee*. London: Michael Joseph, 1964.

Denning, Michael. *Culture in the Age of Three Worlds*. London; New York: Verso, 2004.

Development Aid Committee, *Development Aid Cooperation: 1998 Report*. 1998.

Du Gay, Paul. *Consumption and Identity at Work*. London; Thousand Oaks, Calif.: Sage, 1996.

—— *Doing Cultural Studies: The Story of the Sony Walkman*. Culture, Media and Identities. London; Thousand Oaks, Calif.: Sage, in association with The Open University, 1997.

—— 'Representing "Globalization": Notes on the Discursive Ordering of Economic Life'. *Without Guarantees: In Honour of Stuart Hall*. Eds Paul Gilroy, Lawrence Grossberg and Angela McRobbie. London; New York: Verso, 2000a: 113–126.

—— *In Praise of Bureaucracy: Weber, Organization, Ethics*. London; Thousand Oaks, Calif.: Sage, 2000b.

Du Gay, Paul and The Open University. *Production of Culture/Cultures of Production*. Culture, Media and Identities. London; Thousand Oaks, Calif.: Sage, in association with The Open University, 1997.

Du Gay, Paul and Michael Pryke. *Cultural Economy: Cultural Analysis and Commercial Life*. Culture, Representation and Identities. London; Thousand Oaks, Calif.: Sage, 2002.

Du Gay, Paul, *et al. Identity: A Reader*. London; Thousand Oaks, Calif.: Sage, in association with The Open University, 2000.

During, Simon. 'What Was the West?' *Meanjin* 48.4 (1989): 759–776.

—— 'Popular Culture on a Global Scale: A Problem for Cultural Studies?' *Critical Inquiry* 23.4 (1997): 808–834.

—— *The Cultural Studies Reader*. 2nd edn. London: Routledge, 1999.

Dworkin, Dennis L. *Cultural Marxism in Postwar Britain: History, the New Left and the Origins of Cultural Studies*. Post-Contemporary Interventions. Durham, NC: Duke University Press, 1997.

Dyer, Richard. *White*. London; New York: Routledge, 1997.

—— *The Culture of Queers*. New York: Routledge, 2002.

Ellis, John. *Visible Fictions: Cinema, Television, Video*. Rev. edn. London; New York: Routledge, 1992.

—— 'Scheduling: The Last Creative Act in Television'. *Media, Culture and Society* 22.1 (2000).

Erni, John Nguyet. *Unstable Frontiers: Technomedicine and the Cultural Politics of 'Curing' AIDS*. Minneapolis, Minn.: University of Minnesota Press, 1994.

—— 'Introduction – Like a Postcolonial Culture: Hong Kong Reimagined'. *Cultural Studies* 15.3/4 (2001): 389–418.

Faludi, Susan. *Backlash: The Undeclared War against American Women*. 1st Anchor Books edn. New York: Anchor Books, 1992.

—— *Stiffed: The Betrayal of the American Man*. 1st edn. New York: W. Morrow & Co., 1999.

Fanon, Frantz. *The Wretched of the Earth*. 1st Evergreen edn. New York: Grove Press, 1966.

Feld, Steven. 'A Sweet Lullaby for World Music'. *Globalization*. Ed. Arjun Appadurai. Alternative Modernities. Durham, NC; London: Duke University Press, 2001: 189–219.

Felski, Rita. *The Gender of Modernity*. Cambridge, Mass.: Harvard University Press, 1995.

Fenster, Mark. 'Boxing in, Opening Out: The Boxed Set and the Politics of Musical Production and Consumption'. *Stanford Humanities Review* 3.2 (1993): 145–153.

Ferguson, Marjorie and Peter Golding. *Cultural Studies in Question*. London; Thousand Oaks, Calif.: Sage, 1997.

Fernandez, Raul A., and Jeffrey Grant Belnap, eds. *Jose Marti's 'Our America': From National to Hemispheric Cultural Studies*. Durham, NC: Duke University Press, 1998.

Fèuredi, Frank. *The Silent War: Imperialism and the Changing Perception of Race*. New Brunswick, NJ: Rutgers University Press, 1998.

Fiske, John. 'British Cultural Studies and Television'. *Channels of Discourse: TV and Contemporary Criticism*. Ed. R.C. Allen. Chapel Hill, NC; London: University of North Carolina Press, 1987.

—— *Understanding Popular Culture*. Boston: Unwin Hyman, 1989.

Foucault, Michel. *The Archaeology of Knowledge*. London: Tavistock, 1972.

—— *The History of Sexuality*. 1st American edn. New York: Pantheon, 1978.

Frankenberg, Ruth, ed. *Displacing Whiteness: Essays in Social and Cultural Criticism*. Durham, NC: Duke University Press, 1997.

Franklin, Sarah, Celia Lury and Jackie Stacey. *Global Nature, Global Culture*. Gender, Theory and Culture. London: Sage, 2000.

Friedan, Betty. *The Feminine Mystique*. London: Victor Gollancz, 1963.

Friedman, Jonathan. *Cultural Identity and Global Process*. London: Sage, 1994.

Frith, Simon. *Performing Rites: Evaluating Popular Music*. Oxford: Oxford University Press, 1996.

Frith, Simon and Andrew Goodwin. *On Record: Rock, Pop and the Written Word*. London: Routledge, 1990.

Frith, Simon and Howard Horne. *Art into Pop*. London; New York: Methuen, 1987.

Frith, Simon, Will Straw and John Street. *Cambridge Companion to Pop and Rock*. Cambridge Companions to Music. Cambridge, England; New York: Cambridge University Press, 2001.

Frow, John. *Cultural Studies and Cultural Value*. Oxford; New York: Clarendon Press; Oxford University Press, 1995.

—— 'A Politics of Frozen Time'. *Timespace: Geographies of Temporality*. Eds Jon May and Nigel Thrift. London: Routledge, 2001: 73–89.

Frow, John and Meaghan Morris. *Australian Cultural Studies: A Reader*. Questions in Cultural Studies. St Leonards, NSW: Allen & Unwin, 1993.

Fukuyama, Francis. *The End of History and the Last Man*. New York; Toronto: Free Press; Maxwell Macmillan Canada; Maxwell Macmillan International, 1992.

Fumaroli, Marc. *L'état culturel: une religion moderne*. Paris: Editions de Fallois, 1991.

Fuss, Diana. *Identification Papers*. New York: Routledge, 1995.

Gardiner, Judith Kegan. *Masculinity Studies and Feminist Theory: New Directions*. New York: Columbia University Press, 2002.

Garnham, Nicholas. 'Dominance and Ideology in Culture and Cultural Studies'. *Cultural Studies in Question*. Eds Marjorie Ferguson and Peter Golding. London: Sage, 1997.

—— 'Political Economy and Cultural Studies'. *The Cultural Studies Reader*. Ed. Simon During. London: Routledge, 1999: 492–506.

Garnham, Nicholas and Fred Inglis. *Capitalism and Communication: Global Culture and the Economics of Information*. Media, Culture and Society Series. London; Newbury Park, Calif.: Sage, 1990.

Gauntlett, D. *Moving Experiences: Understanding Television's Influences and Effects*. London: John Libbey, 1995.

Gauntlett, David and Annette Hill. *TV Living: Television, Culture and Everyday Life*. London: Routledge, 1999.

Gendron, Bernard. *Between Montmartre and the Mudd Club: Popular Music and the Avant-Garde*. Chicago: University of Chicago Press, 2002.

Gibson, Lisanne and Tom O'Regan. 'Culture: Development, Industry, Distribution'. *Media International Australia* 102 (2002): 5–8.

Giddens, Anthony. *The Consequences of Modernity*. Stanford, Calif.: Stanford University Press, 1990.

— *In Defence of Sociology. Essays, Interpretations and Rejoinders*. Cambridge, England: Polity Press, 1996.

Gillespie, Marie. *Television, Ethnicity and Cultural Change*. London: Routledge, 1995.

Gilroy, Paul. *There Ain't No Black in the Union Jack: The Cultural Politics of Race and Nation*. London: Hutchinson, 1987.

— *Against Race: Imagining Political Culture Beyond the Color Line*. Cambridge, Mass.: Belknap Press of Harvard University Press, 2000.

Gilroy, Paul, Lawrence Grossberg and Angela McRobbie, eds. *Without Guarantees: In Honour of Stuart Hall*. London; New York: Verso, 2000.

Giroux, Henry. 'Resisting Difference: Cultural Studies and the Discourse of Critical Pedagogy'. *Cultural Studies*. Eds Lawrence Grossberg, Cary Nelson and Paula Treichler. New York: Routledge, 1992.

Gleik, James. 'Days of Future Past'. *New York Times Magazine* (1997): 26–28.

Goldberg, David Theo. *Multiculturalism: A Critical Reader*. Cambridge, Mass.: Blackwell, 1994.

Goodwin, Andrew. *Dancing in the Distraction Factory: Music Television and Popular Culture*. Minneapolis, Minn.: University of Minnesota Press, 1992.

Gordon, Avery and Christopher Newfield. *Mapping Multiculturalism*. Minneapolis, Minn.: University of Minnesota Press, 1996.

Greider, William. *One World, Ready or Not: The Manic Logic of Global Capitalism*. New York: Simon & Schuster, 1997.

Griffin, Susan. *Woman and Nature: The Roaring inside Her*. 1st edn. New York: Harper & Row, 1978.

Grossberg, Lawrence. 'Is Anybody Listening? Does Anybody Care? Talking About the State of Rock'. *Microphone Fiends*. Eds Andrew Ross and Tricia Rose. New York: Routledge, 1994: 40–54.

— 'Toward a Genealogy of the State of Cultural Studies: The Discipline of Communication and the Reception of Cultural Studies in the United States'. *Disciplinarity and Dissent in Cultural Studies*. Eds Cary Nelson and Dilip Parameshwar Gaonkar. New York: Routledge, 1996.

— 'Toward a Genealogy of the State of Cultural Studies'. *Bringing It All Back Home: Essays on Cultural Studies*. Durham, NC: Duke University Press, 1997.

— 'Cultural Studies vs. Political Economy: Is Anybody Else Bored with This Debate?' *Cultural Theory and Popular Theory*. Ed. John Storey. London: Prentice Hall, 1998.

— 'History, Imagination and the Politics of Belonging: Between Death and the Fear of History'. *Without Guarantees: In Honour of Stuart Hall*. Eds Paul Gilroy, Lawrence Grossberg and Angela McRobbie. London; New York: Verso, 2000: 148–164.

— 'Reflections of a Disappointed Music Scholar'. *Rock over the Edge: Transformations in Popular Music Culture*. Eds Roger Beebe, Denise Fulbrook and Ben Saunders. Durham, NC: Duke University Press, 2002: 25–59.

Grossberg, Lawrence, Cary Nelson and Paula A. Treichler. *Cultural Studies*. New York: Routledge, 1992.

Guillory, John. *Cultural Capital: The Problem of Literary Canon Formation*. Chicago: University of Chicago Press, 1993.

Gunter, B. and J. McAleer. *Children and Television*. London: Routledge, 1997.

Habermas, Jürgen. *The Structural Transformation of the Public Sphere: An Inquiry into a Category of Bourgeois Society*. Studies in Contemporary German Social Thought. Cambridge, Mass.; Cambridge, England: MIT Press; Polity Press, 1989.

— 'The European Nation-State: On the Past and Future of Sovereignty and Citizenship'. *Public Culture* 10.2 (1998).

Hage, Ghassan. *White Nation: Fantasies of White Supremacy in a Multicultural Society*. Sydney: Pluto Press, 1998.

Hall, John R. 'The Capital(s) of Culture: A Non-Holistic Approach to Status Situations, Class, Gender and Ethnicity'. *Cultivating Differences*. Eds Michele Lamont and Marcel Fournier. Chicago: University of Chicago Press, 1992.

Hall, Stuart. *Minimal Selves*. ICA Documents; Vol. 6. London: ICA, 1987.

— 'New Ethnicities'. *'Race', Culture and Difference*. Eds James Donald and A. Rattaansi. London: Sage, 1992.

— 'The Problem of Ideology: Marxism without Guarantees'. *Stuart Hall: Critical Dialogues in Cultural Studies*. Eds Stuart Hall, David Morley and Kuan-Hsing Chen. London; New York: Routledge, 1996: 25–46.

Hall, Stuart and Paul Du Gay. *Questions of Cultural Identity*. London; Thousand Oaks, Calif.: Sage, 1996.

Hall, Stuart, David Morley and Kuan-Hsing Chen. *Stuart Hall: Critical Dialogues in Cultural Studies*. Comedia. London; New York: Routledge, 1996.

Hall, Stuart *et al. Policing the Crisis. Mugging, the State and Law and Order*. London: Macmillan, 1978.

— *Without Guarantees: In Honour of Stuart Hall*. New York: Verso, 2000.

Halperin, David M. *How to Do the History of Homosexuality*. Chicago: University of Chicago Press, 2002.

Hannaford, Ivan. *Race: The History of an Idea in the West*. Washington, DC; Baltimore, Md.: Woodrow Wilson Center Press; Johns Hopkins University Press, 1996.

Hannerz, Ulf. *Cultural Complexity: Studies in the Social Organization of Meaning*. New York: Columbia University Press, 1992.

Haraway, Donna Jeanne. *The Haraway Reader*. New York: Routledge, 2003.

Hardt, Michael and Antonio Negri. *Empire*. Cambridge, Mass.: Harvard University Press, 2000.

Harootunian, Harry D. *History's Disquiet: Modernity, Cultural Practice and the Question of Everyday Life*. New York: Columbia University Press, 2000.

Harpold, Terry. 'Hypermedia and the Literary Text'. *Hypermedia and Literary Studies*. Eds Paul Delany and George Landow. Cambridge, Mass.: MIT Press, 1991.

Hartley, John. *The Politics of Pictures: The Creation of the Public in the Age of Popular Media*. London: Routledge, 1992.

— *Popular Reality: Journalism, Modernity, Popular Culture*. London: Arnold, 1996.

Harvey, David. *The Condition of Postmodernity: An Enquiry into the Origins of Cultural Change*. Oxford; Cambridge, Mass.: Blackwell, 1990.

Hayles, N. Katherine. *How We Became Posthuman: Virtual Bodies in Cybernetics, Literature and Informatics*. Chicago: University of Chicago Press, 1999.

Hazan, Hakim. *Old Age: Deconstructions and Constructions*. Cambridge, England: Cambridge University Press, 1994.

Hebdige, Dick. *Subculture, the Meaning of Style*. London: Methuen, 1979.

— *Cut'n'Mix: Culture, Identity and Caribbean Music*. London; New York: Methuen, 1987.

— 'After the Masses'. *Marxism Today* (1989): 48–53.

Held, David and Anthony G. McGrew. *The Global Transformations Reader: An Introduction to the Globalization Debate*. Cambridge, England; Malden, Mass.: Polity Press, 2000.

Herman, Andrew and Thomas Swiss. *The World Wide Web and Contemporary Cultural Theory*. New York: Routledge, 2000.

Hermes, Joke. 'Media, Meaning and Everyday Life'. *1993* 7.3 (1993): 493–508.

Hewison, R. *The Heritage Industry: Britain in a Climate of Decline*. London: Methuen, 1987.

Highmore, Ben. *Everyday Life and Cultural Theory: An Introduction*. London: Routledge, 2002.

Hills, Matt. *Fan Cultures*. Sussex Studies in Culture and Communication. London; New York: Routledge, 2002.

Hirst, Paul and Grahame Thompson. *Globalization in Question: The International Economy and the Possibilities of Governance*. Cambridge, England: Polity Press, 1996.

— 'Globalization – a Necessary Myth?' *The Global Transformations Reader: An Introduction to the Globalization Debate*. Eds David Held and Anthony G. McGrew. Cambridge, England; Malden, Mass.: Polity Press, 2000: 68–76.

Hobsbawm, E.J. and T.O. Ranger. *The Invention of Tradition*. Past and Present Publications. Cambridge, England; New York: Cambridge University Press, 1983.

Hoggart, Richard. *The Uses of Literacy. Aspects of Working-class Life, with Special Reference to Publications and Entertainments*. London: Chatto & Windus, 1957.

Hollinger, David A. *Postethnic America: Beyond Multiculturalism*. New York: Basic Books, 1995.

Homer-Dixon, Thomas F. *The Ingenuity Gap*. 1st edn. New York; Toronto: Knopf, 2000.

Hopkins, A.G. *Globalization in World History*. Pimlico Original. London: Pimlico, 2002.

Horkheimer, Max and Theodor W. Adorno. *Dialectic of Enlightenment*. New York: Continuum, 1988 [1947].

Hughes, Robert. *The Culture of Complaint: The Fraying of America*. New York: Oxford University Press, 1993.

Human Development Report. Oxford: Oxford University Press; United Nations Development Program, 1999.

Hunt, Leon. *British Low Culture: From Safari Suits to Sexploitation*. London: Routledge, 1998.

Hunter, Ian. *Rethinking the School*. Sydney: Allen & Unwin, 1994.

Huntington, Samuel. *The Clash of Civilisations and the Remaking of the World Order*. New York: Simon & Schuster, 1997.

Huyssen, Andreas. *After the Great Divide: Modernism, Mass Culture, Postmodernism*. Theories of Representation and Difference. Bloomington: Indiana University Press, 1986.

Ignatiev, Noel. *How the Irish Became White*. New York: Routledge, 1995.

Ivy, Marilyn. *Discourses of the Vanishing: Modernity, Phantasm, Japan*. Chicago: University of Chicago Press, 1995.

Jagose, Annamarie. *Queer Theory: An Introduction*. New York: New York University Press, 1996.

Jahoda, Gustav. *Images of Savages: Ancients* [sic] *Roots of Modern Prejudice in Western Culture*. London; New York: Routledge, 1999.

James, C.L.R. *The Black Jacobins; Toussaint L'ouverture and the San Domingo Revolution*. 2nd edn. New York: Vintage Books, 1963.

Jameson, Fredric. *Postmodernism, or, the Cultural Logic of Late Capitalism*. Post-Contemporary Interventions. Durham, NC: Duke University Press, 1991.

—— *Signatures of the Visible*. New York: Routledge, 1992.

Jenkins, Henry. *Textual Poachers: Television Fans and Participatory Culture*. Studies in Culture and Communication. New York: Routledge, 1992.

Jenkins, Henry, Tara McPherson and Jane Shattuc. *Hop on Pop: The Politics and Pleasures of Popular Culture*. Durham, NC: Duke University Press, 2002.

Jordan, Glenn and Chris Wheedon. 'When the Subalterns Speak, What Do They Say? Radical Cultural Politics in Cardiff Docklands'. *Without Guarantees: In Honour of Stuart Hall*. Eds Paul Gilroy, Lawrence Grossberg and Angela McRobbie. London; New York: Verso, 2000: 148–164.

Kaliman, Ricardo. 'What Is "Interesting" in Latin American Cultural Studies'. *Journal of Latin American Cultural Studies* 17.2 (1998): 261–272.

Kellner, Douglas. *Media Culture: Cultural Studies, Identity and Politics between the Modern and the Postmodern*. London: Routledge, 1995.

Kipnis, Laura. '(Male) Desire and (Female) Disgust: Reading Hustler'. *Cultural Studies*. Eds Lawrence Grossberg, Cary Nelson and Paula Treichler. New York: Routledge, 1992: 375–392.

Kittler, Friedrich A. *Eine Kulturgeschichte Der Kulturwissenschaft*. Mèunster: Fink, 2000.

Klein, Naomi. *No Logo. No Space, No Choice, No Jobs, Taking Aim at the Brand Bullies*. London: Flamingo, 2000.

Kline, S. *Out of the Garden: Toys and Children's Culture in the Age of TV Marketing*. London: Verso, 1993.

Koselleck, Reinhart. *Futures Past: On the Semantics of Historical Time*. Studies in Contemporary German Social Thought. Cambridge, Mass.: MIT Press, 1985.

—— *Critique and Crisis: Enlightenment and the Pathogenesis of Modern Society*. Studies in Contemporary German Social Thought. 1st MIT Press edn. Cambridge, Mass.: MIT Press, 1988.

Kristol, Irving. *Neoconservatism: the Autobiography of an Idea*. New York: Free Press, 1995.

Landry, C. and F. Bianchini. *The Creative City*. London: Demos, 1995.

Lasch, Christopher. *The Culture of Narcissism: American Life in an Age of Diminishing Expectations*. New York: Norton, 1978.

Latour, Bruno. *We Have Never Been Modern*. Trans. C. Porter. Cambridge, Mass.: Harvard University Press, 1993.

—*Politics of Nature: How to Bring the Sciences into Democracy*. Cambridge, Mass.: Harvard University Press, 2004.

Lazarsfeld, Paul and Robert Merton. 'Mass Communication, Popular Taste and Organized Social Action'. *The Processes and Effects of Mass Communication*. Eds W. Schramm and D. Roberts. Chicago: University of Illinois Press, 1977.

Lefebvre, Henri. *Critique of Everyday Life*. Trans. John Moore; intro. Michel Trebitsch. London: Verso, 1991.

Lembo, Ron. *Thinking through Television*. Cambridge Cultural Social Studies. Cambridge, England; New York: Cambridge University Press, 2000.

Lennon, J. John and Malcolm Foley. *Dark Tourism*. London: Continuum, 2000.

Levine, Lawrence W. *Highbrow / Lowbrow: The Emergence of Cultural Hierarchy in America*. The William E. Massey, Sr. Lectures in the History of American Civilization; 1986. Cambridge, Mass.: Harvard University Press, 1988.

Lewis, Justin. *Art, Culture and Enterprise: The Politics of Art and the Cultural Industries*. London; New York: Routledge, 1990.

— 'Notes on Teaching Youth Culture'. *A Companion to Cultural Studies*. Ed. Toby Miller. Oxford: Blackwell, 2001: 317–330.

Leys, Ruth. *Trauma: A Genealogy*. Chicago: University of Chicago Press, 2000.

Lipsitz, George. 'Listening to Learn, Learning to Listen: Popular Culture, Cultural Theory and American Studies'. *American Quarterly* 42 (1990): 615–636.

— *Dangerous Crossroads: Popular Music, Postmodernism and the Poetics of Place*. London; New York: Verso, 1994.

Long, Elizabeth. *From Sociology to Cultural Studies*. Malden, Mass.: Blackwell, 1997.

Lovink, Geert. *Dark Fiber: Tracking Critical Internet Culture*. Electronic Culture – History, Theory, Practice. Cambridge, Mass.: MIT Press, 2002.

Lury, Celia. *Consumer Culture*. Cambridge, England: Polity Press, 1996.

Lyotard, Jean François. *The Postmodern Condition: A Report on Knowledge*. Theory and History of Literature; Vol. 10. Minneapolis, Minn.: University of Minnesota Press, 1984.

Maddox, Lucy. *Locating American Studies: The Evolution of a Discipline*. Baltimore, Md.: Johns Hopkins University Press, 1999.

Malbon, Ben. *Clubbing: Dancing, Ecstasy and Vitality*. Critical Geographies. London; New York: Routledge, 1999.

Malcolmson, Scott. 'The Varieties of Cosmopolitan Experience'. *Cosmopoltics: Thinking and Feeling Beyond the Nation*. Eds Peng Cheah and Bruce Robbins. Minneapolis, Minn.: Minnesota University Press, 1998: 233–246.

Marcus, George E. 'Cultural Studies and Anthropology'. *A Companion to Cultural Studies*. Ed. Toby Miller. Oxford: Blackwell, 2001: 169–186.

Marcus, Greil. *Lipstick Traces: A Secret History of the Twentieth Century*. Cambridge, Mass.: Harvard University Press, 1989.

Marginson, Simon and Mark Considine. *The Enterprise University: Power, Governance and Reinvention in Australia*. Melbourne: Cambridge University Press, 2000.

Marling, Karal Ann. *As Seen on TV: The Visual Culture of Everyday Life in the 1950s*. Cambridge, Mass.: Harvard University Press, 1994.

Massey, Doreen. *Space, Place and Gender*. Cambridge, England: Polity Press, 1994.

Maxwell, Rick. 'Political Economy within Cultural Studies'. *A Companion to Cultural Studies*. Ed. Toby Miller. Oxford: Blackwell, 2001a: 116–138.

— ed. *Culture Works: Essays on the Political Economy of Culture*. Minneapolis, Minn.: University of Minnesota Press, 2001b.

Mbembe, Achille. 'At the Edge of the World: Boundaries, Territoriality and Sovereignty in Africa'. Trans. Steven Rendall. *Globalization*. Ed. Arjun Appadurai. Alternative Modernities. Durham, NC; London: Duke University Press, 2001: 22–48.

McCarthy, Anna. *Ambient Television: Visual Culture and Public Space*. Console-ing Passions. Durham, NC: Duke University Press, 2001.

McGuigan, Jim. *Cultural Populism*. London; New York: Routledge, 1992.

— *Culture and the Public Sphere*. London; New York: Routledge, 1996.

McLeod, Kembrew. *Owning Culture: Authorship, Ownership and Intellectual Property Law*. Popular Culture and Everyday Life; Vol. 1. New York: P. Lang, 2001.

McRobbie, Angela. *In the Culture Society: Art, Fashion and Popular Music*. London: Routledge, 1999.

— *Feminism and Youth Culture: From 'Jackie' to 'Just Seventeen'*. 2nd edn. Basingstoke: Macmillan, 2000.

Meyrowitz, Joshua. *No Sense of Place: The Impact of Electronic Media on Social Behavior*. New York: Oxford University Press, 1985.

Michaels, Eric. *Bad Aboriginal Art: Tradition, Media and Technological Horizons*. St Leonards, NSW: Allen & Unwin, 1994.

Miller, Daniel and Don Slater. *The Internet: An Ethnographic Approach*. Oxford; New York: Berg, 2000.

Miller, Toby. *The Well-Tempered Self: Citizenship, Culture and the Postmodern Subject*. Parallax. Baltimore, Md.: Johns Hopkins University Press, 1993.

— *Sportsex*. Philadelphia: Temple University Press, 2001.

Miller, Toby and Geoffrey Lawrence. 'Globalization and Culture'. *A Companion to Cultural Studies*. Ed. Toby Miller. Oxford: Blackwell, 2001: 490–509.

Mitchell, Juliet. *Women's Estate*. Harmondsworth: Penguin, 1971.

— *Psychoanalysis and Feminism*. Harmondsworth: Penguin, 1975.

Miyoshi, Masao and Harry D. Harootunian. *Learning Places: The Afterlives of Area Studies*. Durham, NC: Duke University Press, 2002.

Morgan, Robin. *Sisterhood Is Powerful: An Anthology of Writings from the Women's Liberation Movement*. 1st edn. New York: Random House, 1970.

Morley, David. *The Nationwide Audience: Structure and Decoding*. BFI Television Monograph; 11. London: British Film Institute, 1980.

— 'Not So Much a Visual Medium, More a Visible Object'. *Visual Culture*. Ed. Chris Jenks. London: Routledge, 1995.

— *Home Territories: Media, Mobility and Identity*. New York: Routledge, 2000.

227

Morley, David and Kevin Robins. *Spaces of Identity: Global Media, Electronic Landscapes and Cultural Boundaries*. London; New York: Routledge, 1995.

Morris, Meaghan. *The Pirate's Fiancée: Feminism, Reading, Postmodernism*. Questions for Feminism. London; New York: Verso, 1988.

— 'Banality in Cultural Studes'. *Logics of Television: Essays in Cultural Criticism*. Ed. Patricia Mellencamp. Bloomington: Indiana University Press, 1990.

— *Too Soon Too Late: History in Popular Culture*. Theories of Contemporary Culture; Vol. 22. Bloomington: Indiana University Press, 1998.

Morrison, Toni. 'Talk of the Town'. *New Yorker* 3 October 1998: 31–32.

Muecke, Stephen. *Textual Spaces: Aboriginality and Cultural Studies*. Communication and Culture Series. Kensington, NSW: New South Wales University Press, 1992.

Mulgan, Geoff. *Politics in an Antipolitical Age*. Cambridge, England: Polity Press, 1994.

Mulhern, Francis. *Culture / Metaculture*. The New Critical Idiom. London: Routledge, 2000.

Naficy, Hamid. *Home, Exile, Homeland: Film, Media and the Politics of Place*. New York: Routledge, 1999.

Nairn, Tom. *The Break-up of Britain: Crisis and Neonationalism*. 2nd expanded edn. London: NLB and Verso Editions, 1981.

Narayan, Uma. *Dis-Locating Cultures: Identities, Traditions and Third-World Feminism*. Thinking Gender. New York: Routledge, 1997.

Negus, Keith. *Music Genres and Corporate Cultures*. London: Routledge, 1999.

Nixon, Sean. 'Resignifying Masculinity: From "New Man" to "New Lad"'. *British Cultural Studies*. Eds David Morley and Kevin Robins. Oxford: Oxford University Press, 2001: 373–385.

Nora, Pierre and Lawrence D. Kritzman. *Realms of Memory: Rethinking the French Past*. European Perspectives. 3 vols. New York: Columbia University Press, 1996.

Nyers, P. 'Emergencies or Emerging Identities? Refugees and Transformation in World Order'. *Millennium* 28 (1999): 1–26.

O'Regan, Tom. 'Too Much Culture, Too Little Culture: Trends and Issues for Cultural-Policy Making'. *Media International Australia* 102 (2002): 9–24.

Ohmae, Kenichi. *The End of the Nation State: The Rise of Regional Economies*. New York: Free Press, 1996.

Oliver, Kelly. *French Feminism Reader*. Lanham, Md.: Rowman & Littlefield, 2000.

Omi, Michael and Howard Winant. *Racial Formation in the United States: From the 1960s to the 1980s*. New York: Routledge, 1986.

Ong, Aihwa. *Flexible Citizenship: The Cultural Logics of Transnationality*. Durham, NC: Duke University Press, 1999.

Oritz, Fernando. *Miscelanea II of Studies Dedicated to Fernando Oritz (1881–1969)*. 1998. New York Public Library. Available: http://digilib.nypl.org/dynaweb/ortiz/ortizfin. 14 May 2003.

Orwell, George. *Collected Essays, Journalism and Letters*; Vol. 1. London: Secker & Warburg, 1961.

— *Collected Essays, Journalism and Letters*; Vol. 2. London: Secker & Warburg, 1970.

Papastergiadis, Nikos. 'Tracing Hybridity in Theory'. *Debating Cultural Hybridity*. Eds Prina Werbner and Tariq Modood. London: Zed Books, 1997.

— *Dialogues in the Diasporas: Essays and Conversations on Cultural Identity*. London; New York: Rivers Oram Press, distributed in the USA by New York University Press, 1998.

— *The Turbulence of Migration: Globalization, Deterritorialization and Hybridity*. Cambridge, England; Malden, Mass.: Polity Press; Blackwell, 2000.

Pateman, Carole. *The Disorder of Women: Democracy, Feminism and Political Theory*. Stanford, Calif.: Stanford University Press, 1989.

Pater, Walter and Adam Phillips. *The Renaissance: Studies in Art and Poetry*. Oxford; New York: Oxford University Press, 1986 [1873].

Patton, Cindy. *Inventing Aids*. New York: Routledge, 1990.

Patton, Cindy and Benigno Sánchez-Eppler. *Queer Diasporas*. Series Q. Durham, NC: Duke University Press, 2000.

Peterson, Richard A. and David G. Berger. 'Cycles in Symbolic Production: The Case of Popular Music'. *On Record*. Eds Simon Frith and Andrew Goodwin. New York: Pantheon, 1990.

Plant, Sadie. 'The Virtual Complexity of Culture'. *Futurenatural: Nature / Science / Politics*. Eds G. Robertson *et al*. London: Routledge, 1996.

Press, Andrea Lee. *Women Watching Television: Gender, Class and Generation in the American Television Experience*. Philadelphia: University of Pennsylvania Press, 1991.

Raboy, Marc *et al*. 'Cultural Development and the Open Economy: A Democratic Issue and a Challenge to Public Policy'. *Canadian Journal of Communication* 19.3 (1994).

Radway, Janice. *A Feeling for Books: The Book-of-the-Month Club, Literary Taste and Middle-class Desire*. Chapel Hill, NC; London: University of North Carolina Press, 1997.

Rajchman, John. *The Deleuze Connections*. Cambridge, Mass.: MIT Press, 2000.

Rapping, Elayne. 'Daytime Utopias: If You Lived in Pine Valley, You'd Be Home'. *Hop on Pop: The Politics and Pleasures of Popular Culture*. Eds Henry Jenkins, Tara McPherson and Jane Shattuc. Durham, NC: Duke University Press, 2002: 47–65.

Rattansi, Ali and Sallie Westwood. *Racism, Modernity and Identity: On the Western Front*. Cambridge, England; Cambridge, Mass.: Polity Press, 1994.

Readings, Bill. *The University in Ruins*. Cambridge, Mass.: Harvard University Press, 1996.

Reynolds, Simon. *Generation Ecstasy: Into the World of Techno and Rave Culture*. 1st edn. Boston: Little, Brown, 1998.

Robbins, Bruce. *Feeling Global: Internationalism in Distress*. Cultural Front. New York: New York University Press, 1999.

Roediger, David R. *The Wages of Whiteness: Race and the Making of the American Working Class*. London; New York: Verso, 1991.

Rojek, Chris. *Celebrity*. Focus on Contemporary Issues. London: Reaktion, 2001.

Rosaldo, Michelle Zimbalist, Louise Lamphere and Joan Bamberger. *Woman, Culture and Society*. Stanford, Calif.: Stanford University Press, 1974.

Rose, Jonathan. *The Intellectual Life of the British Working Classes*. New Haven: Yale University Press, 2001.

Rose, Tricia. *Black Noise: Rap Music and Black Culture in Contemporary America*. Music/Culture. Hanover, NH: University Press of New England, 1994.

Ross, Andrew. *Strange Weather: Culture, Science and Technology in the Age of Limits*. Haymarket Series on North American Politics and Culture. London; New York: Verso, 1991.

— *The Chicago Gangster Theory of Life: Nature's Debt to Society*. London; New York: Verso, 1994.

— *Science Wars*. Durham, NC; London: Duke University Press, 1996a.

— 'The Future Is a Risky Business'. *Futurenatural: Nature, Science, Culture*. Eds George Robertson *et al*. London; New York: Routledge, 1996b: 7–22.

Ross, Andrew and Tricia Rose, eds. *Microphone Fiends*. New York: Routledge, 1994.

Roy, Arundhati. *The Cost of Living*. Modern Library pbk edn. New York: Modern Library, 1999.

Said, Edward. *Orientalism*. New York: Pantheon, 1978.

Sale, Kirkpatrick. *The Conquest of Paradise: Christopher Columbus and the Columbian Legacy*. 1st edn. New York: Knopf, distributed by Random House, 1990.

Samuel, Raphael. *Theatres of Memory*. London: Verso, 1994.

Sassen, Saskia. *Globalization and Its Discontents: Essays on the New Mobility of People and Money*. New York: New Press, 1998.

— 'Spatialities and Temporalities of the Global: Elements for a Theorization'. *Globalization*. Ed. Arjun Appadurai. Alternative Modernities. Durham, NC; London: Duke University Press, 2001: 260–278.

Savage, Jon and Simon Frith. 'Pearls and Swine: The Intellectuals and the Mass Media'. *New Left Review* 198 (1993): 107–116.

Schramm, Wilbur Lang. *Television in the Lives of Our Children*. Stanford, Calif.: Stanford University Press, 1961.

Schulze, Gerhard. *Die Erlebnisgesellschaft: Kultursociologie Der Gegenwart*. Frankfurt: Campus, 1992.

Schwengell, Herman. 'British Enterprise Culture and German Kulturgesellschaft'. *Enterprise Culture*. Eds Russell Keat and Nicholas Abercrombie. London: Routledge, 1991: 136–151.

Sedgwick, Eve Kosofsky. *Between Men: English Literature and Male Homosocial Desire*. Gender and Culture. New York: Columbia University Press, 1985.

— *Epistemology of the Closet*. Berkeley, Calif.: University of California Press, 1990.

Sen, Amartya Kumar. *Development as Freedom*. Oxford; New York: Oxford University Press, 2001.

Senft, Theresa, M. 'Baud Girls and Cargo Cults: A Story About Celebrity, Community and Profane Illumination on the Web'. *The World Wide Web and Contemporary Cultural Theory*. Eds Andrew Herman and Thomas Swiss. New York: Routledge, 2000: 183–206.

Shumway, David R. *Modern Love: Romance, Intimacy and the Marriage Crisis*. New York: New York University Press, 2003.

Sim, Stuart. *Post-Marxism: A Reader*. Edinburgh: Edinburgh University Press, 1998.

— *Post-Marxism: An Intellectual History*. New York: Routledge, 2000.

Sinha, Indra. *The Cybergypsies: A Frank Account of Love, Life and Travels on the Electronic Frontier*. 1st American edn. New York: Simon & Schuster, 1999.

Smith, Anthony D. 'LSE Centennial Lecture: The Resurgence of Nationalism? Myth and Memory in the Renewal of Nations'. *British Journal of Sociology* 47.4 (1996): 575–598.

Smith, Neil. 'The Production of Nature'. *Futurenatural: Nature, Science, Culture*. Eds George Robertson *et al*. London; New York: Routledge, 1996: 35–54.

Smith, P. *The New American Cultural Sociology*. Cambridge, England: Cambridge University Press, 1998.

Spigel, Lynn. *Make Room for TV: Television and the Family Ideal in Postwar America*. Chicago: University of Chicago Press, 1992.

Spivak, Gayatri Chakravorty. 'Can the Subaltern Speak?' *Marxism and the Interpretation of Culture*. Eds Lawrence Grossberg and Cary Nelson. Urbana, Ill.: University of Illinois Press, 1988: 271–313.

Stallybrass, Peter and Allon White. *The Politics and Poetics of Transgression*. London: Methuen, 1986.

Steedman, Carolyn. *Landscape for a Good Woman: A Story of Two Lives*. London: Virago, 1986.

Steele, Tom. *The Emergence of Cultural Studies, 1945–65: Cultural Politics, Adult Education and the English Question*. London: Lawrence & Wishart, 1997.

Stephens, Michelle A. 'Babylon's "Natural Mystic": The North American Music Industry, the Legend of Bob Marley, and the Incorporation of Transnationalism'. *Cultural Studies* 12.2 (1998): 139–167.

Storey, John. *Cultural Theory and Popular Culture: A Reader*. 2nd edn. New York: Prentice Hall, 1998.

Storey, Robert F. *Pierrots on the Stage of Desire: Nineteenth-Century French Literary Artists and the Comic Pantomime*. Princeton, NJ: Princeton University Press, 1985.

Strathern, Marilyn. 'No Nature, No Culture: The Hagen Case'. *Nature, Culture and Gender*. Eds Carol MacCormack and Marilyn Strathern. Cambridge, England: Cambridge University Press, 1980: 174–222.

Stratton, Jon and Ien Ang. 'On the Impossibility of a Global Cultural Studies: "British" Cultural Studies in an "International" Frame'. *Stuart Hall: Critical Dialogues in Cultural Studies*. Eds David Morley and Kuan-Hsing Chen. London: Routledge, 1996.

Straw, Will. 'Characterizing Rock Music Culture: The Case of Heavy Metal Music'. *The Cultural Studies Reader*. 2nd edn. Ed. Simon During. London: Routledge, 1998: 451–462.

Streeter, Thomas. *Selling the Air: A Critique of the Policy of Commercial Broadcasting in the United States*. Chicago: University of Chicago Press, 1996.

Sullivan, Andrew. *Virtually Normal. An Argument About Homosexuality*. New York; London: Alfred A. Knopf; Picador, 1995.

Supiot, Alain. 'Dogma and Rights'. *New Left Review* NS 21 (2003): 118–136.

Takahiko, Tsubouchi. *Look East Policy and Oshin*. 1997. Available: http://www.iijnet.or.jp/asia/database/mw9510_1txt.

Taylor, Charles. 'The Politics of Recognition'. *Multiculturalism: A Critical Reader*. Ed. David Theo Goldberg. Oxford: Blackwell, 1994: 75–106.

Todorov, Tzvetan. *On Human Diversity: Nationalism, Racism and Exoticism in French Thought*. Cambridge, Mass.: Harvard University Press, 1993.

Tomlinson, John. *Cultural Imperialism*. London: Pinder, 1991.

Tsing, Anna Lowenhaupt. *In the Realm of the Diamond Queen: Marginality is an Out-of-the-Way Place*. Princeton, NJ: Princeton University Press, 1993.

Turner, Graeme. *British Cultural Studies*. 2nd edn. London: Routledge, 1996.

UNESCO. *International Flows of Selected Cultural Goods 1980–1998*. Paris: UNESCO, 2001a.

—— *Draft UNESCO Declaration on Cultural Diversity*, 2001b.

United Nations Development Programme. *Human Development Report*. UNDP, 1999.

Urry, John. *The Tourist Gaze*. 2nd edn. London; Thousand Oaks, Calif.: Sage, 2002.

Wallerstein, Immanuel. *The End of the World as We Know It: Social Science for the Twenty-First Century*. Minneapolis, Minn.: University of Minnesota Press, 1999.

Warner, Michael. *The Trouble with Normal: Sex, Politics and the Ethics of Queer Life*. New York: The Free Press, 1999.

— *Publics and Counterpublics*. Cambridge: Zone Books, 2002.

Williams, Raymond. *Culture and Society*. London: Chatto & Windus, 1958.

— *The Long Revolution*. London: Chatto & Windus, 1961.

— *Television: Technology and Cultural Form*. New York: Schocken Books, 1975.

— *Marxism and Literature*. Oxford: Oxford University Press, 1977.

— 'Ideas of Nature'. *Problems in Materialism and Culture: Selected Essays*. London: Verso, 1980a: 67–85.

— *Problems in Materialism and Culture: Selected Essays*. London: Verso, 1980b.

Williamson, Judith. *Decoding Advertisements: Ideology and Meaning in Advertising*. Ideas in Progress. London: Boyars, distributed by Calder & Boyars, 1978.

Willis, Paul E. *Learning to Labour. How Working Class Kids Get Working Class*. Farnborough, Hants: Saxon House, 1977.

Wilson, Alexander. *The Culture of Nature: North American Landscape from Disney to the Exxon Valdez*. Cambridge, Mass.: Blackwell, 1992.

Wimsatt, William. *Bomb the Suburbs*. Chicago: Soft Skull Press, 2001.

Winston, Brian. *Media Technology and Society: A History: From the Telegraph to the Internet*. London; New York: Routledge, 1998.

Wolf, Naomi. *The Beauty Myth: How Images of Beauty Are Used Against Women*. 1st edn. New York: W. Morrow, 1991.

— *Promiscuities: The Secret Struggle for Womanhood*. 1st edn. New York: Random House, 1997.

Woolgar, Steve. 'Five Rules of Virtuality'. *Virtual Society? Technology, Cyberbole, Reality*. Ed. Steve Woolgar. Oxford: Oxford University Press, 2002: 1–23.

Wright, Handel. 'Dare We Decentre Birmingham? Troubling the "Origin" and Trajectories of Cultural Studies'. *European Journal of Cultural Studies* 1.1 (1998): 33–56.

Young, Robert. *Colonial Desire: Hybridity in Theory, Culture and Race*. London; New York: Routledge, 1995.

Yudice, George. 'Comparative Cultural Studies Traditions: Latin America and the US'. *A Companion to Cultural Studies*. Ed. Toby Miller. Oxford: Blackwell, 2001: 217–231.

Zielinski, Siegfried. *Audiovisions: Cinema and Television as Entr'actes in History*. Film Culture in Transition. Amsterdam: Amsterdam University Press, 1999.

Zizek, Slavoj. 'Multiculturalism, or, the Cultural Logic of Multinational Capitalism', *New Left Review* 225 (September–October 1997): 28–51.

Index

aboriginal culture 26
abortion 171
absolute culture 20
academic training 15, 16
ACT UP 183
activism 40–1
Adorno, Theodor 115, 209
advertising: analysis of 120–1; branding
  and marketing 199, 202, 210; on television 111–12
Africa 98, 158, 183
African Americans: cultural history 57;
  identity and 147, 148; in movies 202;
  multiculturalism and 153; 'race laws'
  164; stereotypes 165
African Studies 98
Against Race (Gilroy) 166–7
Agamben, Georgio 29
agency 22, 29, 32
aid 88
AIDS 41, 183, 187
alienation 28
Althusser, Louis 31–2, 43
'American Family' (TV show) 120
American studies 24, 26–7

'America's Funniest Home Videos' (TV show)
  119
analytic methodology 5
Anderson, Benedict 99–100
androgyny 182
Ang, Lin 26
anthropology 31, 36
anti-positivism 8
Appadurai, Arjun 94
architecture, post-modernism and 67
area studies 25
Arnold, Matthew 36, 69, 195
art see also avant-garde: for art's sake 195;
  commercialism 200; cultural studies
  9–10; fiction 132; post-modernism 64,
  67–8
arts de faire 29
Asia: Asianisation of 97; caste system 161;
  dam-building 70; high and low culture 196;
  queer culture 183; stereotypes 165; universities 12
Association for the Taxation of Financial
  Transactions to Aid Citizens (ATTAC) 89
Australia: Aboriginal 'stolen generation' 60;
  'black armband' history 54–5; class and

233